Economic
Development
and the
Labor Market
in Japan

Studies of the
East Asian Institute
Columbia
University

Economic Development & the Labor Market in Japan

Koji
Taira

Columbia University Press

1970

New York & London

Koji Taira is Professor of Economics and Industrial Relations
at the University of Illinois.

Copyright © 1970 Columbia University Press
Library of Congress Catalog Card Number: 78-111459
ISBN: 0-231-03272-2
Printed in the United States of America

The East Asian Institute
of Columbia University

The East Asian Institute of Columbia University was established in 1949 to prepare graduate students for careers dealing with East Asia, and to aid research and publication on East Asia during the modern period. The faculty of the Institute are grateful to the Ford Foundation and the Rockefeller Foundation for their financial assistance.

The Studies of the East Asian Institute were inaugurated in 1962 to bring a wider public the results of significant new research on modern and contemporary East Asia.

to young Okinawans
for an intelligent use of the Japanese Labor Market

Preface

SURPRISINGLY, THERE ARE ONLY a few Western-language books by Japanese authors on the history of the labor market, industrial relations, and social policy in modern Japan. Only three books may be considered as predecessors to this one. These are widely spaced in time. The earliest is *La protection ouvrière au Japon* (Paris, 1898), by a Japanese official of the then Ministry of Agriculture and Commerce, Kashiro Saito. The historical importance of this book was immediately recognized by an eminent English economist, Ernest Foxwell, who contributed a substantial summary and evaluation of the Saito volume to the *Economic Journal* in 1901. Thirty years after Saito, Columbia University Press published Shuichi Harada's dissertation, *Labor Conditions in Japan* (1928). In 1963, nearly thirty years after Harada, an extremely illuminating and comprehensive volume on the social history of Japan's industrialization was written by Professor Mikio Sumiya (*Social Impact of Industrialization in Japan*). The thirty-year intervals in the stream of classics are striking. Although it is not yet thirty years—indeed, far from it—since Sumiya's book, one may feel that the importance of the subject calls for consideration in addition to the classical evaluations.

The subject of this book is the labor market, but the real heroes and heroines are the people who offer their services for pay and thereby constitute one of the two important segments of the labor market, the supply side. The labor market process means the totality of interrelations and interactions of all the individual expectations, strategies, and activities of workers and employers in relation to the evaluation and allocation of human resources. In order to get at the focal points and leading forces in this immensely complicated process of the labor market and to put them in proper perspective with a tolerable degree of expository efficiency, I have followed the practice of labor economists who have placed at the center of their attention what the labor market is supposed to achieve, that is, the equalization of net advantages of different occupations. This viewpoint has guided the presentation and analysis of data in Part I.

If Part I is "analytical," Part II is "institutional." Another way of characterizing the two parts is to call one "economic" and the other "Japanologist." The interpretation of Japanese data in Part I is based on economic theory. Among the Western scholars who take an interest in Japan, there are those who insist that the behavioral postulates of economic theory are "culture-bound" to the West and that Japan is not in or of the West. The desire to appreciate the subtle and particular elements of Japanese life is commendable. In some cases, however, there seems to be a theory that Japan is different and requires certain unique interpretations. If reactions to my past publications and to an early version of this book are any guide to the general attitude toward Japan, it is clear that people consider it a great heresy to say that in the ordinary business of life the Japanese follow the law of supply and demand like any other people. There are many versions of this attitude, ranging from romanticism to antagonism. When the view that Japan is different is frustrated by facts of economic life as, for example, Japan's adherence to the law of supply and demand in the international markets, the habit of thinking that has always sought after unique interpretations specific to Japan follows its own logic by turning a disproportionate amount of attention and emphasis to "peculiarities" of Japanese practices in production, distribution, and marketing. These peculiarities with their mystic and mystifying forces intensify the sentiment against the competition of Japanese products in the international markets. The ramifications of the traditional Japanologists' central doctrine that Japan is and must be different therefore have grave practical consequences. In Part II of this book, I use an alternative approach. The behavioral postulates of economic theory and the logic of the labor market process are not "culture-bound" to the West. Part II demonstrates their usefulness for the understanding of Japanese experience.

The articles on which I "moonlighted" during the early 1960s had accumulated to the size of a small book by 1965. I then toyed with the idea that I should put them together in book form in order to reach a wider reading public, and expressed this wish rather timidly to Professor Ronald Dore. Encouraged by kind words and sympathetic comments from a man whose thorough scholarship and marvelous insights had always been the objects of my admiration, I began to put some of the papers together, coordinating style, correcting errors, eliminating duplications, and adding new data where necessary. The manuscript was read at this stage by Professors James I. Nakamura, Henry Rosovsky, and T. C. Smith, all of whom delighted me with favorable responses. In the meantime, from different quarters came the charge that the manuscript suffered from too much of the "Chicago School" type of approach and that I might have been falsifying the data and information to prove at all costs that the market was always right. I was not able to fathom the implications of charges of this kind but thought that spending some time in learning the recent history of economic thought would be a good idea. While I was doing this, time passed quickly and there was a definite need for updating some of my data. At the same time, Japanese scholars on the other side of the Pacific were pouring out quantities of new materials on the labor history of Japan. When I went over the manuscript in the fall of 1968 I therefore revised it substantially by deleting earlier findings and incorporating new ones, as well as adding the latest data and rerunning statistical experiments. As for my ideological contamination, while I cannot recall when and where I was infected, I have at least tried to behave respectably and respectfully by revising expressions which I suspected had given rise to misgivings. But then one could never be sure about the total ideological effect of the present version since new chapters had replaced some of the old ones. If I still fall short of the expected standards of recantation, I only ask for the reader's indulgence on that score.

I have incurred enormous debt to numerous persons in the course of all the years since 1960 during which my thoughts and observations on Japan have appeared in bits and pieces in America, Europe, and Japan. However, since I have expressed my profound gratitude to them in my previous publications, and in view of the awkward ideology and methodology that allegedly characterize this book, it would be unforgivably ostentatious to repeat acknowledgments here. I might even say that it would be unethical to implicate my benefactors by doing so.

My biennial "home leaves"—my Tokyo friends jokingly call them my "sankin kōtai"—have helped me keep abreast of changing events in Japan and developments in research activities in various places, although these sojourns in Japan have never been directly related to the preparation of this book. For the last two leaves, I am glad to acknowledge the financial help received from the East Asian Studies Committee of Stanford University. The institutions and organizations in Japan which have kindly allowed me to use their facilities in recent years include the following: the Japan Economic Research Center, the Institute of Economic Research of Hitotsubashi University, the Tokyo Branch of the International Labor Office, the Central Labor Relations Commission, the Japan Institute of Labor, the Japan Productivity Center, the Social Development Research Institute, the National Institute of Research on Living Conditions, the Japan Association for Industrial Training, the Research Institute for Industrial Labor, and the University of the Ryukyus.

I am grateful to numerous scholars, officials, research workers, managers, unionists, community leaders, and journalists who over the years have been of great help to me through gifts of their publications, and by communications and visits. I regret that the sheer number of my benefactors precludes the possibility of mentioning them all. Some to whom I am especially indebted are Dr. Saburo Okita, Professor Isamu Yamada, Professor Mataji Umemura, Dr. Konosuke Odaka, Professor Mikio Sumiya, Dr. Takeshi Takahashi, Mr. Goro Omiya, Mr. Rokuro Hotani, Mr. Yasuhiko Torii, Mr. Haruo Shimada, Professor Yuzo Yamada, Professor Makoto Sakurabayashi, Professor Hisao Kumagai, Professor Ichiro Nakayama, and Mr. Yutaka Kosai.

Although words hardly suffice, I am particularly grateful to Mr. Ryohei Magota of the Central Labor Relations Commission for the full personal charge he took of me in the summer of 1968, instructing me in the history and development of the Japanese wage structure, taking me to important conferences and seminars where practical and academic problems of wage determination were discussed, introducing me to research officers in several major companies in Tokyo, and making my leave of that year especially meaningful and fruitful in general.

The following organizations have kindly granted me their permission to use substantial portions of my articles previously published by them: the American Farm Economic Association, the Industrial Relations Research Association, the International Labour Office, the London School of Economics and Political Science, the New York School for Social Research, the New York State School of Labor and Industrial Relations, the University of Chicago, the University of the Ryukyus, and the Western Economic Association.

KOJI TAIRA

February 1970

Contents

Part I   Relative Wages in the Equilibrating Process

Part II   Institutions in the Labor Market Process

Abbreviations

AER	*American Economic Review*
ASCMJ	*Aspects of Social Change in Modern Japan,* ed. by R. P. Dore (Princeton: Princeton University Press, 1967)
BJIR	*British Journal of Industrial Relations*
CH	*Chingin hakusho* (White Paper on Wages) by Japan Productivity Center
CKC	*Chingin kihon chōsa* (Basic Surveys of Wages), ed. by Ichiro Nakayama (Tokyo: Tōyō keizai, 1956)
ELTES	*Estimates of Long-Term Economic Statistics of Japan Since 1868,* ed. by Kazushi Ohkawa, Miyohei Shinohara, and Mataji Umemura (Tokyo: Tōyō keizai, different years)
EPA	Economic Planning Agency
GROJES	*The Growth Rate of the Japanese Economy Since 1878* by Kazushi Ohkawa and Associates (Tokyo: (Kinokuniya, 1957)
HJE	*Hitotsubashi Journal of Economics*
ILR	*International Labor Review*
ILRR	*Industrial and Labor Relations Review*
JAS	*Journal of Asian Studies*
KH	*Keizai hakusho* (White Paper on the Economy) by the EPA
KKN	*Kōjō kantoku nenpō* (Annual Report on Factory Supervision) by the Ministry of Agriculture and Commerce, and the Ministry of Commerce and Industry
KTH	*Kōjō tōkei hyō* or *Kōgyō tōkei hyō* (Factory Statistics or Census of Manufacture) by the Ministry of Agriculture and Commerce, the Ministry of Commerce and Industry, and the MITI
MGZ	*Mita gakkai zasshi* (Journal of the Mita Academy)
MITI	Ministry of International Trade and Industry
MLSRB	*Monthly Labor Statistics and Research Bulletin*

NCKK   *Nihongata chingin kōzō no kenkyū* (Studies on Japanese
                    Wage Structure), ed. by Miyohei Shinohara and
            Naomichi Funahashi (Tokyo: Rōdō hōgaku kenkyūjo, 1961)
NKKSK   *Nihon keizai kenkyū sentā kaihō* (Bulletin of the
                                Japan Economic Research Center)
NKTS   *Nihon keizai tōkei shū* (A Collection of Japanese
                                Economic Statistics), ed. by Hyoe Ouchi
                                (Tokyo: Nihon hyōron shinsha, 1958)
NRKZ   *Nihon rōdō kyōkai zasshi* (Monthly Journal of
                                the Japan Institute of Labor)
NRUS   *Nihon rōdō undō shiryō* (Historical Materials on the
            Japanese Labor Movement), ed. by Rōdō undō shiryō iinkai
                                (Tokyo, different years)
NTN   *Nihon (teikoku) tōkei nenkan* (Statistical Yearbook
                                of [the Empire of] Japan)
PDIMJ   *Political Development in Modern Japan,* ed. by
            Robert E. Ward (Princeton: Princeton University Press, 1968)
RH   *Rōdō hakusho* (White Paper on Labor)
                                by the Ministry of Labor
RTJCH   *Rōdō tokei jitchi chōsa hōkoku* (Field Surveys of Labor
                                Statistics) by the Prime Minister's Office
RUN   *Rōdō undō nenpō* (Annual Report
                                on the Labor Movement)
SEEJ   *The State and Economic Enterprise in Japan,*
                                ed. by W. W. Lockwood (Princeton:
                                Princeton University Press, 1965)
SSU   *Saikin no shakai undō* (The Social Movements in
                                Recent Years) by Kyōchō kai (Tokyo, 1930)
WCKNSK   *Wagakuni chingin kōzō no shiteki kōsatsu* (Historical
            Studies of Japanese Wage Structure) by Shōwa dōjin kai
                                (Tokyo: Shiseidō, 1960)
YLS   *Yearbook of Labor Statistics*

Economic
Development
and the
Labor Market
in Japan

Introduction

The Concept of Labor Market

IN COMMON PARLANCE, "labor market" is a disagreeable expression. "Market" is the concept that originates in the sale and purchase of a commodity, but "labor" is not a commodity. "Labor" is inseparable from the person who works. Man surely cannot be bought or sold, at least in the modern world which has outlawed slavery. So goes the argument against labor market. One would agree that the idea of a labor market as a mechanism for resource allocation is one of the most difficult applications of the market concept one can visualize. But, as M. W. Reder points out, "properly utilized, the idea of a labor market can be used as a partial explanation of wage determination." [1] It is the task of this book to observe the working of the labor market in the course of Japanese economic development and to relate the market forces and other factors that bear upon the rates of pay for various activities and in different firms, industries, and geographical areas of Japan.

A labor market exists if there are people who work for pay. As implied in the "anti-market" argument mentioned above, however, "working for pay" is not necessarily a preferred way of earning a living if there are other ways of securing the same level of living such as self-employment or cooperatives. The difference between working for pay and working on one's own is that in the former case work is specified and directed by the employer. E. H. Phelps-Brown observes that "men who can spend the hours of their working days at their own discretion regard it as an indignity to put themselves under the orders of another man." He continues: "The issue is not how hard they shall work or how much they shall get, but whether they shall work as they choose or as they are told." [2] For these reasons, paid work is clearly subject to a negative premium vis-à-vis self-employment for the same level of earning and for the same kind of working conditions. "Being one's own boss" not only is a pleasant rhetoric but also reflects substantive rationality in occupational choice.

The margin of preference for self-employment over paid work decreases in the course of economic development. In less developed economies where a great majority of able-bodied persons are self-employed, the predominant kind of occupational choice—if there is room for choice at all—is between self-employment and participation in the labor market. In highly developed economies choice is usually among alternative opportunities for paid work. The discussion of the labor force in developed economies can be carried on without specific reference to the labor market, for the allocation of human resources usually goes through the market anyway. But it is fatal to disregard the shifting importance of the labor market in the discussion of labor force utilization in less developed economies.[3]

Labor Market Participation

Anyone who works for pay is a participant in the labor market. The size of the labor market in a national economy is therefore commonly represented by the proportion of the labor force in paid employment. Table 1 shows the development of the Japanese labor market for the economy as a whole and by sector. Participation in paid employment shows a rising secular trend as may be expected in a developing economy. By 1920, when the first exhaustive census of population was taken, paid employment in Japan had reached a moderately high level in the nonagricultural sectors. Paid employment in agriculture has always been low. The weight of the agricultural labor force, though decreasing relative to nonagriculture, has been large until recently, and the low labor market participation of the agricultural labor force has kept the average for the whole economy low.[4]

Detailed comments on the development of the labor market in Japan are deferred to appropriate chapters in this book. For the moment suffice it to note that paid employment in Japan has expanded rather slowly by the standards of industrialized countries in the world. In 1920, after one half century of economic development, the industrial sector was still small and the labor market participation rate of the labor force was modest. Japan in the 1920s was still predominantly a country of family farms, family workshops, and family stores.[5] This implies two things which are of great importance to the understanding

TABLE I

THE LABOR MARKET PARTICIPATION RATE IN JAPAN
BY SECTOR, 1872–1966[a]

(PERCENT)

Year	Total	Primary	Secondary	Tertiary
1872	8.6	1.7	33.2	36.8
1920	29.5	4.5	65.5	48.8
1930	32.3	4.9	60.2	57.8
1940	41.9	4.8	79.0	61.7
1950	39.6	6.2	76.5	66.9
1960	49.0	5.2	82.0	65.4
1966	60.0	5.2	84.0	72.8

Sources: For 1872–1950, Tadao Ishizaki, "Sangyō kōzō to shūgyō kōzō" (Industrial and Employment Structures), in Wagakuni kanzen koyō no igi to taisaku (Full Employment in Japan: Significance and Policy), edited by Showa Dojin Kai (Tokyo: 1957). For 1960 and 1966, YLS (1960, 1966).

[a] The ratio of paid employment to total employment.

of the Japanese labor market process. First, it implies a deep-seated antipathy to paid employment as a way of living. People would offer themselves in the market only as the last resort and would get out of it as soon as prospects improved for proprietorship. Second, employers either had to offer enough to make up for the negative premium on paid work in order to secure stable work forces of good qualities or were compelled to suffer from the consequences of their failure to do so by being able to employ only the least desirable, least skilled, and least educated workers in the nation.

The barrier between self-employment and paid employment was particularly high in the early stage of Japan's development. Employers, constrained by capital shortage and thin financial reserve, were in no position to be generous or far-sighted in their hiring policy. Many of them did not even grasp the logic of the labor market. By failing to adjust wages and working conditions upward to make up for the transfer cost between self-employment and paid work, they were stuck with the perennial problems of instability and low morale of the work force. The relatively stiff supply price of labor resulting from the low valuation of paid employment and the failure of many employers to meet it brought about an extremely fluid labor market in which the participants were largely short-term migrants (*dekasegi* workers).[6]

In strict definition, the dekasegi worker always returns to his home after some months or years of outside work to resume his normal activities or operates intermittently in the labor market from the gravitation center of his home. But in view of the steady progress of urbanization and the considerable geographical movements of population, dekasegi from farms alone could not have accounted for the whole bulk of the paid labor force. The second and third sons of farmers in most cases left the land for good and, for the sheer necessity of balancing the sexes, nature and society expelled an equal number of girls from the land. Many of these youngsters became wage-earners as an initial step in the life of the city. After having gained experience in some trades, they would settle down to operate their own stores or workshops. Thus year in and year out, workers left the land at a rate that kept the number of farm households constant during the whole period before the Second World War, but most of them shunned paid employment.

It was generally considered desirable that older persons should own and operate their own enterprises. The scales of operation in many activities were almost infinitely divisible, and each person was able to pick his scale of production matching his luck and ability. Large-scale operations employing tens, hundreds, and even thousands of paid workers did increase in number. But prewar Japan was a country of small craftsmen and shopkeepers surrounded by masses of even more minute enterprises of roadside stands for *sake*, tobacco, noodles, candies, and what not, and millions of urban and rural households burning the midnight oil under putting-out arrangements. This was the economic scene of Japan's famous (or was it notorious?) labor-intensive development widely celebrated as a classic example of indigenous and endogenous economic development in the literature.[7]

The Leisurely Pace
of Japanese Development

One might suspect that an economy which had as much difficulty as Japan in developing its paid labor force would fail in achieving a rapid expansion of the aggregate output. One is right in this regard despite the exaggerated emphasis on Japan's *rapid* economic development that is in wide circulation. The truth is that there was not anything so spectacular about Japanese development before the Second World War. Lest this might sound too audacious, I shall review the current state of Japanese studies in this respect.

The renowned *rapidity* of Japanese development has so far stemmed from the preliminary work of the Hitotsubashi University Institute of Economic Research, *The Growth Rate of the Japanese Economy Since 1878,* published in 1957 (to be abbreviated as *GROJES* hereinafter). The methods and results of this work have been challenged by a few critics, however. The most formidable of the critiques is James I. Nakamura's challenge to the estimate of agricultural production in *GROJES.*[8] The Hitotsubashi economists themselves have been revising all their previous estimates and expect to complete the series of the *Estimates of Long-Term Economic Statistics of Japan Since 1868 (ELTES) in* the near future. Several volumes in this series devoted to particular sectors and industries have already been published, but one still waits for the crucial volume on the aggregate output estimates.

Nakamura rejects the data on agricultural production used in *GROJES* on the grounds that they grossly underestimate the actual production. Nakamura's estimates put the value of agricultural production for the period 1878–1882 at a level 80 percent above the *GROJES* estimates.[9] After adjustments are made in the figures for all other years, the average annual rate of increase in the value of agricultural production in constant prices between 1878 and 1882 and 1918 and 1922 comes down to 1 percent per annum from the previous 2.4 percent. Nakamura has not attempted to revise the production statistics of the other sectors but rightly suspects that they may also be underestimates so far as the Meiji period is concerned. The *GROJES* estimates of nonagricultural output together with Nakamura's agricultural output reduce the average annual rate of increase in the net national product in constant prices between 1878 and 1882 and 1918 and 1922 from 4 percent to 2.8 percent.[10] If the correct estimates of nonagricultural output were obtained, the aggregate growth rate would come down farther. Adjusted for population increases, the rate of growth of net national product per capita must have been less than 1.8 percent per annum. The rate of economic growth that is less than 2.8 percent for the aggregate output and 1.8 percent on a per capita basis is not a spectacular affair in the light of the growth experience in other countries.

However, it is only fair to add that the Nakamura correction of the agricultural output for the early Meiji years is regarded as somewhat excessive even by those who agree with Nakamura on the imperfections of earlier production statistics.[11] The Hitotsubashi economists themselves have come up with their own revisions and concede the point of earlier underestimates to Nakamura without accepting his results.[12] The new Hitotsubashi estimates, *ELTES,* give a range of growth rates and put the median rate at 1.8 percent per annum for the period of 1880 to 1900, and at 2.0 percent per annum for the period of 1900 to 1920.[13]

At the same time, one of the Hitotsubashi economists, Yuichi Shionoya, has completed his revision of the index of industrial production for the prewar period.[14] He has discovered technical inadequacies and outright computational errors in the Index of Industrial Production constructed by the Nagoya Commercial College researchers (known as the Nagoya Index) which was used in *GROJES* for the industrial sector. The removal of the inadequacies and errors raises the index number for 1874 on the base of 1935 from 0.31 to 0.53, an upward correction of no less than 68 percent. Eliminating electricity and gas, which were included in the original Nagoya Index, and using weighted arithmetic averages in lieu of the weighted geometrical averages used in the Nagoya Index, Shionoya obtains a revised Nagoya Index which yields the index number of 1.49 (1935 = 100) for 1874, nearly five times as high as the index number for the same year in the original Nagoya Index. Shionoya's own index of industrial production, at which he has arrived after laborious experiments, gives 4.27 (1935 = 100) as the index number of 1874, nearly 14 times as high as the index number for the same year given by the original Nagoya Index!

Shionoya's revision of the index of industrial production leaves no doubt that the production data for early Meiji years grossly under-estimated the actual production. Compared with the Nagoya Index, the Shionoya Index reduces the average annual growth rate of indus-trial production from 11.7 to 4.5 percent for the period of 1874 to 1905, from 8.2 to 6.1 percent for the period of 1905 to 1935, and from 9.9 to 5.3 percent for the entire period of 1874 to 1935.[15] Shionoya's international comparisons for the decades preceding the First World War show that Japan's industrial expansion was slower than Sweden's, at about the same rate as Germany's, Italy's, and the United States', but faster than Great Britain's and France's.[16]

The above reference to statistical details of agricultural and indus-trial production has been necessary to make the unconventional point that Japan's industrialization and economic development at least be-fore the First World War were leisurely affairs unworthy of descriptions connoting rapidity and amazement which have so far characterized the discussion of Japanese experience. Leisurely industrialization also fits better with the slow growth of the labor market. One almost feels that Japan's prewar development was limited by the lack of paid labor suit-able to large-scale, capital-intensive factories.

The "Feudal" Legacy

There is one extremely important point to note in connection with Japan's "slow" economic development before the First World War, that is, that the level of economic development at the beginning of Japan's modernization was considerably higher than has hitherto been supposed. Modern Japan had inherited that level of economic develop-ment from the preceding Tokugawa period. Although money and com-merce were anathema to the organizational principle of feudal society, the economic system at the end of the feudal period was reasonably commercialized. Emphasizing the market as an indispensable institu-tion for economic development, Charles P. Kindleberger advances an admittedly "strong" argument for "the proposition that economic development through industrialization should be preceded by com-mercialization, and the industrial by the commercial revolution." [17] While Kindleberger claims Japan as an exception to this rule, pre-

Meiji Japan, for all her feudal characteristics in political structure, had an economy oriented to and regulated by the market. Reviewing the available evidence and estimates, E. Sydney Crawcour feels that in the 1860s the Japanese peasantry must have marketed 20 to 25 percent of their rice after the payment of the tax in rice. Counting the tax rice as something similar to marketed rice—indeed, much of it eventually found its way to the market because of the feudal lords' demand for cash balances—and using the usual tax rate during the feudal period, Crawcour raises the proportion of rice marketed to 70 to 80 percent. He further suggests that for all agricultural crops the average proportion marketed would have been 60 to 70 percent in the 1860s.[18] This was a very high degree of commercialization for the agricultural sector of a "feudal" economy.

Thus one feels that toward the end of the Tokugawa period the productivity of Japanese agriculture was far above the subsistence requirements of the peasantry. That agriculture was above the subsistence level at the beginning of modern Japan calls into question all the attempts to apply W. Arthur Lewis's concept of "unlimited supplies of labor" to Japanese experience.[19] I shall have something to say on this point in relation to the intersectoral labor transfer in Chapter 3. For the moment, what is important is to note that, while the Japanese economy at the beginning of modernization was a commercial economy, the labor market had seen only a modest beginning. When four fifths of output were marketed, only less than one tenth of the labor force was available in the labor market. Preindustrial Japan was par excellence a "commercialized household economy" in which families worked on their own and marketed their products. This was the initial state of the Japanese economy, and the subsequent history of Japan's modern economic growth has in important degrees been the story of an expanding labor market.

The Organization of the Book

This book consists of two parts. In Part I, I shall discuss the working of the labor market by following the statistical indicators for the principal function of the labor market, namely, wage determination. The central question in Part I is that of labor market efficiency in the adjustment of relative wages so as to equalize the net advantages of different occupations. In the presentation of the data and analysis of the underlying forces, I shall follow the method commonly used by labor economists under the heading of wage structure or wage differentials. Although the excavation of wage data over as long a period as possible is claimed to be an important contribution of Part I, I have tried to go beyond mere statistical archeology. I have followed the practice of economic analysis to instill a new life into data so that they "speak for themselves" as chronicles of labor market events. In analysis, my emphasis is on the question of how the changes in the whole economy filter through different sectors and industries and penetrate the labor market. By asking this question and providing answers, I hope to show as best I can how integrated the Japanese economy has been as a market system.

In Part II, fortified by the analytical unity of the Japanese economic system, I shall venture to look into its institutional characteristics with a view to obtaining a balanced view of the working of the economic system. With institutional knowledge, one may also increase the understanding of labor market phenomena in relation to the individual aspirations of workers, employers' techniques of work force management, the raison d'être of power groups, and the consequences of public policy. The arrangement of chapters in Part II is historical. Chapter 5, the first chapter in this part, is devoted to the period preceding the First World War. The emphasis is on the state of the early labor market and employers' responses to its dictates. Chapter 6 takes up similar events during the interwar period, adding descriptions and analyses of new events such as the labor movement and social legislation. Chapter 7 examines the labor market structure in the period after the Second World War, focusing attention on the hero of the age, the trade union. Chapter 8 evaluates the degree of social and political respectability that workers have achieved after a century of economic development, by looking into the role of the labor movement in economic planning and public policy vis-à-vis the place of business and bureaucracy.

Part I

Relative Wages
in the
Equilibrating Process

1

Japanese
Wage Differentials
before the Second World War

THE FUNCTION OF THE LABOR MARKET is to equalize the net advantages of different occupations throughout the economic system.[1] For purposes of observation, it is quite unwieldy to try to consider how rates of pay for all the different jobs within the economy change relative to one another. To reduce the task to manageable proportions, labor economists have conventionally adopted a certain intermediate level of aggregation of paid activities and have observed the relationships among these broad wage groups. These relationships are called relative wages or wage differentials.

There are five broad groups of wage differentials: (1) interindustry, (2) occupational, (3) geographical, (4) personal, and (5) interfirm. The interindustry wage differentials may, in turn, be classified into (a) the intersectoral wage differential (between agriculture and nonagriculture), and (b) wage differentials among branches of nonagriculture (such as manufacturing, construction, mining, trade, transportation, and services), or among several subdivisions of manufacturing. The special reference to the intersectoral wage differential is based on the recognition of its possible importance in relation to labor transfer between sectors in the course of economic development. This chapter presents Japanese data on all these six groups of wage differentials for the period of 1880 to 1940.

A conclusion drawn by L. G. Reynolds and Cynthia H. Taft from their study of wage differentials in the West may serve as an advance notice of the shape of things to expect from a study of Japanese experience. Reynolds and Taft state: "The long-run tendencies are the process of industrialization itself and the secular increase in the money wage level, both making for a shrinkage of wage differentials. Within this long-term movement, cyclical fluctuations in aggregate demand produce an alternating dilation and contraction of the wage structure." [2]

Two findings are therefore expected. (1) Since a good deal of industrialization has occurred in Japan in the last one hundred years, Japanese wage differentials should have been subject to trends of secular narrowing. (2) Since the Japanese economy is a variant of capitalism and has fluctuated from time to time, wage differentials should have been associated with general economic conditions so that they narrowed (or widened) under prosperous (or depressed) economic conditions. The tasks required to test these expectations are two: (1) collection of data on wages and construction of appropriate measures of wage differentials, and (2) demonstration of relationships between wage differentials and economic conditions. This chapter presents the results of the first task. Some of these results are shown on Chart I. The following text comments on the sources of data and methods of data handling used in making the chart, together with data and topics not shown on the chart but related to each of the major groups of wage differentials mentioned above.[3]

Intersectoral
Wage Differentials

The intersectoral wage differential is defined as the ratio of the average industrial wage to the average agricultural wage. In the data used here, "wage" refers to a daily wage rate, which until the end of the Second World War was the most widely practiced method of reckoning compensation for paid labor. The agricultural wage, which is the denominator of the intersectoral wage ratio presented here, is a simple average of the daily wage rates for male and female workers hired daily in farming and sericulture. Chart I shows two series of the intersectoral wage differential. The differences in the size and movement over time of the two series arise from different average wages used for industry. From the average daily wage rates of eight manufacturing industries which I have put together from diverse sources for the whole period under review, I have calculated two average wages for manufacturing and compared them with the agricultural wages. One of the two series of the average manufacturing wages is calculated with fixed weights (employments in different industries in 1925) for the entire period. The other series of wages is weighted with actual employments in various industries for each year. Both the industrial and the agricultural wages are smoothed by five-year moving averages before the ratio of one to the other is calculated.[4]

The two series of the intersectoral wage differential on Chart I show conflicting trends over time. This is unfortunate because, as I shall show on appropriate occasions later, trends in the prewar Japanese economy have been implicated in doctrinal controversies between different schools of thought. Those who prefer seeing something peculiar in the Japanese economy would attach greater importance to series 1-b which reveals a single increasing trend and can be taken as an indicator of increasing structural rigidities in the Japanese economy despite continued economic growth. These may be called "Structuralists." Series 1-a would be preferred by those who are more inclined to consider economic growth and market expansion as factors that in the long run equalize net advantages of alternative employment opportunities. The great reversal in this trend during the 1930s could be attributed to the extraordinary circumstances of the current depression which had very little to do with the long-run structural characteristics of the Japanese economy. Those who take this view may be called "Neoclassicists" as distinct from the "Structuralists" just mentioned. The labor market analysis presented in this book will be useful for evaluating the relative merits of the two different views.

Putting the trend aside, one should now note the existence of systematic long swings in the time series of the intersectoral wage differential. There is at least one full swing from trough to trough, 1896 to 1924, ranging over nearly thirty years. Although it is not clear from Chart I, the period of 1886 to 1896 may well have been a decreasing phase of the wage differential coinciding with improvements in general economic conditions (described in Chapter 2). This was a half swing of ten years. The swing that started in 1924 reached its peak in the mid-1930s and, in view of other data which will be introduced later in this book, in all likelihood reached its trough in 1945. This swing lasted for a period somewhat longer than twenty years. As a preview of what will be elaborated with further evidence, it may be stated at this point that the prewar wage differentials in Japan fluctuated in a manner similar to the well-known Kuznets cycles. Since the cycles in wage differentials

CHART I

JAPANESE WAGE DIFFERENTIALS, SELECTED SERIES,
1881–1940

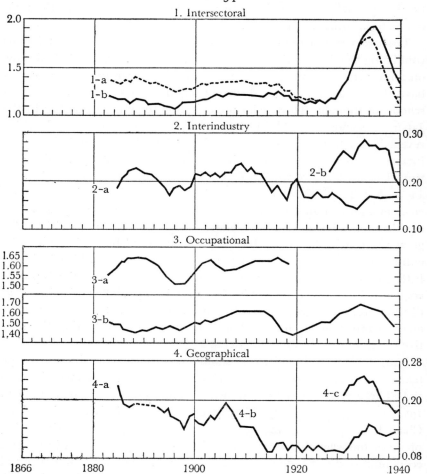

1-a. The ratio of the average daily wage rate in industry to the average daily wage rate in agriculture, when the former is an average of daily wage rates in eight manufacturing industries (see 2-a below) weighted by the constant weights which are the proportions of employment in these industries to total manufacturing employment during the decade 1920 to 1930. Scale is on the left. For further explanations please see the text. *Sources:* Ministry of Agriculture and Commerce, *Nōshōmu tōkei hyō* [*Statistics of Agriculture and Commerce*], 1882–1924; Ministry of Agriculture and Forestry, *Nōrinshō tōkei hyō* [*Statistics of the Ministry of Agriculture and Forestry*], 1925 et seq.; and Ministry of Commerce and Industry, *Shōkōshō tōkei hyō* [*Statistics of the Ministry of Commerce and Industry*], 1925 et seq.

1-b. The ratio of the average daily wage rate in industry to the average daily wage rate in agriculture, when the former is an average of daily wage rates in eight manufacturing industries weighted by the proportions of employment in these industries to total manufacturing employment in each year. Scale is on the left.

2-a. The coefficient of average deviation from the simple average of the daily wage rates in eight manufacturing industries. These are (1) textiles, (2) metals and machinery, (3) ceramics, (4) lumber and wood products, (5) printing and bookbinding, (6) food and drink, (7) chemicals, and (8) apparel and accessories. Scale is on the right. *Sources:* Same as for 1-a.

2-b. The coefficient of average deviation from the simple average of the daily earnings in eleven manufacturing industries. These are (1) textiles, (2) clothing, (3) food and drink, (4) lumber and wood products, (5) printing and bookbinding, (6) chemicals, (7) precision instruments, (8) shipbuilding, (9) machinery, (10) metals, and (11) ceramics. Scale is on the right. *Source:* Surveys of wages undertaken by the Bureau of Statistics, Prime Minister's Office, re-collected in *NKTS*, pp. 280–81.

3-a. The simple average of the ratios between the high-grade and low-grade wages in thirty-five manual occupations. Scale is on the left. *Sources:* In addition to materials listed under 1-a above, Tōyō keizai shimpō sha, *Meiji taishō kokusei sōran* [*A Comprehensive Survey of the State of the Nation during the Meiji and Taisho Periods*] (Tokyo, 1926).

3-b. The ratio between the simple average of daily wage rates for several skilled workers in building trades (such as carpenters, painters, plasterers, stone masons, shingle-roof layers, tile-roof layers, bricklayers, and paper hangers) and the daily wage rate for male common labor. Scale is on the right. *Sources:* Same as for 3-a.

4-a. The coefficient of average deviation from the simple average of the daily wage rates in forty-six prefectures. In turn, the average daily wage rate in a prefecture is a simple average of daily wage rates for all the non-agricultural manual occupations reported for that prefecture in the source materials used. Scale is on the right. *Source: NTN*, 1885–1900.

4-b. The coefficient of average deviation from the simple average of the daily wage rates in thirteen cities. The daily wage rate in a city is a simple average of the daily wage rates for all the occupations reported for that city. Scale is on the right. *Source:* Ministry of Commerce and Industry, *Chingin tōkei hyō* [*Statistics of Wages*], 1930, 1933–1939.

4-c. The coefficient of average deviation from the simple average of hourly factory earnings in forty-six prefectures. Scale is on the right. *Source: KTH*, 1929–1942.

are inversely associated with those in economic conditions, the pattern of the time series of wage differentials suggests that there should have been authentic Kuznets cycles in Japanese economic history. This "prediction" will be discussed further in Chapter 2.

Using the same sources as those I have been using, but processing them differently, Mataji Umemura has calculated average industrial and agricultural wage rates for male and female workers separately. Table 2 summarizes the results he has obtained. I have inverted Umemura's ratios of agricultural to industrial wages to meet my definition of the intersectoral wage differential. The male wage differential shows rather neat Kuznets-type variations, supporting my observa-

TABLE 2

UMEMURA'S INTERSECTORAL WAGE DIFFERENTIAL,
SELECTED YEARS, 1880–1939

Male			Female		
Cycle Position	Date	Differential	Cycle Position	Date	Differential
...a	1880	109.1	...a	1882	114.2
Peak	1885	146.7	...b	1894	109.0
Trough	1898	124.1	Trough	1905	86.4
Peak	1909	149.0	Peak	1915	114.2
Trough	1923	124.3	Trough	1925	77.8
Peak	1934	238.0	Peak	1932	116.3
...c	1939	148.6	...c	1939	75.3

Source: Mataji Umemura, Chingin, koyō, nōgyō [Wages, Employment, and Agriculture] (Tokyo: Daimeido, 1961), pp. 193–95.
a Initial dates in Umemura's time series.
b No corresponding peak is observable for female wages.
c Final dates in Umemura's time series for the prewar period.

tions based on Chart I. Umemura's female wage differential has two characteristics that differ from the male wage differential and from my intersectoral wage differential with male and female wages taken together. First, swings prior to 1920 in the female wage differential are not synchronized with those in the male wage differential. Second, there were times when female wages in industry actually sank below those in agriculture. This is certainly an extraordinary fact to observe in a growing economy which has succeeded in transferring a good deal of the female labor force from agriculture to industry. This enigma and its consequences call for several chapters for a full treatment, analytical as well as institutional, although I have been able to devote only an equivalent of two chapters to the problem in this book.

Although not shown on the chart, there are data that indicate an interesting relationship between wages for agricultural employment of long-term nature (contracted for a full year or more) and wages for agricultural workers hired on a day-to-day basis. Table 3 shows this relationship. The series that runs from 1928 to 1945 is based on daily

TABLE 3

WAGE DIFFERENTIALS BETWEEN ANNUAL EMPLOYMENT
AND DAY LABOR IN AGRICULTURE,
SELECTED YEARS, 1886–1945

Year	Series A[a] (Times)	Year	Series B[b] (Percent)
1886	126	1928	56
1888	132	1930	55
1892	120	1936	59
1895	124	1939	57
1900	99	1943	62
1912	115	1945	51
1918	102		

Sources: Same as for Chart I. (See pp. 16–17.)

[a] Ratios of annual wages for annual employment to daily wages for day labor.

[b] Ratios of daily equivalents of annual wages for annual employment to daily wages for day labor.

equivalents of annual wages; the one that runs from 1886 to 1918 is based on the annual wages themselves. In the 1880s and 1890s annual wages decreased from the equivalent of 130 days of daily wages to only 100 days. They increased relatively between 1900 and 1910 but were back again on the low level by 1920.

The source materials I have been using do not show how annual wages were converted to their daily equivalents during the period from the mid-1920s to the mid-1940s, so that the size of the annual-daily differential in the latter period cannot be compared with the size in the earlier period. But some rough estimates can be ventured by multiplying the absolute level of the differential in the latter period by an estimated number of working days in agriculture. It is estimated that the working days in agriculture per year are about 60 percent of those in industry.[5] If so, the working days in agriculture are about 180 days per year. The annual-daily wage differential in the period of 1928 to 1945 averages 0.58, which, when multiplied by 180, is equivalent to 103. The annual wages equivalent to 103 days of daily wages are among the lowest in the years prior to 1920. In short, wages for long-term farm employment have tended to decrease relative to those for day-to-day employment in the course of Japanese economic development.

Incidentally, this observation presents an interesting contrast to the historical trend in the wage differentials between long-term and short-term farm employments during the pre-industrial period as discovered by T. C. Smith.[6] During most of the hundred-year period from 1718 to 1820, the average annual wages of farm servants hired on an annual basis did not increase as rapidly as wages of servants contracted for longer periods, although wages of the former were always higher than those of the latter in absolute terms. Moreover, according to Smith, there was a decided shift in agricultural employment from long-term to short-term service in the eighteenth and nineteenth centuries. One explanation may well be that there was a shift in the servants' preferences from long-term to short-term employment, while the employers' preferences for long-term employment relationships remained constant. It is remarkable that during the depth of Japan's "feudalism" something akin to the labor market was already at work. The inverse association between wage increases and employment expansion implied in Smith's data has occurred frequently during Japan's modern period, as this book will show. This relationship is almost the "karma" of the Japanese economy whose transformations through time have spelled a neoclassical course of economic development for Japan.

Interindustry
Wage Differentials

The measure of wage differentials among several industries commonly used is dispersion. For my purpose, I have adopted what may be called "coefficient of average deviation," which is the average of the absolute values of deviations from the mean as a percentage of the mean.[7] As can be seen from Chart I, variations in the interindustry wage rate dispersions are similar to those in the intersectoral wage differentials. But the similarity holds only up to a point, and that point is the middle of the 1920s. The interindustry wage rate dispersion shows a marked decrease between 1927 and 1931, when most of the other differentials are found to be increasing. On the other hand, this peculiar behavior of the wage rate dispersion in the early 1930s is contradicted by that of the earnings dispersion (Chart I, series 2-b), which increases distinctly between 1926 and 1933 and decreases in the rest of the 1930s and early 1940s.

The inconsistency of the dispersion of rates and the dispersion of earnings during the 1930s is rather puzzling. The compression of wage rates is also at variance with the behavior of the wage-rate differential between the highest-wage and lowest-wage industries in the same period. What occurred, at least statistically, was a marked reduction of rate differentials among all other industries, overriding the divergence between metal (highest) and textile (lowest) wage rates.

The evidence of a widening of interindustry *earnings* differentials during the early 1930s and a subsequent narrowing is overwhelming. Using data on the average hourly factory earnings in *Kōjō tōkei hyō* [*Factory Statistics*], Miyohei Shinohara discovered that among nine subdivisions of manufacturing there was an inverse association of rates of change in hourly earnings for the period 1929 to 1932, during which wages decreased in all industries, with rates of change for the period 1932 to 1937, during which wages increased in most industries. He also found that wages decreased proportionately more in low-wage than in high-wage industries during 1929–1932, resulting in a widening of interindustry wage differentials, and increased proportionately more in the former than in the latter during 1932–1937, resulting in a narrowing of differentials.[8]

Limited data are available on the earnings of some major divisions of economic activities, such as manufacturing, mining, construction, utilities, and transportation.[9] The earnings dispersion among these five divisions shows a distinct increase between 1928 and 1932 (from 10.5 to 17.9) and an equally distinct decrease between 1932 and 1940 (from 17.9 to 9.5).

It might be pointed out at this time that the peculiar narrowing of the interindustry wage rate dispersion (series 2-a) between 1927 and 1931, during which period it should have widened, is not without a parallel in the experience of other countries. D. E. Cullen's examination of the interindustry wage structure for manufacturing in the United States showed an unexpected *decrease* in the interindustry wage dispersion (interquartile range as a percentage of the median in this case) between 1927 and 1935. In this connection Cullen observes: "In spite of the several apparent inconsistencies in the cyclical variations of this [inter-industry] wage structure, a generalization might still be hazarded that inter-industry wage differentials have tended to narrow during periods of prolonged full employment . . . and periods of very severe unemployment. . . ." [10] That wage differentials tend to narrow during prosperity is theoretically to be expected. That they also tend to narrow during a depression of a special kind is something for which theoretical justification is not immediately clear. However, in the case of Japanese interindustry wage differentials during the early thirties, it is not necessary to go so far in generalization as Cullen did in relation to differentials in the United States.

In order to use a measure of dispersion as a measure of wage differentials, so that we may identify an increase or a decrease in dispersion with the widening or narrowing of wage differentials, it is necessary to show that the ranking of various industries by the level of wages is stable over time. For if the relative positions of industries change so radically that the high-wage industries of one time became low-wage industries of another, a measure of dispersion alone will be a poor guide to the understanding of the nature of change in the interindustry wage differentials. The stability or instability of the interindustry wage structure can be tested by the method of rank correlation, comparing the ranks at one time with those at another, and expressing the degree of disturbance in ranking by the coefficients of rank correlation. By selecting the intervals marked by the turning points in the time series of interindustry dispersion in Chart I, the rank correlation coefficients shown in Table 4 have been obtained. Generously

TABLE 4

RANK CORRELATION COEFFICIENTS
FOR EIGHT MANUFACTURING INDUSTRIES,
SELECTED PAIRS OF YEARS, 1885–1939

1885 and 1888	0.963	1885–1888 average	
1888 and 1895	0.572	and	1895	0.788
1895 and 1909	0.715	or	1909	0.643
1909 and 1922	0.572	or	1922	0.785
1922 and 1932	0.785	or	1932	0.572
1932 and 1939	0.715	or	1939	0.500

Note: The rank correlation coefficients are calculated by M. G. Kendall's method, in his *Rank Correlation Methods* (London: Charles Griffin, 1948). The lowest coefficient among the above (0.500) is acceptable at a little more than 10 percent level of probability, and the next lowest (0.572) at a 7 percent level.

interpreted, these coefficients indicate the stability of the ranking of industries over time. When the rankings of the eight manufacturing industries for selected years are compared with their ranking during the initial years (Table 4, Col. 4), the rank correlation coefficient tends to decrease as the period of comparison lengthens. This suggests that the relative positions of various industries increasingly changed over time.

Occupational
Wage Differentials

Occupational wage differentials are usually related to skill differences, although there are difficulties in measuring the work content of different occupations by a single scale of skill. There are also differences in skill within each occupation. From the point of view of a potential worker on the threshold of entrance into the labor force, the interoccupational skill differences may be more important. But from the point of view of a worker already engaged in a given trade, the question whether he should strive to improve himself in that trade might be just as important a question as whether he should change his trade. In other words, the skill difference has intra- as well as interoccupational dimensions.

On the intraoccupational dimensions, the Japanese Government collected wage rates for three grades of labor (high, average, and low) in each of more than thirty manual occupations during the period of 1881 to 1920. I took the ratio of "high-grade" to "low-grade" wage rates in each occupation and averaged these ratios over all occupations with a view to showing the behavior of the average intraoccupational skill margins over time. According to series 3-a, Chart I, the high-grade low-grade wage differential widens in the 1880s, narrows in the 1890s, and widens again in the early 1900s. The pattern of fluctuation thus far conforms to that of the other differentials. The subsequent movement of this differential seems to be somewhat out of line. On the whole this differential fluctuates within narrow limits (the highest being 164 and the lowest 150), so that one may conclude that the margins of excellence in these manual trades remained roughly constant over time.

A common example of occupational wage differentials is the skilled-unskilled wage differential in the building trades. Series 3-b, Chart I, shows this differential. One peculiarity of this series is the narrowing that took place in the 1880s, when most other wage differentials tended to widen. During the rest of the period under consideration it behaved much the same way, widening in the 1900s, narrowing in the 1910s, widening in the 1920s, and narrowing in the 1930s.

The wage differential between office and manual workers in manufacturing establishments is another interesting type of occupational wage differential. Data are available only for government-owned factories. Table 5 summarizes the time series of the office-manual wage differential calculated from the available data, together with another type of occupational wage differential. A distinctive feature of the office-manual wage differential is its marked diminution from 1884 to 1925.

TABLE 5

OCCUPATIONAL WAGE DIFFERENTIALS,
OFFICE-MANUAL AND TEXTILES-DOMESTICS,
SELECTED YEARS, 1883–1932[a]

(PERCENT)

Year[b]	Office-Manual Differential[c]	Textiles-Domestics Differential[d]
1883	. . .	226
1887	340	255 (Peak)
1892	255	234 (Trough)
1897	243 (Trough)	247
1899	261 (Peak)	250 (Peak)
1906	234 (Trough)	214
1910	255	194 (Trough)
1914	291 (Peak)	209
1917	262	225 (Peak)
1922	177	182 (Trough)
1932	. . .	200

[a] Differential is the ratio of higher to lower wages.

[b] Years are selected, except for the initial and terminal dates, by the occurrences of peaks or troughs in one or both of the time series shown here.

[c] Based on annual earnings in government-owned factories calculated from NTN for relevant years.

[d] Based on the daily wage rate of the textile industry and the daily equivalent of the monthly rate in domestic service. The sources are the same as those mentioned in relation to intersectoral wage differentials.

Another example of occupational wage differentials is the differential between the textile factory operative and the domestic servant, which can be obtained for the period 1881 to 1933. During this period the differential measured by the ratio of textile to domestic wages decreased from 250 percent of the 1880s to 190 percent of the 1920s. The decline in this differential over time, indicating the relative rise in the attractiveness of domestic service, accords with the long-run trends in some other wage differentials. But what seems to be of historical and international importance is that the wages of domestic servants were still markedly inferior to those of textile factory operatives in Japan during the 1920s. According to Colin Clark's data,[11] domestic wages in the twentieth century have always been higher in Australia, England, and the United States. But if we move sufficiently back in time, we find in England that domestic wages began to overtake factory wages around 1880 and that back in seventeenth-century England the ordinary laborer was paid two and a half times as much as the male servant. From these figures it can be inferred that the improvement of the domestics' position relative to other kinds of labor is intimately related to social and economic progress. The gross inferiority of the domestics' position in Japan might therefore be regarded as part of Japan's relative backwardness.

Geographical
Wage Differentials

Other wage differentials for which time series over a long stretch of time are available are the geographical. I have calculated the average wage rates for prefectures for the period 1885 to 1900 based on the prefectural reports on wage rates on key jobs in representative establishments, and the average wage rates for thirteen major cities for the period 1900 to 1939 from similar wage data reported for these cities. The thirteen cities are widely scattered over Japan in a manner representative of various parts of Japan. From north to south, they are Otaru, Nigata, Sendai, Tokyo, Yokohama, Nagoya, Kanazawa, Kyoto, Osaka, Kobe, Kochi, Hiroshima, and Fukuoka. Prefectural average hourly earnings for the period 1929 to 1942 are available from the *Factory Statistics* of the Ministry of Commerce and Industry. From these data I obtained the coefficients of average deviation as indicators of geographical wage differentials (see Chart I, series 4-a, 4-b, and 4-c).

The prefectural dispersion of wages decreased between 1885 and 1898 and increased from 1898 to 1900. The intercity dispersion of wages increased from 1900 to 1906, decreased from 1906 to 1914, remained at about the 1914 level for the next fifteen years, increased from 1929 to 1934, and decreased during the remainder of the 1930s. The intercity dispersion of wages was larger in the 1930s than in the 1910s and 1920s, but smaller than in the 1900s. From this information it is seen that the geographical wage differentials narrowed during the first four decades of this century. Moreover, the prefectural wage differentials decreased in the 1880s and 1890s. From the joint consideration of the decrease in the prefectural wage differentials in the nineteenth century and the decrease in the intercity wage differentials in the decades of the twentieth century prior to 1940, it may be said that the Japanese geographical wage differentials narrowed over the course of nearly six decades up to 1940. This suggests that the process of wage equalization among geographical areas proceeded rather steadily over several decades in Japan. The fluctuations in the intercity dispersion of wage rates during the 1930s are confirmed by those in the prefectural dispersion of factory earnings, which also indicates an increase in the early 1930s and a decrease in the rest of the decade.

Since I have been using a measure of dispersion as a measure of wage differentials, the question of the positions of various prefectures or cities relative to one another still remains to be clarified. The disturbances in the rankings of prefectures or cities by the level of wages over time have not been great enough to invalidate the assumption of the stability of the geographical wage structure over time. The rank correlation coefficients (according to Kendall's method)[12] between the rankings of prefectures or cities for several paired years are significant at a 1 percent level of probability in most cases and at a 5 percent level in the worst cases, as for cities between 1900 and 1939. The pairing of years for the comparison of ranks of prefectures or of cities is done according to the turning points in series 4, Chart I. The coefficients of rank correlation are as follows:

	Prefectures			*Cities*	
1886–1887 : 1896–1900	0.495		1900 : 1906	0.693
1896 : 1929	0.526		1906 : 1914	0.693
1929 : 1933	0.670		1914 : 1922	0.513
1933 : 1942	0.584		1922 : 1929	0.718
			1929 : 1934	0.564
			1934 : 1939	0.820
			1900 : 1939	0.462

Although the significance test of rank correlation does not negate the long-run stability of the geographical wage structure, the decrease in rank correlation over time indicates that the longer the period, the more frequently transpositions tend to occur in the ranking of various areas. Because of the joint occurrence of the decrease in the geographical dispersion of wages and the changes in the ranking of various areas by wage level, the geographical equalization of wages over time must have been more extensive than suggested by the measure of dispersion or the rank correlation alone.

It is of some interest to note at this point that in 1886 the national and private railroads were not so extensive as they are today. According to a well-known historical atlas,[13] there were some railroads sprawling about in the prefecture of Fukuoka, but they did not extend to the south into less developed parts of Kyushu. In Honshu a railroad started somewhere near the end of the prefecture of Yamaguchi and carried passengers as far east as Osaka. The Tokyo-Osaka route was just being completed but was not yet in good condition in the vicinity of Osaka. On the other hand, the whole route in the northeastern part of Honshu from Tokyo to Aomori had been completed by 1886. Isolated beginnings had also been made in Hokkaido at various points. By 1900 the trunk line from Tokyo to Shimonoseki had been completed, while the road which started from Moji extended as far south as Kumamoto. There was still no railroad to the south of Kumamoto. By the end of the Russo-Japanese War (1904–1905), however, the whole line had been completed from Kagoshima on the southern end of Kyushu to Aomori on the northern end of Honshu.

When one reflects upon the enormous difficulties which must have attended geographical movements in the nineteenth century, it does not seem strange that the subsequent development of transportation facilities should have reduced the geographical wage differentials that had obtained in the earlier years of modern Japan.

Personal
Wage Differentials

Differences in the wages that individual workers receive arise in part from natural and social differences in personal attributes, such as ability, aptitude, age, appearance, education, nationality, race, sex, status, and the like. There are customary rules, peculiar to a given economy or common to many economies, that provide at least some basis for determining an average price for the given complex of personal attributes with which a worker presents himself for employment. A full appreciation of the nature and magnitude of problems which arise from the peculiarities of these rules is impossible without extensive inquiries into the cultural, social, and economic factors that make one person more or less valuable than another. But I cannot go beyond an observation of changes in the undifferentiated effects of all these factors.

The distribution of workers on some scale that measures the economic desirability of given bundles of personal attributes embodied in various individuals can be represented by some kind of frequency distribution. The distribution of workers by size of wages they receive is a convenient summary of the net effect of all kinds of personal attributes and their economic values. These distributions are available for 1924, 1927, 1933, and 1939. I have calculated the degree of dispersion for each of these years by the difference between the first and ninth deciles as a percentage of the median. The results are tabulated in Table 6, which indicates that the dispersion of wages increased from 1924 to 1933 but decreased from 1933 to 1939.

Chotaro Takahashi has investigated variations in the dispersion of wages over time as part of his broader project of research into income distribution in Japan. His findings are similar to mine for the years 1924, 1927, and 1933. On the increase in the dispersion of wages between 1924 and 1933, Takahashi notes:

> . . . since the inequality of wage rates increased remarkably in 1933, the year of depression in Japan, it may be possible to say in general that the wage distribution becomes more equal in boom and more unequal in depression, though the evidence is not complete. Furthermore, increased inequality of female wage rates was clearly observed in 1933, but the sensitivity of the inequality of the female wage distribution to business cycles, it must be noticed, is less than that of the male equivalent.[14]

Takahashi is right about the relationship between personal wage distribution and business cycles. Table 6, however, does not particularly indicate greater cyclical sensitivity of male wages than female wages. If

TABLE 6

DISPERSION OF EARNINGS, BY SEX,
SELECTED YEARS, 1924–1939[a]

(PERCENT)

Year	All Workers	Male	Female
1924[b]	194	123	106
1927[b]	203	128	110
1933[b]	279	151	138
1939[c]	185	132	80

[a] The measure of dispersion is the range between the first and ninth deciles as a percentage of the median.

[b] RTJCH (1924, 1927, 1933). These reports cover male and female workers in establishments employing 30 or more workers, with exceptions of a few industries for which establishments with 300 or more, 100 or more, or 15 or more were surveyed.

[c] Average hourly earnings in manufacturing (Ministry of Welfare, Rōdōsha chingin chōsa hōkoku [Investigation of Wages], 1939), covering experienced workers in establishments employing 10 or more workers.

anything, the reverse seems to be the case. The logic of labor supply would also suggest the reverse, that is, greater sensitivity of female wages to economic conditions.

The wage differential between male and female workers is a species of personal wage differential in which one personal attribute, sex, plays a central role. Table 7 summarizes three kinds of male-female wage differentials. The male-female wage differential in agriculture remained roughly stable at the level of 170 percent preceding the First World War, but decreased to a little over 130 percent from 1916 to 1922. The male-female wage differential has remained undisturbed ever since at this lower level. The male-female earnings differential in factories was stable at the level of more than 200 percent preceding the First World War, decreased during the war, but increased to a phenomenal height

TABLE 7

MALE-FEMALE WAGE DIFFERENTIALS IN AGRICULTURE,
MANUFACTURING, AND DOMESTIC SERVICE,
SELECTED YEARS, 1883–1940[a]

(PERCENT)

Year[b]	Agriculture[c]	Manufacturing[d]	Domestic Service[e]
1883	165	...	175
1887	169 (Peak)	...	192
1888	168	...	193 (Peak)
1896	164 (Trough)	...	179
1901	177	...	163 (Trough)
1902	178 (Peak)	204	172
1905	171	205	172 (Peak)
1911	167	206	150 (Trough)
1913	165	208 (Peak)	155
1915	166	207	159 (Peak)
1920	150	186 (Trough)	142
1928	132 (Trough)	225	129
1933	135	294	...
1935	134	304 (Peak)	...
1940	131	273	...

[a] Differential is a ratio of male to female wages or earnings.
[b] Selected, except for initial and terminal dates, by the occurrences of peaks or troughs in one or more of the time series.
[c] Based on daily wage rates.
[d] Based on factory earnings.
[e] Based on monthly wage rates.

of 300 percent in 1935. It then decreased, but even so stood at the level of 273 percent in 1940. The male-female wage differential in domestic service showed a secular narrowing from around 190 percent to 130 percent during the period 1881 to 1933.

Interfirm
Wage Differentials

Just as differences in the personal attributes of workers give rise to a frequency distribution of workers by wages they command, differences in the characteristics of firms or establishments with respect to efficiency, experience, credit standing, and so on, are reflected in differences in the wages they pay. Data on the frequency distribution of factories by the level of wages (average wage bill per worker) are available for the period 1919 to 1927 in *Factory Statistics,* first published by the Ministry of Agriculture and Commerce and later by the Ministry of Commerce and Industry. Table 8 presents the coefficients of interfactory dispersion of wages based on this source.

TABLE 8

INTERFACTORY DISPERSION OF WAGES, BY SEX, 1919–1927[a]

(PERCENT)

Year	Male	Female
1919	74	83
1920	77	82
1921	98	84
1922	97	79
1923	94	74
1924	93	78
1925	92	76
1926	95	74
1927	96	78

[a] Based on the total wage bill per worker per day in factories with five or more operatives. The measure of dispersion is the first–ninth decile range as a percentage of the median.

The changes in dispersion of wages for male workers between 1919 and 1921 in Table 8 are somewhat puzzling, but the dispersion of wages for both male and female workers after 1921 behaves in much the same way as the other wage differentials that have been considered in previous sections, decreasing till the middle of the 1920s and increasing thereafter.

There is a special kind of interfirm wage differential which is of considerable significance, namely, wage differentials by size of firm. In many countries large firms tend to pay higher wages than small ones, although the sizes of the differentials vary from country to country. In Japan, after the Second World War, these interfirm wage differentials in manufacturing have been so large by international comparison that they are often attributed to some peculiarly Japanese socioeconomic forces. This subject is discussed in Chapter 7 and is also referred to on a number of occasions in other chapters.

Some aspects of wage differentials by size of firm or establishment can be illustrated by different wage data which are collected from different groups of firms or establishments. There are three representative sets of wage data for prewar Japan, collected by different methods and concepts for different purposes. First, I have been using the data of the Ministry of Agriculture and Commerce (1882–1925), which was succeeded by the Ministry of Agriculture and Forestry and the Ministry of Commerce and Industry.[15] These data cover key jobs in "representative" firms or establishments in each industry, or "representative" villages in each prefecture in the case of agriculture. The ministries determined the industrial and occupational categories to be investigated and the elements to be included in a daily wage, but left the selection of firms, establishments, or villages to the prefectural governments, chambers of commerce and industry, or agricultural associations. It is impossible to know what criteria the local data-collecting agencies used in selecting the "representative" firms or villages. The intent of these wage surveys was to obtain a general notion of the daily wage *rate* at which the ordinary worker on a given job was being paid. In other words, the motivation was a price concept of wages. The average industrial wage rates that emerge from these sources are shown in the second column of Table 9. (This series is the same as the series of the average industrial wage rates with variable weights assigned to eight subdivisions of manufacturing as previously mentioned in relation to the intersectoral wage differentials.)

Second, there are data on factory *earnings* covering manufacturing establishments obtained by adding the wages bills of all the reporting units and dividing the sum by total man-days. The representative sources are *Factory Statistics* and *Census of Manufacturing* (abbreviated *KTH* from their Japanese titles hereafter), covering establishments with five or more operatives. This series of data began in 1909. It was in-

TABLE 9

WAGE RATES AND EARNINGS FROM THREE DIFFERENT SOURCES, SELECTED YEARS, 1902–1940

| Year | Money Values in Yen[a] | | Earnings in Large Factories[d] (3) |
	Factory Earnings[b] (1)	Average Wage Rate[c] (2)	
1902	0.27	0.30	...
1908	0.32	0.39	...
1916	0.47	0.56	...
1920	1.13	1.29	...
1925	1.35	1.62	1.75
1930	1.22	1.46	1.98
1932	1.16	1.40	1.90
1937	1.35	1.79	1.92
1940	1.75	...	2.11

[a] Five-year moving averages.

[b] Earnings in factories with five or more operatives, calculated from Tohata and Ohkawa, eds., *Nihon no keizai to nōgyō* [*The Japanese Economy and Agriculture*] (Tokyo: Iwanami shoten, 1956), I, 197.

[c] Weighted average of wage rates of eight manufacturing industries. For sources, see Chart I, notes 1 and 2.

[d] Earnings in factories with fifty or more operatives. Data collected by the Bureau of Statistics, Prime Minister's Office, quoted in *CKC*, p. 1274. This series began in 1923.

tended to be quinquennial but became annual beginning in 1919. Kazushi Ohkawa has estimated average daily earnings for male and female workers separately from factory statistics and other interim reports of the government for the period of 1900 to 1945.[16] From his estimates, the weighted average daily earnings of the factory worker can be obtained. This series of earnings is shown in Column 1 of Table 9.

Third, there are data on average daily earnings covering establishments with fifty or more workers collected by the Bureau of Statistics, Prime Minister's Office, for the period of 1923 to 1941. This series of earnings is shown in the third column of Table 9.

As may be seen from this table, in the period that is common to the three wage series the average wage rate is higher than the average earnings in factories with five or more operatives. It is lower than the average earnings in factories with fifty or more workers. This ranking of the three kinds of wages is understandable, for it can be regarded as corresponding to the differences in pay in large, medium, and small factories. Especially relevant to the question of interfirm wage differentials is the relationship between the first and third columns, according to which the earnings differential between the large and small factories widened in the late 1920s and early 1930s, but narrowed in the rest of the 1930s.

Konosuke Odaka presents an interesting kind of interfirm wage differentials. He compares wages in two large firms in Northern Kyushu with market wages in the same area for comparable occupations. The firms used for the purpose are the Yawata Iron and Steel Works and the Mitsubishi Shipbuilding Yard in Nagasaki. Relative wages in these firms decreased during the first two decades of the century but turned up at the end of the First World War, continuing to outpace the market wages in the 1920s and 1930s. The movements of wage differentials between large firms and the labor market in the North Kyushu industrial area were thus part of what was happening in the whole economy.[17]

Conclusion

The profile of the Japanese wage structure preceding the Second World War painted in this chapter does not permit any strong general statement about the trend for the entire period. Evidently, one epoch which started in the 1880s came to an end in the 1920s. During the forty-year period from 1885 to 1925 there were trends toward narrowing in most of the wage differentials examined in this chapter. The economic crises and a major crisis during the period of 1925 to 1935 reversed these trends, bringing about an unprecedented widening in many wage differentials. How to interpret this event is an unresolved issue which divides "Structuralists" and "Neoclassicists." Any period can claim its historical individuality, but in terms of the general logic of economic process, there seems to be no compelling reason to treat the interwar period as a structurally different stage in Japanese economic development. I hope to offer a balanced argument on this point in Part II.

As for variations in wage differentials, the general picture becomes clearer than that of trends. Here one can speak, with reasonable confidence, of the dominant pattern of variations, and specify exceptions to the rule. Exceptions are fewer than the cases that fall into line with the dominant pattern. In ascertaining the latter, one might apply a rough majority rule, decade after decade, to the group of wage differentials reviewed in this chapter, to be able to say that wage differentials *on the whole* widened during some periods and narrowed during others. By this rule, the following periodization of variations in Japanese wage differentials arises:

1881–1886 (5 years): widening
1886–1896 (10 years): narrowing
1896–1910 (14 years): widening (with some intraperiod variations in several wage differentials)
1910–1924 (14 years): narrowing
1924–1934 (10 years): widening
1934–1946 (12 years): narrowing

The foregoing periodization suggests an interesting point. The hypothesis that relates economic conditions and wage differentials states that the narrowing of wage differentials is associated with prosperous economic conditions and the widening with depressed conditions. One now knows how wage differentials behaved over a period of time in prewar Japan. This knowledge, through the medium of the hypothesis mentioned, leads to a "prediction" of similar variations in general economic conditions in prewar Japan. This is the task to which I devote the next chapter.

2   Wage Differentials and Economic Conditions

THIS CHAPTER CONSISTS of three sections. In the first section, the validity of the hypothesis that variations in wage differentials are systematically associated with those in economic conditions is tested. In the second section, interrelationships among several economic variables are explored with a view to sketching the functioning of the Japanese economy during its fluctuating growth prior to the Second World War. In the third section, the behavior of wage differentials is discussed in relation to the level of wages and relative factor prices.

Economic Conditions[1]

Chart II shows some of the representative time series adjusted for their respective trends. There are long swings as well as short fluctuations in these series. One would have to strain one's eyes to detect long cycles in some series, however. For example, it is difficult to see long cycles in the midst of saw-toothed fluctuations of the national income and output series in earlier years. Nevertheless, one would notice that the movements of the two series are upward during the 1880s and the 1890s and downward during the first decade of this century. It may not be wide of the mark to say that the early sections of the income and output series (the first two series in Chart II) contain a Kuznets cycle running from the trough of 1889, through the peak of 1898, to the trough of 1910. This is a cycle twenty-one years in length. The trend-adjusted series of the real per capita national income (series 1) after 1910 shows a rather clear Kuznets cycle running, say, from 1910 to 1931, that is, for another twenty-one years. However, the real national output per

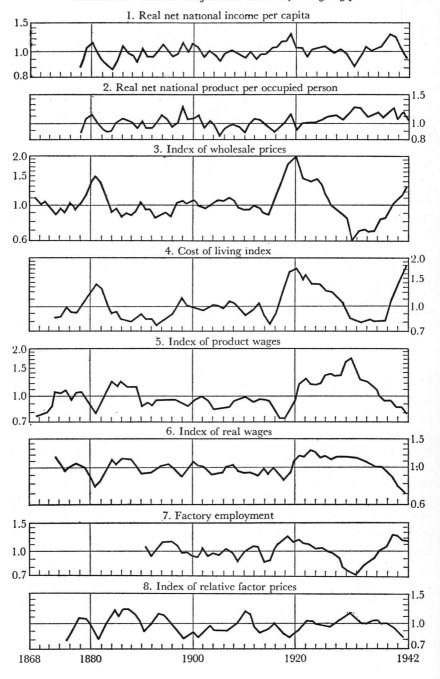

CHART II: INDICATORS OF JAPANESE ECONOMIC CONDITIONS,
SELECTED TREND-ADJUSTED SERIES, 1869-1942

1. Real net national income per capita

2. Real net national product per occupied person

3. Index of wholesale prices

4. Cost of living index

5. Index of product wages

6. Index of real wages

7. Factory employment

8. Index of relative factor prices

1868   1880   1900   1920   1942

gainfully occupied person (series 2) does not show a similar cycle after 1910. It even seems to suggest an inverse swing between 1920 and 1930 in comparison with variations in the first series of Chart II.

The wholesale price index and the index of the cost of living show two periods of extraordinary increases and decreases. The length of time surrounding each peak in these series is similar to that of a Kuznets cycle. For example, one cycle in the wholesale price index around the peak of 1881 lasted fifteen years from trough to trough; another cycle in the same series, centering around the peak of 1920, lasted sixteen years. Between the end of the earlier cycle (1888) and the beginning of the later cycle (1915) there are no clear Kuznets cycles either in the wholesale price index or in the cost-of-living index. However, considering that both these series tended to increase faster during the 1890s and more slowly from 1905 to 1915 than their long-run trend

---

NOTES TO CHART II

Most of the time series used for this chart, unless otherwise specified, are from *GROJES*. Trend was fitted to each series by the least squares method for the entire prewar period ending in 1942 wherever possible. Where more than one trend were applicable, it is mentioned under appropriate headings below.

1. Real net national income per capita, that is, net national product per head of population deflated by the cost-of-living index.

2. Real net national product per gainfully employed person, that is, net national product per gainfully employed person deflated by the index of wholesale prices.

3. The index of wholesale prices. No trend prior to 1885, secular rise after 1885.

4. The cost-of-living index.

5. The index of product wages, that is, money wages deflated by the index of wholesale prices.

6. The index of real wages, that is, money wages deflated by the cost-of-living index. Downward trend up to 1895 and upward trend thereafter.

7. Factory employment. Two series are available, one referring to employment in factories with ten or more workers for the period of 1889 to 1920, and another to employment in factories with five or more workers for the period of 1909 to 1942. Earlier employment figures were estimated from various issues of *NTN* and *Nihon teikoku tōkei zensho* (Collection of the Statistics of the Empire of Japan), 1928, p. 50. Factory employment for later years is from *KTH*. Trend was fitted to the two series separately and deviations from trend were averaged over the overlapping years.

8. The index of relative factor prices, that is, the index of product wages (see 5 above) divided by the series of interest rates on short-term bank loans in Tokyo. Data on the latter are from *NKTS*, pp. 214–15.

rates of increase, one might regard the period of 1890 to 1915 as one swing in series 3 and 4 of Chart II.

While trend-adjusted annual data on output and prices do not readily suggest clear-cut Kuznets cycles, further adjustments of the data might, in some manner, produce such cycles. Noting that the national income series estimated by Ohkawa does not produce Kuznets cycles when deflated by the wholesale price index (as shown by series 2, Chart II) while the cost-of-living index is more helpful for that purpose (as shown by series 1, Chart II), Miyohei Shinohara constructs his own national income deflator by averaging the two indices with a greater weight assigned to the cost-of-living index (7 against 3 for the wholesale price index). Average annual rates of increase in the successive five-year averages of national income figures deflated by this deflator show clear-cut Kuznets cycles.[2] Ohkawa and Rosovsky identify long swings by smoothing the annual series with a seven-year moving average and then computing the growth rates in overlapping seven-year intervals.[3]

A disturbing fact is that the dating of turning points in the Kuznets cycles strictly depends on the method used for the detection of these cycles. For example, the turning points in the trend-adjusted series come after those in the rates of change in the same series. When the successive averages over a specified number of years are used (as is done by Shinohara), the cycle dates will have to be the midpoints of the arbitrarily chosen intervals. The peaks and troughs of these cycles also have different economic contents depending on different methods. The peaks in the rates of change indicate that the economic activities are being most accelerated but have not yet reached their absolute maxima, which would have been the peaks if some other method of cycle identification had been used. However, these are details that have to be borne in mind only in interpreting the economic conditions corresponding to different phases of the cycles.

With the aid of findings of other students of the Japanese long cycles, such as mentioned above, and keeping in mind that the "cycles" relevant to the method of this chapter are in terms of deviations from long-run trends of various economic indicators (not in rates of change), one might propose that Japanese economic conditions preceding the Second World War were broadly subject to Kuznets cycles according to the following periodization:

I {	1875–1881	Upswing, 6 years
	1881–1892	Downswing, 11 years
II {	1892–1900	Upswing, 8 years
	1900–1914	Downswing, 14 years
III {	1914–1920	Upswing, 6 years
	1920–1932	Downswing, 12 years
IV {	1932–1938	Upswing, 6 years
	1938–1945 (conjectural)	Downswing, 7 years

The periodization of the Japanese Kuznets cycles shown above roughly corresponds to that of cycles in Japanese wage differentials previously shown. After the price inflation was checked in 1881, the 1880s were a generally depressed period. Although there was a sharp recovery in 1886, it was not sustained for long. The widening of wage differentials in the 1880s took place against the background of this generally depressed state of the economy.[4] Most time series in Chart II suggest that the 1890s were a period of considerable prosperity, while a good part of the 1900s was comparatively quiet. Wage differentials significantly narrowed during the 1890s and widened during the 1900s.[5] The strong boom reaching its peak in 1920 was no doubt due in large part to the First World War. After a severe crisis in 1920–1921, the Japanese economy inched forward in protracted stagnation throughout the 1920s, eventuating in the severe slump of 1932. Following, though with lags, the transition of economic conditions during the 1910s and 1920s, wage differentials narrowed during the 1910s and early 1920s, but began to widen around 1925. The recovery of economic conditions after 1931 again accompanied, with lags, the narrowing of wage differentials.

The Behavior of the Japanese Economy

In addition to showing the relationships between wage differentials and general economic conditions, the time series in Chart II also suggest interesting interrelations among major variables that constitute an economic system, such as output and prices, wages and employment, and interest and investments. As a point of entry into the exploration of the internal logic of the Japanese economic system in its fluctuating growth, one might start with the peculiar relationship between prices and real wages. There are two kinds of real wages: money wages deflated by the index of wholesale prices and the same money wages deflated by the cost-of-living index. Series 3 to 6 in Chart II suggest that the prices and real wages are inversely associated. Trend is upward in both prices and real wages, but in trend-adjusted subperiods real wages fall (or rise) against their long-run trend in association with a rise (or fall) in prices against their trends. Table 10 summarizes the movements

TABLE 10

DEVIATIONS FROM TRENDS; PRICES AND WAGES,
SELECTED YEARS, 1877–1942

Year	Whole-sale Prices	Direction of Change	Product Wages	Direction of Change	Retail Prices	Direction of Change	Real Wages	Direction of Change
1877	92.0	...	105.4	...	90.3	...	103.6	...
1881	150.3	+	78.8	−	140.0	+	76.2	−
1886	83.7	−	122.3	+	81.0	−	113.2	+
1890	97.6	+	88.7	−	88.3	+	93.4	−
1894	82.5	−	97.3	+	79.5	−	102.2	−
1898	100.1	+	90.4	−	111.5	+	87.6	−
1902	93.2	−	98.2	+	95.8	−	105.3	+
1907	108.8	+	87.9	−	103.5	+	98.6	−
1910	93.4	−	98.6	+	88.1	−	109.3	+
1913	94.9	+	94.1	−	102.2	+	89.3	−
1915	86.8	−	93.7	−	77.7	−	90.5	+
(1918)	(159.0)	(+)	(72.3)	(−)	134.5	(+)	(85.2)	(−)
1920	203.8	+	93.1	+	171.3	+	108.5	+
1931	61.8	−	171.6	+	82.7	−	116.7	+
1942	150.4	+	72.0	−	182.0	+	50.4	−

Sources: Same as for Chart II. (See pp. 38–39.)

of prices and real wages for selected years. Most of these years are the turning points of the cycles in the time series shown in Chart II. Table 10 shows rather impressively that changes in prices and real wages in prewar Japan were overwhelmingly in opposite directions. To mix some a priori reasoning as a device for weaving different time series together, one might say that a rise in prices in association with a fall in real wages would increase profits, while the larger profits would induce entrepreneurs to expand output and to increase demands for factors of production. Thus more (or less) employment and more (or less) investment should be observed in conjunction with a rise (or fall) in prices and a fall (or rise) in real wages. Fluctuations in factory employment (series 8), which can be considered representative of changes in all paid employment, are seen to be inversely associated with those in real wages.[6] This is an old orthodox relationship between employment and real wages that drew the attention of economists in considerable amount during the 1930s. However, there is no need to rehash the old controversy.[7]

Another factor of production for which demand increases under the stimulus of increasing profits is capital. One of the indicators for changes in demand for capital is the ratio of investment to the aggregate output. From Rosovsky's study of Japanese capital formation,[8] one gains the impression that the ratio of capital formation to national output moved in an expected fashion after 1910, that is, rising in prosperity and falling in depression. Although judgment depends on the exact indicator of the investment ratio (gross domestic capital formation to gross domestic product or net national capital formation to net national product, for example), Rosovsky's estimates show that the investment ratio either stayed constant or tended to fall during the prosperous 1890s. This leads to the question of why rapid economic growth after 1910 accompanied increases in the rate of capital formation, while rapid growth during the 1890s, although probably not so impressive as after 1910, was possible with the declining rate of capital formation. Economic theory suggests an hypothesis: increases in output during the 1890s must have been brought about by capital-saving techniques, while they were possible only by capital-using techniques in later years.

Although a given increase in the aggregate demand leads to increases in the derived demands for factors of production such as labor and capital, a relatively larger increase in demand for one or the other depends on how the relative factor prices change in the meantime. In a growing economy the price of labor (real wages) rises not only relatively to the price of capital (the rate of interest) but also absolutely while the price of capital falls absolutely. Therefore the index of relative factor prices, which may be represented by the ratio of the index of real wages to rates of interest, is subject to a steeply rising trend. This index adjusted for trend is shown as series 8 in Chart II. This series of relative factor prices shows rather clear Kuznets-type swings inversely associated with swings in general economic conditions. This indicates that real wages relative to the rate of interest tend to fall during upswings and increase during downswings.

The introduction of the relative factor prices into the bundle of time series and the kit of analytical tools is helpful for clarifying the peculiarities of relative factor uses for the period prior to 1910, although it raises other questions (namely, about the relationships between relative factor prices and relative factor uses for the period after 1910). It should be noted that the cheapening of labor relative to capital during the 1890s was associated with greater employment of labor and a lower investment ratio and that the cheapening of capital relative to labor during the 1900s was associated with greater investment and smaller employment of labor. For the same reason, however, it is disturbing to find that this plausible relationship between relative factor prices and relative factor uses did not obtain in the years following 1910. Thereupon three hypotheses suggest themselves: (1) the elasticity of substitution between factors may have become smaller in the second period than in the first; or (2) the fluctuation of the aggregate demand may have increased so much in the second period that the substitution effect on relative factor uses of changes in relative factor prices was swamped under predominant income effect; or (3) both of these (that is, reduced substitution effect and increased income effect on relative demands for factors) may have reinforced each other during the second period.

Indeed, there is a view advanced that the elasticity of factor substitution became lower after 1910.[9] Its implication appropriate to our problem is that the scope of activities which could obtain output expansion by the application of more labor became narrower after 1910 than before, so that a given rate of cheapening of labor relative to capital could not have resulted in as much relative use of labor as before. While the reduction in the relative factor prices during the 1890s accompanied an increase in employment and a decrease in investment, their similar reduction following 1910 and during the 1930s accompanied increases in both employment and investment.

Now, as for the income effect when the increase in the aggregate demand is modest, the stimulus it conveys to demands for factors will also be modest. If labor cheapened considerably (relative to capital) in the meantime, even a modest increase in the aggregate demand might be associated with a substantial increase in employment and with a small increase or even a decrease in investment. The relationships between the income effect and the substitution effect on relative factor use must have been like this during the 1890s. On the other hand, a very large increase in the aggregate demand, despite a substitution effect, might lead to some increase in the demand for the relatively expensive factor which had been adversely affected by the substitution effect. This might have been the case after 1910 and during the 1930s.

Real Wage Level and Wage Differentials

It has been noted that real wages fall during prosperity when paid employment rises and rise during depression when paid employment falls. Wage differentials are seen to narrow during prosperity and widen during depression. In other words, the real wage level falls when wage differentials are narrowing and rises when they are widening. Is this relationship theoretically plausible? To answer this question, one needs a theoretical guidance on the relationship between wage differentials and economic conditions, for the relationship has so far been only an empirically observed phenomenon. M. W. Reder's theory of occupational wage differentials seems to supply the needed guidance.[10]

Briefly, the theory runs somewhat like this. The labor force of a given economy consists of employed wage earners and a labor reserve. Wage earners are further structured into different grades of labor from the highest to the lowest skills, each grade being guarded by a given set of hiring standards. One grade of labor is highly substitutable with immediately neighboring grades of labor through changes in hiring standards, and these substitutions form the avenue of "upgrading" or "downgrading" workers as occasion demands.

The supply of labor of a given grade to a firm increases (or decreases) with a rise (or fall) in wages if hiring standards are held constant, or with a fall (or rise) in hiring standards if wages are held constant. The firm's responses to the need for replenishing or contracting its work force are also ordered in the sequence of manipulating hiring standards first and wages next. Assume, for instance, that there are two grades of labor (skilled and unskilled) inside the firm and a labor reserve outside the firm. Under the impact of increasing demand for all grades of labor during a period of prosperity, each firm increases the skilled work force by upgrading some of the unskilled, and then replenishes the unskilled work force by new hirings from the labor reserve. Since total labor force is relatively fixed in the short run or does not increase as fast as economic conditions change, there is no way to replenish the labor reserve as more and more of it is drawn into active employment. Exhaustion of the labor reserve will be felt as a greater shortage of labor for unskilled jobs than for skilled, and this tends to push up unskilled wages proportionately more than skilled. Thus the skilled-unskilled wage differentials tend to narrow during periods of high employment.

For the sake of symmetry, the reverse of the foregoing process can be expected to take place during periods of low employment. The firm responds to the downward changes in economic conditions by tightening the hiring standards for all grades of labor with a view to pushing out the inefficient workers at each grade. As workers descend along the skill gradient, worker competition for jobs intensifies at lower ends of the gradient, and unskilled wages are pressed down proportionately more than skilled. The skilled workers who are unemployed at their customary skill levels crowd into markets for low-skilled jobs, while the unemployed unskilled workers are hauled into the labor reserve. As is so often the case, the neat symmetry of economic events expected by pure theory becomes considerably lopsided in practice. For instance, Reder abandons the symmetry of his theory in relation to the response of wage differentials to the decrease in the aggregate demand, for wage differentials in practice do not increase in periods of low employment as much as might be expected in theory. The intervention of ethical and institutional forces in the economic process is particularly acute during depressed periods.

The behavior of the firm postulated by Reder in regard to wages and hiring standards has been criticized by some writers.[11] But what seems to be important and is often ignored by the critics is that the postulated behavior of the firm is above all a logical device for explaining what is happening in the skilled and unskilled markets. Reder states:

> It cannot be *deduced* from this consideration [of the behavior of the firm] that wage rates paid on the lowest grade of jobs would rise proportionately more than the rates on others. But if for other reasons we knew that this did occur, then the relatively greater reduction in the supply of workers available for these jobs would afford an important clue to the explanation of its occurrence. . . . *Accordingly, we offer the hypothesis that the association of short-period variations in skill margins with the level of aggregate employment is due to the fact that a rise in the level of employment for all grades of labor reduces the supply of labor available for unskilled jobs (at initial wage rates) proportionately more than it reduces the supply available for others* [italics mine].[12]

The last sentence deserves special attention. A change in the wage differential between skilled and unskilled jobs can be seen to be the net result of interactions of differences characteristic of these jobs in relation to (1) the income-elasticity of demand for labor, (2) the wage-elasticity of demand for labor, (3) the elasticity of supply of labor with respect to hiring standards, and (4) the wage-elasticity of supply of labor.

The foregoing hypothesis of relative changes in demands for and supplies of labor for skilled and unskilled jobs in the labor markets can be applied to the analysis of any pair of high-wage and low-wage groups of workers. The "group" may be a sector, industry, firm, occupation, sex, or anything that distinguishes some workers from others. One then assumes that the wage differential between the high-wage and low-wage groups, whatever concrete designation "group" may take, behaves in relation to the general economic conditions as predicted by the Reder theory, that the supply of labor to the high-wage group increases (or decreases) proportionately more than that to the low-wage group in response to good (or poor) economic conditions and the rise (or fall) in the level of aggregate employment.

It may now be noted that the hypothesis of inverse association between wage differentials and economic conditions is theoretically compatible with the orthodox, inverse relationship between real wages and paid employment. According to the hypothesis on the behavior of wage differentials, the increased demand for each skill category of labor during prosperity is met in part by lowering hiring standards (or, in popular parlance, by "watering" skills). In other words, the average efficiency of labor in each skill category (aside from the long-run trend of productivity which is due more to technical change than to work performance) falls during prosperity. This cannot but result in a lower average real wage rate for every skill category. Having noted that wholesale prices usually rise faster than money wages during prosperity, the late W. C. Mitchell added an observation which, despite its date and place, is highly relevant to the relationship between hiring standards and wage differentials. Mitchell said:

> If humanitarian motives are not allowed to interfere with business policy, the less efficient employees are the first to be discharged after a crisis. Hence the relatively small working forces of depression are the picked troops of the industrial army. When revival has ripened into full prosperity, on the contrary, employers are constrained to accept any help to be had. They must take on men who are too old, and boys who are too young, men of irregular habits, men prone to malinger, even the chronic "trouble makers." Raw recruits of all sorts must be enlisted and trained in a hurry at the employer's expense. The average efficiency of the working forces is inevitably impaired.[13]

To close the circuit of economic logic in a manner appropriate to this book, I would like to recall at this point the implications of variations in relative factor prices in relation to wage differentials. The movement of relative factor prices (the ratio of real wages to the rate of interest) is inversely associated with variations in general economic conditions. The fact that labor becomes less expensive relative to capital when economic conditions improve and more expensive when they deteriorate is entirely consistent with the specific pattern of association between wage differentials and economic conditions predicted by the Reder theory. It has already been noted that the inverse association between real wages and economic conditions is a suitable context for bringing about the narrowing or widening of wage differentials in response to changes in economic conditions. In addition, to the extent that relative factor prices influence the entrepreneurial decision, the decrease (or increase) in the cost of labor relative to that of capital in association with good (or poor) economic conditions would further intensify the increase (or decrease) in the demand for labor as a whole. At the same time, the incidence of the increase (or decrease) in the total demand for labor on various grades of labor is such that pressures for wage increases (or decreases) are greater on low-grade labor than on high-grade. It can be concluded that the behavior of wage differentials observed in Chapter 1 conforms to what is theoretically expected about it from the nexus of changes in relative factor prices, price-wage relationships, and the relative demand and supply forces affecting different kinds of labor in the Japanese context of economic fluctuations.

Conclusion

The periods of swings in the Japanese wage differentials are like those of the Kuznets cycles and are systematically associated with the genuine Kuznets cycles in general economic conditions. That variations in wage differentials are related to variations in economic conditions is an empirical fact widely observed in American and European economies. It has been found that this observation also applies to Japanese experience, though with one difference: although variations in wage differentials are associated with ordinary business cycles in other countries, they are associated with the Kuznets cycles in Japan. The Kuznets cycles are also observed in the economic conditions of the other countries. This being so, wage differentials in these countries, upon closer examination, might also show variations similar to the Kuznets cycles. This is an hypothesis that the study of Japanese wage differentials offers for the study of wage differentials in other countries.

In this chapter variations in wage differentials have been explored in a fashion of one-way causation by changes in general economic conditions. It cannot be denied that wage differentials are variables in the general system of economic interdependences in which they are as much causes for as effects of, economic conditions, a point suggested long ago by J. R. Hicks:

As economic conditions vary, they bring about changes in the [wage] system, but external changes have to reach a certain magnitude and a certain duration before they can break down the internal resistance [of the wage system]. Some of these changes in economic conditions . . . arise from the fact that a particular wage-system has effects peculiar to itself on the slow-moving ground-swell of the economic world—that it influences the distribution of labour, and stimulates or discourages the accumulation of capital, in a way of its own. Any change in the wage-system must influence these slow-moving tendencies, and they in turn react on the wage-system.[14]

Japanese experience substantiates two interrelated characteristics of the "wage system" (which can be taken to stand for the totality of wage differentials) mentioned in the above quotation from Hicks; namely, (1) resistance and (2) pliability of the wage system. First, the wage system in the sense of the rankings of industries, occupations, and regions is stable over time, exhibiting a very high degree of internal resistance to changes in economic conditions. Second, the wage system in the sense of relative wages is pliable to a notable degree, widening and narrowing in response to changes in economic conditions of "a certain magnitude and a certain duration." The flexibility of relative wages in Japan is an aspect of the general economic process which is fundamentally neoclassical.

3   The Intersectoral and Interindustry Wage Differentials before the Second World War

In the preceding chapters a systematic inverse association between wage differentials and general economic conditions has been ascertained. An analytical interpretation has also been attempted as to why such a specific relationship should exist. This chapter pursues the same question in relation to the intersectoral and interindustry wage differentials. Data on these differentials have already been presented in Chapter 1.

The growth of the industrial labor force relative to the agricultural and the growth of paid employment relative to self-employment are central features of the evolution of the labor force in economic development. This chapter first explores the place of the intersectoral wage differential in relation to the aggregate demand and intersectoral transfer of labor. Then the behavior of the interindustry wage differentials is discussed in the context of interactions between paid labor and self-employment. Finally, this chapter examines the applicability of a well-known "structuralist" view of economic development to Japanese experience.

The Intersectoral Wage Differential [1]

At one time there was widespread inclination among economists to regard relative prices as independent variables, and movements of economic resources as dependent variables. It was generally taken for granted that the larger the intersectoral wage differential, that is, the higher the industrial wages relative to the agricultural, the larger would be the movement of labor from agriculture to industry. However, available data indicate the relationship between wage differentials and labor mobility to be the other way around; that is, migration from agriculture to industry tends to increase (or decrease) in association with a narrowing (or widening) of the intersectoral wage differential. According to a study by H. L. Parsons, for example, when the intersectoral wage differential (the ratio of the industrial to agricultural earnings in this case) in the United States was above (or below) its trend, gross migrants to and from farms were below (or above) their respective trends.[2]

There are two ways of resolving the conflict between the theoretically expected direction of causality running from relative prices to resource transfer and the actually observed relationship between them. One is simply to abandon the intersectoral wage differential as a relevant variable, since it is not performing the function of allocating labor between sectors. For example, Parsons states that "it seems safe to conclude that variations in relative earnings were not a significant cause of variations in migration from farms for the years 1920 to 1945."[3] He also remarks that "increased movement of labor has occurred even in the face of decreasing relative earnings of city workers."[4] D. Gale Johnson was once troubled by the same question. Noting that "farm labor income per worker rose relative to the income of employed industrial workers between 1910 and 1919" but that farm employment did not increase during the same period, Johnson asked why farm labor employment failed to increase. Then he answered that "the evidence available is inconclusive in indicating what rational conduct would have been for farm workers" and that "a rise in relative earnings when the absolute differences increase may or may not indicate that real returns to farm workers increased relatively."[5]

Another method of handling the conflict between theory and fact is to explore whether the relative wages as actually observed between sectors are really the same as the theoretical variables which are said to influence the worker's choice of occupation. If the question is why a widening of the intersectoral wage differential fails to move labor from agriculture to industry, and if the explanation should be consistent with the economic rationality of the worker, one answer is suggested by M. W. Reder: if the intersectoral wage differential were weighted by the relative probabilities of getting employed in industry and agriculture, the relevant intersectoral wage differential might well be moving in the same direction as the flow of labor actually observed between these sectors. Thus, in times of depression when the intersectoral wage differential widens, "unemployment so reduces expected actual earnings in urban centers that the higher hourly rates of pay obtainable cease to induce much (if any) net migration." [6]

This chapter tries a different approach to the problem. Reversing the ordinary chain of causation from relative wages to allocation of labor, I treat the intersectoral wage differential as a dependent, and migration as an independent, variable, relating migration, in turn, to something else than the wage differential. My suggestion is that the movement of workers from agriculture (in response to some third factor) reduces the supply of labor in agriculture, while increasing it in industry, and consequently raises the agricultural wages relative to the industrial. [7]

The interdependence between sectors

There are two particularly important factors that respectively condition the direction of migration in the long run and determine the volume of migration in the short run. First, the net absolute advantages of industrial employment persist over agricultural, as determined by two economic forces unfavorable to agriculture: the low-income elasticity of demand for agricultural products relative to industrial, and higher birth rates in rural than in urban areas. [8] Second, the employment opportunities in industry, which fluctuate in response to changes in aggregate demand, determine the volume of labor to be absorbed from agriculture in the short run. Thus, accordingly, as employment opportunities in industry increase or decrease, the net flow of labor from agriculture to industry increases or decreases, and consequently the intersectoral wage differential narrows or widens. [9]

In the paragraph above, aggregate demand was related to the intersectoral wage differential through migration of labor, that is, through changes on the supply side of the labor market. Aggregate demand also affects the intersectoral wage differential through the demand side of the labor market. There are three forces that jointly determine the relative effects on wages of a given change in aggregate demand through changes in the demand for labor in industry and agriculture. The first is the income effect that shifts the demand curve for labor. The second and third are the elasticities of demand for and supply of labor with respect to wages.

Since the income elasticity of demand for agricultural products is usually lower than that for industrial products, what can correspondingly be called "income elasticity" of demand for labor will be lower in agriculture than in industry. Thus the income effect by itself is a force that widens or narrows the intersectoral wage differential in direct association with a rise or fall in aggregate demand. But if the labor demand and supply curves are more inelastic in agriculture than in industry (a proposition yet to be demonstrated), a small proportionate shift in agriculture's demand (with the supply curve remaining fixed) might change agricultural wages proportionately more than a large proportionate shift in industry's demand for labor changes industrial wages. Thus the net effect on the intersectoral wage differential of changes in aggregate demand through the demand side of the labor market depends upon the relative strength of the income elasticity of demand for labor on the one hand and the wage elasticities of demand for and supply of labor on the other.[10]

There seems to be little doubt that the wage elasticity of labor supply is lower in agriculture than in industry, as illustrated by the combination of rigid employment and flexible wages in agriculture and that of flexible employment and rigid wages in industry during a business cycle.[11] There is also reason to believe that demand for labor is less elastic in agriculture than in industry. On this point, one can fully depend on Marshall's four laws on the elasticity of derived demand for productive factors. According to Marshall, the demand for a factor is the more elastic, the more elastic the demand for the product, the more elastic the substitution between the factor in question and other factors, the more elastic the supply of other factors, and the larger the cost of the factor in question in the total cost of production.

Provided that the income elasticity of demand for labor is not markedly lower in agriculture than in industry, the foregoing considerations suggest that the intersectoral wage differential should be inversely associated with aggregate demand and intersectoral labor transfer.

The Japanese experience

The data presented in the preceding chapters can be used to examine the suggested relationship between the intersectoral wage differential on the one hand and aggregate demand and intersectoral labor transfer on the other. For the dependent variable, series 1-b on Chart I is used. As an indicator of the aggregate demand, national income per capita in constant prices adjusted for trend (series 1 on Chart II) is used after the annual values are smoothed by five-year moving geometric averages. Two types of relationship are observed between intersectoral wage differential and aggregate demand. For the period of 1883 to 1914, the two series are inversely correlated on the basis of the corresponding annual values ($r = -0.81$). Between 1915 and 1944, however, the best association is obtained when the wage differential is lagged behind income by five years ($r = -0.87$).

The intersectoral labor transfer is inferred from the average numbers of gainfully occupied persons in different sectors supplied in publications such as *GROJES*. Following the practice of the Hitotsubashi economists, I have estimated net migration from the primary to non-primary sector on the basis of these data: one first estimates by how much the agricultural labor force would have increased in the absence of out-migration between years t and $t + 1$, assuming that the natural rate of increase in the agricultural labor force is the same as in the total labor force, and then subtracts the actual increase in the agricultural labor force from the expected increase to obtain the size of net migration from agriculture between t and $t + 1$ (to be recorded for $t + 1$) in number of persons.

Estimated in this fashion, net out-migration from the primary sector shows a steady upward trend but no fluctuations around the trend for the period prior to 1915. The net intersectoral labor transfer in thousands of persons increases from 130 of the 1880s to 200 of the 1910s. It goes up sharply to 250 toward the end of the First World War and decreases to the point of virtual extinction around 1930. Waves of out-migration from the primary sector are renewed in the latter part of the 1930s. For the period of 1915 to 1944, the best association between intersectoral wage differential and labor transfer ($r = -0.80$) is found when the differential is lagged behind migration by five years.

The foregoing exploration of the relationships among the intersectoral wage differential, aggregate demand, and net migration in prewar Japan can be summarized by two regression equations appropriate to the two periods just mentioned.

(1) $D_t = 193.22 - 0.74Y_t$ $\qquad$ $\bar{R}^2 = 0.6450$
$\qquad$ (19.65) (7.52) $\qquad$ t: from 1883 to 1914

(2) $D_t = 453.33 - 2.86Y_{t-5} - 0.15M_{t-5}$ $\qquad$ $\bar{R}^2 = 0.7881$
$\qquad$ (8.78) (5.06) $\qquad$ (2.92) $\qquad$ t: from 1920 to 1944

D, Y, and M, respectively, stand for the ratio of the industrial to agricultural wages in percentages, the annual values of the per capita real national income as percentages of its trend values, and net out-migrants from the primary sector in thousands of persons. The t ratios shown in parentheses in the equations indicate that the coefficients are highly significant.

Before the First World War, according to Equation 1, "normal" economic conditions ($Y = 100$ percent) were associated with the intersectoral wage differential equal to 119.5 percent. This was just about the average value of the differential during the period of 1883–1914. Under "normal" economic conditions during this period the aggregate demand was increasing at its long-term trend rate and there was steady, autonomous migration from the primary sector in the order of 130,000 to 200,000 persons. One may say that the "normal" differential of industrial over agricultural wages before the First World War was about 20 percent. During the interwar period, according to Equation 2, slightly prosperous conditions ($Y = 105$ percent, for example) coupled with a moderate degree of out-migration from the primary sector ($M = 100,000$ persons, for example) would have been associated with industrial wages 38 percent above agricultural. This was roughly the situation that obtained in the late 1920s. A fairly advanced state of prosperity ($Y = 110$ percent), if accompanied by the maximum migration before the First World War ($M = 200,000$ persons), would have wiped out the differential entirely. This was the direction of economic forces after 1938. The numerical exercises one can do on the basis of the regression equations suggest that there was essentially no difference in the labor market process between the period before the First World War and the interwar period in so far as the strength of the market to equilibrate wages in different sectors was concerned.

An interpretation

All the analytical elements for a proper interpretation of the Japanese experience just summarized were stated in the first subsection devoted to the mechanism of interdependence between sectors. I would now like to identify the realistic counterparts of some of these analytical elements in the characteristics of the Japanese labor market. I start with the period during which the intersectoral wage differential was influenced only by aggregate demand working through the demand side of the labor market. Before the First World War the intersectoral wage differential varied in inverse association with aggregate demand, but net migration from agriculture showed no variations. A formal interpretation of this case is (1) that in the short run the labor demand curves shifted in both sectors while the labor supply curves remained fixed and (2) that although the income effect shifted agriculture's demand for labor proportionately less than industry's, agriculture's demand and supply curves were sufficiently more inelastic than industry's to raise or lower agricultural wages proportionately more than industrial.

Now, the question is whether it is possible to back up this claim on the relative elasticities of demand and supply curves for labor with the relevant facts of the Japanese labor market. To study the claim that agriculture's demand for labor is less elastic than industry's, one merely falls back upon the Marshallian laws of derived demand, as stated earlier. It can be accepted without further ado that in Japan, as in other countries, the demand for products, the substitution between labor and capital (including land), and the supply of other factors are all more elastic in industry than in agriculture and that the share of labor in the total cost of production is larger in industry than in agriculture. It then follows that agriculture's demand for labor is less elastic than industry's.

The supply side of the labor market is somewhat more complicated than the demand side. "Supply" in this case is understood to be the supply of "paid" labor. During the period from 1890 to 1915, the total labor force in mining and manufacturing showed no short-run variations, while the employment of paid labor in mines and factories varied in response to changes in aggregate demand. But there was no overt unemployment. This relationship between paid labor and total employment in these industries suggests that paid labor was drawn from or returned to self-employment as more or less labor was needed in mines and factories under the varying impact of aggregate demand. In other words the supply of paid labor to industry was highly elastic in the short run because of the readiness of the self-employed segment of the labor force to supply needed workers and absorb discharged ones.

If the foregoing sounds meaningful from the point of view of paid employment in industry, the economic rationality of self-employment is not immediately clear.[12] The question is what technical or economic factors account for the behavior of the self-employed segment in industry as a flexible buffer for paid labor in industry.[13]

The crucial difference between paid labor and self-employment is that the wage rate is equated to the marginal value product of labor, while the self-employed person appropriates all his product as his income after payments for the other factors of production. He then consumes some of the net revenue and saves the rest. When several persons employ themselves jointly, they appropriate the total net product of their enterprise and, having put aside a certain portion of the product for ploughing back into the enterprise or investing outside, distribute the rest among themselves according to whatever rules they have set up for the purpose. One of the most common rules of distribution is the rule of marginal product phrased in ways like "each member is rewarded according to what and how he has contributed to the group." If the group is a family, the decision-making may be concentrated in the family head. But the logic of production, consumption, and saving in the family is essentially the same as in any enterprise.

Two complications arise, however. One is that the family consists of productive and nonproductive members and that whether a family member is a worker within the family enterprise or a pure consumer is not a question that can be rigorously defined and answered. Another complication is that a person may be a member of the family in consumption only, paying for his consumption with his earnings from employment outside. In this case, the family is engaged in the business of furnishing room and board for someone who does not belong to the family's principal enterprise but who happens to be a family member. Another phenomenon of the same category is a family member who lives and works in a distant area but remits a portion of his earnings to the family. He occasionally comes back to the family for visits or other purposes and consumes what he has built up with the family through his past remittances. This family is like a savings bank or an insurance business. The nature of all these "businesses" is of course considerably blurred in reality. But the family is clearly informed of one basic factor in its economic strategy, that is, the relative advantage of having some of its members earn from outside sources vis-à-vis employing them within the family enterprise. If someone can do better outside than inside, he or she is usually prevailed upon to take the job outside. In other words, the family always keeps a watchful eye on the marginal products of its members inside the family enterprise and the wage rate in the external labor market.

Given the nature of a self-employed family as a multibusiness unit, one may now spell out what happens to the self-employed sector in interaction with the paid sector. When economic conditions turn adverse, the paid sector lays off some of its workers. They return to their families for temporary support or for temporary participation in the family enterprise. So long as there are things to do, they will be put to work. But these are the times when the market for the family's product has also shrunk, so that the marginal value product schedule for labor has shifted to a lower position. Even without the addition of the returning workers, the depressed economic conditions may have lowered the marginal value product of labor within the family enterprise so much that the consumption level of the working members of the family may have become higher than their marginal value products. The returning workers aggravate the situation further. Since they have most probably built up their claims on the family's resources through past remittances, however, their share in the current consumption of the family is fully justified. The economic logic of this situation is extremely delicate. Although the marginal product rule of distribution of the *current* output within the family is evidently suspended, the marginal rules of costs and benefits in other family businesses like saving and social insurance are in full operation.

A heuristic illustration of how the suspension of the marginal product rule works in the family enterprise during a depression is presented in Figure 1. The family has a labor force equal to ON_2, of which N_1N_2 is ordinarily employed for pay outside. The family work force ordinarily within the family is ON_1. During prosperity the average and marginal value products of labor are as high as AVP_1 and MVP_1. Consumption per capita during prosperity is OW_1 which is equal to the marginal value product of labor. Under adverse economic conditions, the average and marginal value products of labor go down. Suppose that the price of the product of this family enterprise relative to all

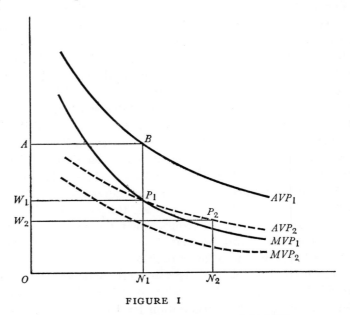

FIGURE I

LABOR INPUT IN A HOUSEHOLD ENTERPRISE

ON_1	Labor input of the resident members of the household
N_1N_2	Labor input of the migrant members who return home during depression
AVP	Average value product of labor
MVP	Marginal value product of labor
1	Prosperity
2	Depression

other prices in the system decreased by the amount which lowered the AVP from B to P_1 at the ON_1 level of employment within the family. (This is an event too precise to be likely in reality but it at least serves the illustrative purpose.) The marginal value product has gone down to MVP_2. The level of consumption to which the family was accustomed during the last prosperity cannot now be maintained by adhering to the rule of allowing consumption only within the bounds of the marginal value product. In addition, the mobile members of the family laid off from the paid sector return to live and work with the family. After savings are exhausted, the best level of consumption per capita that the family can afford depends solely upon the average value productivity, which is OW_2.

The wage rate in the paid sector that remains above OW_1 during depression is an inducement for the mobile workers who would return to work in the paid sector as soon as economic conditions improve and hiring increases. But the point is that the ease with which the paid sector can release its workers and maintain its wage level depends upon what level of living awaits the discharged workers at home. If the addition of the mobile workers to the family economy should reduce the family's consumption standard drastically, the mobile workers would rather try to stay employed in the paid sector with reduced pay instead of going home. This suggests that the stability of wages and the elasticity of labor supply in the paid sector depend upon the flexible average value productivity in the family enterprise which can absorb additional labor without too great a reduction in production and consumption, as deliberatly drawn into Figure 1. In experience a good deal of paid labor was dismissed from mines and factories during depressions before the First World War with only moderate reductions in the wage rate, while the dismissed workers were absorbed into self-employment with apparent ease. This would not have been possible without flexible average value productivity in the family enterprise.

However, the flexibility of the average value productivity of labor and the amplitude of its shifts between prosperity and depression vary from sector to sector. In agriculture the average value product of labor on the family farm drops more drastically during depression, while being less flexible at the same time than in the family enterprise in industry.[14] A large downward shift of the average value productivity coupled with its low flexibility would precipitate the farm family's consumption standard so much if more persons should be added that the mobile agricultural workers would rather take pay cuts and stay in the labor market. This contrast between agriculture and industry is consistent with the greater downward flexibility of agricultural wages during the down-turn of economic conditions than industrial wages. The intersectoral wage differential, therefore, widens during depression.

What has been said on the relationship between paid labor and self-employment during the decreasing phase of aggregate demand can be applied *mutatis mutandis* to its rising phase. As hiring increases in factories and mines in response to an increase in aggregate demand, the workers who have been sheltered under self-employment or family labor during the preceding depression return to paid jobs. Thus the supply of paid labor in the industrial labor market increases without an appreciable rise in the level of industrial wages. In agriculture no such additional workers are forthcoming into the labor market, while those already in paid employment may even be induced to till the land on their own unless wages improve quickly in pace with the upward shift in the average net value productivity of labor in agricultural self-employment.

During the period from 1915 to 1944, the intersectoral wage differential varied in inverse association with aggregate demand and with net migration from agriculture. The interpretation is essentially the same as that offered for the period before the First World War. An additional explanatory element is that the supply curves for paid labor in industry and agriculture, which it is safe to regard as fixed in the short run for the period before the First World War, must now be allowed to shift in opposite directions in the two sectors.[15] When the demand curves for paid labor in both industry and agriculture shift to the right in response to the increase in aggregate demand, the supply curve for paid labor in agriculture is shifting to the left while that in industry is shifting to the right.

In experience, paid employment in factories and mines during the interwar period fluctuated violently around its trend and was inversely associated with the intersectoral wage differential.[16] Furthermore, according to the population censuses of 1920, 1930, and 1940 paid employment in absolute numbers increased by only 3 percent in industry but by 8 percent in agriculture between 1920 and 1930, while it increased by 84 percent in industry but decreased by 3 percent in agriculture between 1930 and 1940. It is remarkable that paid labor in agriculture increased between 1920 and 1930 despite the adverse effect of aggregate demand during this period and against its long-run trend. The price for the increase in the supply of paid labor in agriculture was a sharp reduction in agricultural wages relative to industrial ones.

The Interindustry
Wage Differentials

There are two sources of labor for paid employment in industry: (1) self-employed labor force of the industrial sector itself and (2) the agricultural labor force. Interactions between agriculture and industry were discussed in the preceding section of this chapter. Theoretical considerations were also offered about the interactions between paid labor and self-employment in a sector. This section presents some data on interactions between paid employment and self-employment in manufacturing.

"Self-employment" is represented by gainfully occupied persons in manufacturing other than those employed in factories. They include self-employed persons, unpaid family workers, and even paid employees in manufacturing establishments that are too small to be defined in the official statistics as "factories." The "factories" are manufacturing establishments with five or more operatives. The whole of self-employment certainly cannot be identified with "labor reserve." But one can imagine that much of it can be regarded as such and that the quantum of "labor reserve" which is important in the analysis of wage differentials varies with self-employment.

Table 11 compares the movement of self-employment in manufacturing and that of the interindustry wage differentials over time. In 1880 four fifths of the manufacturing labor force were engaged in manufacturing activities in workshops that were too small to be called factories. In 1939, after half a century of economic development, factory employment accounted for two thirds of the manufacturing labor force. Against this trend of long-term industrial employment, there were short-term fluctuations in the ratio of self-employment to the total labor force. According to Table 11, self-employment tended to increase (or decrease) relative to paid labor in factories when the interindustry wage differentials increased (or decreased). If self-employment can be considered a proxy for the theoretical notion of "labor reserve," the relationship between changes in self-employment and those in the interindustry wage differentials shown by Table 11 may be considered another verification of the relationship between wage differentials and

TABLE 11

SELF-EMPLOYMENT AND INTERINDUSTRY WAGE DIFFERENTIALS,
SELECTED YEARS, 1882–1939[a]

Year	Proportion of Labor Force Self-employed[b] (percent)	Average Annual Change in Self-employment Ratio[c] (percentage points)	Interindustry Wage Differentials[d]
1882	80.0		
1888	85.0	+0.83	Widening
1895	72.3	−1.81	Narrowing
1909	73.8	+0.11	Widening
1923	57.0	−1.20	Narrowing
1933	59.0	+0.20	Widening
1939	33.5	−4.25	Narrowing

[a] Years are selected by the turning points in the time series of the interindustry wage differentials shown on Chart I and discussed in Chapter 1 under "Interindustry Wage Differentials."

[b] The ratio of the "nonfactory" employment to total employment in manufacturing. "Factory" is a manufacturing establishment with five or more operatives.

[c] The difference between two successive figures in the second column divided by the number of years between them.

[d] See Chapter 1.

economic conditions in which "labor reserve" plays an important role as in the theory discussed at the end of Chapter 2.

Table 12 is helpful for showing how the manufacturing sector draws labor from different sources. The official inquiry which has given rise to this table covers the newly established factories or factories which had expanded after the outbreak of the First World War. The data suffer from one serious omission, that is, the reports from the Prefecture of Osaka which arrived too late for tabulation by the Japanese government. The original source also complains about the other possible omissions because factories were suffering from very high labor turnover at the time. It may be pointed out that the total hiring during the three-year period (450,000 persons) was smaller than the net increase in the average number of persons employed in factories with five or more operatives between 1914 and 1917 (540,000). Ordinarily,

TABLE 12

SOURCES OF NEW HIRING IN NEWLY ESTABLISHED
AND IN EXPANDED FACTORIES, 1914–1917

(NUMBER OF PERSONS)

Employers	Sources					
	Agr. and Fishery	Same Mfg. Industries	Other Mfg. Industries and Mining	Trade	Others	Total
Textiles	103,036 (49.5)[a]	61,332 (29.4)	6,832 (3.2)	6,986 (3.3)	29,754 (14.1)	207,940 (100)
Metals and machinery[b]	34,404 (26.9)	45,078 (35.2)	15,714 (12.3)	6,356 (5.1)	26,254 (20.5)	127,806 (100)
Chemicals	23,328 (41.6)	11,980 (21.5)	4,241 (7.6)	3,715 (6.6)	12,573 (22.6)	55,837 (100)
Food and drinks	8,006 (52.4)	2,293 (15.0)	758 (4.9)	755 (4.9)	3,491 (22.8)	15,303 (100)
Other manufacturing	14,365 (33.6)	13,910 (32.6)	2,458 (5.7)	3,007 (7.0)	8,987 (21.0)	42,727 (100)
TOTAL	183,139 (40.7)	134,593 (30.0)	30,003 (6.7)	20,819 (4.6)	81,059 (18.0)	449,613 (100)

Source: Ministry of Agriculture and Commerce, *Jikyoku no kōjō oyobi shokkō ni oyoboshi-taru eikyō* (The Influence of the War on Factories and Workers) (1917). See *NRUS*, Vol. III, pp. 51–54, and MITI, *Shōkō seisaku shi* (A History of Commercial and Industrial Policies) (Tokyo, 1962), VIII, Table 7, pp. 70–71.

[a] Figures in parentheses are percentages.

[b] This combines "kikai kigu kōjō" (machinery and tool-making) and "tokubetsu kōjō" (special factories—iron works and arms production).

one would expect the new hiring in any year to be larger than the net increase in employment for that year. Nevertheless, Table 12 is useful as an indicator of the state of the labor market during a prewar boom period.

According to Table 12, the factories covered in this particular survey drew 41 percent of their workers from the primary sector and 37 percent from the secondary sector. The importance of the primary sector as a source of factory labor is not surprising, as this is to be expected in a less well developed economy like Japan of fifty years ago. What is interesting from the point of view of this section is the manufacturing sector as a significant source of labor for itself. This intrasectoral movement of labor reflects the interfactory job changes and labor transfer from self-employment to factories. Job changes were enormous during the First World War as will be described in Chapter 6. But the participation of self-employed persons in paid work must also have been considerable. This is collaborated by another set of data. The labor force statistics which have given rise to Table 11 show a net decrease of 273,000 persons in self-employment between 1914 and 1917 and a net increase of 543,000 factory workers during the same period.

One might also note that the role of agriculture and fishery as sources of labor for metals and machinery industries is much smaller than for other industries. The fact that many of the newly hired workers in these industries were those with employment experience in the same industries may indicate that employer competition for labor and commensurate labor mobility were keener in these than in other industries. The metals and machinery industries, which paid the highest wages in the manufacturing sector, were surrounded by more elastic labor supplies, coupled with a relatively wider range within which to vary hiring standards, than other industries. Further details are discussed in Part II of this book.

Metals and machinery, together with textiles, presented an interesting feature of the employment structure of the prewar Japanese industrial sector. These two industries (treating metals and machinery as one industry) accounted for a constant 70 percent of the paid labor force in the manufacturing sector as a long-run tendency. Employment in metals and machinery tended to increase relative to that in textiles over time, while in the short run the relative weights of these two branches of manufacturing in terms of employment fluctuated systematically in relation to general economic conditions and the wage differential between them. Of several manufacturing industries for which the interindustry wage differentials were discussed in Chapter 1 and in the paragraphs above, metals and machinery paid the highest wages and textiles the lowest. Thus the wage differential between metals-and-machinery and textiles may be expected to vary in relation to general economic conditions in the pattern specified by the hypothesis on the behavior of the wage differential between the high-wage and low-wage groups of workers. The hypothesis implies that paid employment increases (or decreases) proportionately more in the high-wage than in low-wage industries when the wage differential between the two groups narrows (or widens) in association with good (or poor) economic conditions.

Table 13 puts together the relevant phases of relative wages and of relative employment in metals-machinery and textiles against the background of general economic conditions (represented by characteristics described by Chart II). The movements of total factory employment and average money wages in industry are added as further indicators of economic conditions in the aggregate. The figures in this table are average annual rates of change in the variables enumerated. Given lower wages in textiles than in metals and machinery, when textile wages increase at a faster (or slower) rate than metals-machinery wages, the wage differential between the two branches of manufacturing tends to narrow (or widen). There are lags between the wage differential and changes in employment, which also conforms to the general pattern of economic process in prewar Japan.

Changes in the quantitative variables in Table 13 show short-run variations in conformity with changes in general economic conditions. The rapid increase in factory and textile employment during the 1880s, despite the generally poor economic conditions, was because factory production in the initial stage started from practically nothing. A similar observation applies to the extraordinary growth of the metals and machinery industries during the 1890s; the base of the initial date was very small. Otherwise, employment figures show a rather neat association with the movement of economic conditions. Changes in money wages can be said, without reservations, to be in accord with changes in economic conditions.

The most interesting point demonstrated by Table 13 is, of course, the relationship between variations in the metals-textiles wage differential and relative changes in paid employment in the two industries. It should be noted that employment is subject to more marked short-run variations in the metals and machinery industries than in textiles, while wages tend to oscillate more violently in textiles than in metals and machinery. Furthermore, when wages in textiles gain (or lose) relative to those in metals and machinery, employment in the metals and machinery industries tends to lose (or gain) relative to employment in the textiles industries. The inverse association between wage in-

TABLE 13

CHANGES IN WAGES AND EMPLOYMENT IN TEXTILES AND METALS-MACHINERY COMPARED WITH CHANGES IN ECONOMIC CONDITIONS, 1882-1941[a]

(PERCENT)

	1882-1892	1892-1900	1900-1909	1909-1920	1920-1930	1930-1940
Economic conditions	Poor	Good	Poor	Good	Poor	Good
Total factory employment	19.5	15.4	6.0	9.6	0.7	1.4
Average industrial money wages	-2.1[b]	11.1	4.6	20.8	1.4[c]	5.0[d]
Textiles employment	17.0	12.5	7.2	8.3	0.4	1.1
Metals-machinery employment	0.2	58.8	2.0	15.8	-0.8	5.9
Textiles wages	-3.8[b]	11.0	3.7	21.3	-1.1[c]	9.7[d]
Metals-machinery wages	4.3[b]	9.0	4.6	17.4	1.8[c]	0.9[d]
Textiles-metals wage differential	Widening[b]	Narrowing	Widening	Narrowing	Widening[c]	Narrowing[d]

a "Change" is the simple annual average of the percentage rate of increase (or decrease) in a variable between the initial and terminal dates of each period.

b 1883-1892. c 1920-1935. d 1935-1941.

creases and employment expansion that appears in the comparison of textiles and metals-machinery is a form of manifestation of the Japanese "karma" in the economic process.

Flexible Wage Differentials and "Unlimited Supplies of Labor"

In this chapter one has once again ascertained the orthodox characteristics of the Japanese labor market. It is remarkable that real and relative wages have been sensitive to changes in economic conditions ever since the beginning of Japan's modern period. This evidently contradicts the widely accepted hypothesis that modern Japan had a prolonged period of "unlimited supplies of labor" to the paid sector à la W. Arthur Lewis, for this concept implies a rigid constancy of real wages over time.

The Lewisian notion of labor supply has stirred up a considerable controversy concerning the interpretation of the intersectoral relationship in Japanese development.[17] Many agree that the period of modern Japan preceding the First World War was Lewisian. One is ambivalent about the character of the interwar period, or about the first ten or fifteen years of the period after the Second World War. One is again sure that the Japanese economy of the 1960s is no longer Lewisian. By "Lewisian economy" I mean an economy characterized by "unlimited supplies of labor" to the paid sector. I feel that there has never been a Lewisian period in the history of modern Japan. In the first place, the degree of commercialization that characterized pre-Meiji agriculture already suggests a sensitive marginalist calculus on the part of the peasant household unlike the subsistence sector in the Lewisian economy. Modern Japan accentuated this tendency for finer economic rationality already evident during the Tokugawa period. But there are more direct empirical reasons for rejecting the applicability of the Lewisian concept to Japanese development.

Four characteristics of the Lewisian period can be tested by resorting to experience: (1) the real wage rate remains constant; (2) it is higher than the marginal product of labor in the self-employed sector; (3) the marginal product of labor catches up with the wage rate in the course of economic development; and (4) after the turning point, the wage rate and the marginal product of labor increase *pari passu*. Ryoshin Minami has used these criteria to detect the Lewisian period in Japanese development, although with more emphasis on some than on others.[18] Between 1895 and 1913 the daily wage rate for male day labor deflated by the index of prices for agricultural products remained roughly constant although there were cyclical variations. During the same period Minami shows that there was an increasing trend in the marginal product of labor in agriculture. The first and third characteristics of the Lewisian period just mentioned are therefore easily fulfilled.

The second characteristic is "overfulfilled" to such an extent that one doubts the plausibility of the comparison of wages and marginal products of labor in this case. If it is assumed that the average working days in agriculture are 150 per year, a conservative assumption, Minami's daily wage rate for male agricultural workers at 0.7 or 0.8 *yen* during the period of 1894 to 1913 would result in 105 or 120 *yen* per year in the prices of 1934–1936. The annual marginal product of a person employed in agriculture was less than 30 *yen* in 1895 and barely 40 *yen* in 1914, considerably lower than the presumed annual earnings from paid work in agriculture. The maximum value of the marginal product was reached in 1933 and again in 1939, but it still was no higher than 50 *yen*. Thus, throughout the prewar period, the marginal product of labor in agriculture (labor measured in man-years) never caught up with the earnings from paid work in agriculture. Even the maximum marginal product of labor for the whole period was lower than the earnings from paid work which obtained at the beginning.

In principle, therefore, it seems that even if the real wage rate had stayed constant at its level of the 1890s throughout the prewar period, there would have been no difficulty in drawing labor to paid work. Two questions may be asked about this extraordinary situation. The first question is how such a disproportionate wage rate had ever come into being. The second question is why real wages had to rise in the face of this seemingly enormous advantage of paid labor over self-employment in agriculture. Before answers to these questions are explored, it is desirable to mention what is really meant by the measured marginal product of labor in Minami's framework. Minami obtains the marginal product of labor as a constant fraction of the average product of labor, which in turn is obtained by dividing total output by the number of gainfully employed persons. The whole series of operations is full of hazards. As mentioned in the Introduction to this book, one cannot be too sure about the absolute level of agricultural output. The number of persons gainfully employed in agriculture is another hurdle, but for this, one can depend on Minami; he has done more about agricultural employment than anyone else. After reliable figures are obtained for average products, the next big question has to do with the fraction that is applied to average products to obtain marginal products. The fraction Minami uses is an average of coefficients showing the elasticity of output with respect to labor in cross-section production functions that Kazushi Ohkawa has obtained for the years between 1937 and 1941. The coefficients average at 0.24, that is, the marginal product is assumed to be uniformly 24 percent of the average product for each year of the prewar period. Although one feels somewhat uneasy about this value as applied to the entire period, one cannot but pass over this point merely noting that the level of the marginal product critically depends upon the accuracy of this fraction.

The gainfully employed persons used for obtaining average products include males and females, so that it may not be wholly appropriate to use only the male wages for comparison with the marginal product of labor. More appropriate wage data would include female wages. The agricultural wages used in the first chapter of this book were simple averages of four kinds of wages: male and female wages in farming and sericulture. Table 14 puts together average products, marginal products, and wage rates for a re-examination of the presumed Lewisian period of Japanese development. My wage series deflated by the price index for farm products (row 4) shows a secular increase between the early 1890s and early 1910s, in contrast to the product wages for male workers used by Minami (row 3). I have added on the table data on money wages and the index of farm prices for comparison (rows 7 and 8). Somewhat fortuitously, the rate of increase in my product wages is almost the same as that in Minami's average and marginal products. Thus one of the conditions for the Lewisian notion of "unlimited supplies of labor," that is, the constancy of real wages, is not fulfilled according to my wage series for the period before the First World War. Furthermore, in view of Nakamura's rate of growth of agricultural output, which is 1 percent per annum between 1874 and 1920, the

TABLE 14

AVERAGE PRODUCT, MARGINAL PRODUCT,
AND WAGE RATE IN AGRICULTURE, 1894–1914

Item	A 1894–98	B 1910–14	$\frac{B}{A}$	Annual Compound Rate of Increase
(1) Average product	116 ¥	150 ¥	129%	1.6%
(2) Marginal product	28 ¥	36 ¥	129%	1.6%
(3) Product wage, male per day	0.75 ¥	0.77 ¥	103%	negligible
(4) Product wage, male and female average, per day	0.42 ¥	0.53 ¥	126%	1.5%
(5) (3) × 150 days	112 ¥	115 ¥	103%	negligible
(6) (4) × 150 days	63 ¥	81 ¥	126%	1.5%
(7) Money wage, male and female average, per day	0.184 ¥	0.362 ¥	197%	4.3%
(8) Farm product prices (1934–36 = 100)	43.99	68.42	155%	2.8%

(1), (2), (3). See Ryoshin Minami, "The Turning Point in Japanese Economy," *Quarterly Journal of Economics*, Vol. 82 (August 1968), pp. 380–402.

(4), (7). See Koji Taira, *The Dynamics of Japanese Wage Differentials, 1881–1959* (Unpublished Ph.D. thesis, Stanford University, 1961), p. 235.

(8). *ELTES*, Vol. 9, p. 164.

rates of increase in the more plausible average and marginal products would be lower than the rates shown in Table 14. If so, the product wages might have risen faster than the marginal products of labor in Japanese agriculture before the First World War. That real wages can keep increasing over time is not consistent with the simultaneous existence of "unlimited supplies of labor."

Under the previous assumption of 150 days worked per year in agriculture, the average annual earnings from paid work on the basis of my wage figures would still be higher than the annual marginal products of labor. The gap between the two is still too great to be readily acceptable. One suspects that there are some enormous data problems involved here.

However, the estimated earnings from paid work are lower than the average products of labor according to Table 14, although they are higher than the marginal products. This situation is at least susceptible to rational interpretations. Although each working member's consumption within the farm family may be limited to his or her marginal product, it is recognized automatically that he or she is entitled to the average product if need for justifiable extra expenses should arise. In other words, the working member of the family is saving the difference between average and marginal products when the marginal product rule of distribution is followed by the family. Suppose that the farm family in this situation faced the opportunity of paid work which would fetch cash earnings per person higher than the marginal product but lower than the average product of labor within the family enterprise. How would the individuals and the family react to this opportunity?

First, from the individual point of view, paid work under the direction of someone else may be more strenuous than normal work within the family, so that the cash earnings do not appear so very attractive. On the other hand, with larger cash earnings, a person can afford a higher level of consumption. Furthermore, since he will be the sole decision-maker about his earnings, he will gain an additional sense of freedom. But then this freedom may be exercised too much in favor of present consumption, so that his savings may actually fall below the difference between the average and marginal product of labor within the family despite the larger cash earnings from paid work. By preferring the present consumption too much and saving too little, the person outside the family may be losing his claim to a part of the family savings to which he would be automatically contributing if he stayed with the family.

From the family's point of view, it will benefit the economic well-being of all concerned if some members go out to earn from paid work and the average and marginal products of the remaining family members are increased consequently. The family may therefore "bargain" with the eligible members for a fraction of their earnings from outside employment to be remitted to the family in exchange for full protection and help in case of need. This fraction may be fixed in such a way as to permit a higher level of consumption after the remittance than the level of consumption that has been customary within the family. In other words, under the conditions hypothesized in this logical exercise, the family members who go out to work for pay can enjoy higher standards of living for themselves without impairing the customary protection that the family has always accorded to them. Since paid work is subject to certain negative preferences, there must be some minimum differential between the rate of pay outside and the marginal product of labor within the family in order for the family and individuals to opt in favor of sending some members out to paid employment.[19]

According to Table 14, the differential between the rate of pay for outside employment and the intrafamily marginal product of labor seems to have been enormous in prewar Japan. It is questionable, however, that there was so much differential as that in reality. Whatever the differential, it was not sufficient to render self-employment into a pool of "unlimited supplies of labor" because the rate of pay had to increase from time to time despite the large initial differential suggested by the present data. From these considerations I feel that the period before the First World War cannot be as comfortably regarded as Lewisian as many have so far been willing to assume. I shall take up the Lewisian theory again in connection with another "structuralist" view of Japanese economy at the end of Chapter 4.

Conclusion

This chapter explores theoretical aspects of interrelations between the aggregate demand and intersectoral wage differential. Then statistical experiments are made on testing the hypotheses derived from these considerations. The results are satisfactory.

Second, this chapter advances an elementary economic analysis of the self-employed household enterprise in relation to job opportunities in the labor market. The sensitivity of interactions between self-employment and paid employment and the elasticity of the productivity curves in the household enterprise are seen to be among the determinants of the elasticity of labor supply for paid employment.

Third, the variations in the interindustry wage differentials are related to changes in the ratio of self-employment to total employment in industry. The role of self-employment in manufacturing in relation to the manufacturing labor market is also consistent with the working of economic forces in a broader context that determines the intersectoral wage differential.

Fourth, fortified by the plausible rationality of the household economy, this chapter questions the applicability of the concept of "unlimited supplies of labor" to any stage of economic development in modern Japan. One feels that Japanese development has been neoclassical throughout.

4   Japanese Wage Differentials after the Second World War

POSTWAR JAPAN is now more than twenty years old. In length of time the period since the end of the Second World War is comparable to the interwar period. When measured by the pace of economic expansion, however, the twenty years of the postwar period would be an equivalent of forty years of the prewar period. In 1946 GNP per capita in constant prices was back to the level of the early 1920s. In less than ten years, the prewar peak of 1939 was regained. The first ten years were equivalent to seventeen prewar years. After 1955 each year was filled with economic growth comparable to two years' growth by the prewar standard. One would therefore expect that the labor market had also gone through enormous changes during the postwar period. This is what I would like to discuss in this chapter.[1]

Following the pattern of Chapter 1, I have presented representative pieces of wage differentials together with comments on the nature of data and economic factors that may have been responsible for shaping the course of wage differentials over time. Discussion of interfirm and intrafirm wage relativities is deferred to Chapter 8 because a considerable amount of institutional information is necessary for a reasonable appreciation of this group of wage phenomena. In this chapter my emphasis will be on the intersectoral and interindustry wage differentials in the context of changing economic conditions. Finally, I shall look into another structuralist viewpoint, namely, the concept of "dual structure" in Japanese development.

Intersectoral
Wage Differentials

Different kinds of nonagricultural wages are related to agricultural wages and presented as series 1 on Chart III. The agricultural wage is the lowest wage of paid labor. The wages of unskilled workers in the construction industry are slightly better than those of day laborers in agriculture (series 1-d). The "contractual" wages in manufacturing are considerably higher than agricultural wages (series 1-c). The average earnings in nonagricultural industries including manufacturing are still higher (series 1-a). Series 1-e is the ratio of Ryoshin Minami's marginal product of labor in agriculture to the male wage rate. Because I have commented extensively on the relationship between the marginal product of labor and wages in agriculture in Chapter 3, I pass over it here without comment. It may be noted that an interesting stratification of wages is erected on the base of the marginal product of labor in agriculture.[2]

The average agricultural wage for any year used here except for series 1-e is a simple average of daily wages for the male and female farm workers hired by day as in the case of agricultural wages used in Chapter 1. One difference is that the prewar agricultural wages included wages in sericulture. Although data on sericultural wages are not available for the postwar period, their presence or absence would have made very little difference to the level of agricultural wages. Unskilled wages in construction are also simple averages of male and female unskilled workers engaged in light menial tasks (*keisagyō ninpu*) in this industry.

"Contractual" wage in industry is the official Japanese translation of a somewhat complicated concept of pay. Literally, the original term means "the wage that is surely paid" (*kimatte shikyūsuru kyūyo*). It is not a "guaranteed" monthly salary, however. Only for the white-collar workers, the "contractual" wage approximates a "guaranteed" wage. In most cases it is the wage that a worker understands that he can earn under normal circumstances specified in individual contracts, collective agreements, or rules of wage payments of the firm to which he has agreed. "Total earnings" are the sum of the "contractual" wage and

CHART III

JAPANESE WAGE DIFFERENTIALS, SELECTED SERIES,
1945–1966

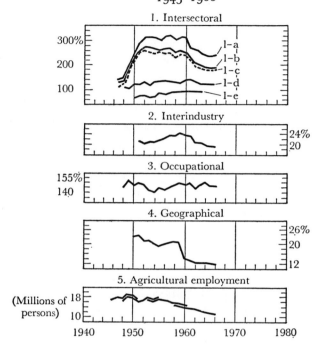

1. Intersectoral

2. Interindustry

3. Occupational

4. Geographical

5. Agricultural employment

1. The intersectoral wage differentials express nonagricultural wages as percentages of agricultural wages. Except for series 1-e, the agricultural wage used is the simple average of daily wages for male and female farm workers. The nonagricultural wages for different series are as follows:

1-a. Daily equivalent of the total monthly earnings in nonagricultural establishments employing 30 or more regular workers. The monthly earnings are divided by the average number of days worked per month reported in the same source (see below).

1-b. Daily equivalent of the contractual monthly wages in the same establishments as in 1-a. For definitions of terms, see text.

1-c. Daily equivalent of the contractual monthly wages in manufacturing establishments of the sames scales as above.

1-d. Daily wages of male and female unskilled workers engaged in light work in construction.

Source: YLS, various years.

1-e. Marginal product of labor in agriculture on an annual basis as a percentage of the annual equivalent of the daily wages for male farm workers.

"special" payment. The latter should rather be called "unexpected" payment, for it is the payment made to the worker temporarily, unexpectedly, or erratically at the discretion of the employer or independently of the stipulations for the "contractual" wage. For example, when back pay is agreed upon at the time of the renegotiations of a collective agreement, it is included as "special" in the pay for the month when it is actually paid to the worker.[3] The weights of "contractual" and "special" components in total earnings may be seen by comparing series 1-a with series 1-b on Chart III. It is also useful to bear in mind that the nonagricultural wages have to do with the regular workers in establishments with thirty or more of them. The proportion of the nonagricultural labor force in these establishments was 45 percent in 1960. In manufacturing, employment in establishments with thirty or more regular workers in 1960 was 64 percent of the total employment of this sector. This was roughly the proportion of the manufacturing labor force employed in "factories" with five or more operatives in 1939. This indicates how the average size of establishment in manufacturing had grown in these twenty-one years.

According to Chart III the intersectoral wage differentials had run one long cycle between 1945 and 1966 quite similar to prewar Kuznets cycles in wage differentials. The differential between total nonagricultural earnings and agricultural wages (series 1-a) increased rapidly

---

Source: Ryoshin Minami, "The Turning Point in Japanese Economy," *Quarterly Journal of Economics,* Vol. 82 (August 1968).

2. The coefficient of average deviation for 20 or 21 subdivisions of manufacturing on the basis of data obtained from establishments of the same scales as for series 1-c. *Sources:* same as for series 1-c above.

3. The wages of skilled workers to those of unskilled workers in construction. *Source: YLS,* various years.

4. The coefficient of average deviation for 46 prefectures (including Hokkaido). Average prefectural wages are usually based on data from establishments of scales mentioned for series 1-a. In some prefectures smaller establishments are also included. *Source: YLS,* various years.

5. The differences in agricultural employment among segments of this series arise partly from changes in the definition of the labor force and partly from adjustments in the light of the population census. The first segment was based on the labor force 15 years old or older by the old Japanese counting of age. The second segment was based on the labor force 14 years old or older by the new (Western) counting of age. The last two segments were based on the labor force 15 years old or older by the new counting of age. The difference between the two is due to the latest adjustments. *Source: YLS,* various years.

during the early postwar years, and after a slight decrease between 1953 and 1955 increased to an all-time high in 1957. The narrowing of this differential was first halting and then precipitous during the early 1960s. The differential between industry's "contractual" wages and agricultural wages followed a similar course to the case of total earnings but reached its peak in 1953 (series 1-b). This pattern is particularly marked in the differential between the contractual wages in manufacturing and agricultural wages (series 1-c). Later in this chapter I shall use this differential between manufacturing and agriculture for an experiment with statistical explanations in the way suggested in Chapter 3. One of the explanatory variables is the number of persons employed in agriculture, which is shown as series 5 on Chart III. Frequent changes in the definition of the labor force require adjustments to obtain one series for the whole period for the purpose of statistical analysis. Series 5 presents data on agricultural employment as it is defined from time to time.

A brief preliminary remark on the course of labor supplies in postwar Japan may be useful at this point. The Second World War, which ended in Japan's defeat, altered factor proportions drastically. With the disappearance of the defense needs and the repatriation of service personnel and overseas Japanese, there were suddenly a large number of redundant workers. Capital and jobs were scarce in industry, and there were massive movements of population back to agriculture. A normal historical pattern of intersectoral labor mobility in a growing economy was reversed for a time during the early postwar years.[4] The increase in the war-induced labor surplus in agriculture was brought to an end as the economy recovered and agricultural employment decreased after 1949, first haltingly and then in a sustained fashion especially after 1955. The migration of labor into and out of agriculture worked on the intersectoral wage differential in the way that was hypothesized in the preceding chapter. The result was the widening and narrowing of the differential as depicted by various elements of series 1 on Chart III.

It is useful to recall that the agricultural wages have to do with casual labor hired by day in agriculture and that the nonagricultural wages are for the regular workers, manual and nonmanual, in establishments employing thirty or more of these workers. It may be plausible to assume that the parity of wages between these different groups of workers will never reach unity because of the quality differences. Just how much of the observed intersectoral wage differential should be charged to quality differences is a difficult question. One wonders whether the "contractual" wages in manufacturing 50 percent above the daily wages in agriculture may not be near the parity of intersectoral wage relationship. If so, the intersectoral wage differential today may be quite close to an equilibrium level. But more on this later.

Interindustry
Wage Differentials[5]

The coefficient of average deviation is again used as an indicator of interindustry wage differentials. Series 2 on Chart III depicts the course of movement of this coefficient since 1951. The Ministry of Labor adopted a new standard industrial classification in October 1950 expanding, or rather disaggregating, the manufacturing sector into twenty subdivisions and limiting the coverage of wage survey to establishments with thirty or more regular workers. Given the nature of the wages used for the calculation, it is not surprising that the peak should have been reached in 1959. For the whole decade of the 1950s there was some uncertainty as to the relative strengths of various factors involved in wage determination and labor market process. In the 1960s, however, the labor market has decidedly been in a state of intensified labor shortage. In keeping with the state of the labor market, the interindustry wage differentials have narrowed considerably since 1959. The wide interindustry wage differentials during the 1950s have often been taken as signs of structural characteristics peculiar to the postwar Japanese economy such as "dual structure." It may be useful to see the alleged "peculiarity" of the industrial structure of the 1950s in historical perspective.

Proper historical comparisons have long been hindered because of changes in the industrial classification over time. Since the new standard industrial classification dates back only to 1950, it takes an enormous reshuffling of wages by industry for earlier statistical data in order to obtain a comparable series of interindustry wage differentials. The Shōwa Dōjin Kai, the research group previously introduced, has undertaken this type of operation on the basis of prewar *Factory Statistics* (*KTH*) and postwar *Census of Manufacture* (also abbreviated *KTH*). The coefficients of variation (standard deviation as a percentage of the mean) in wages among twenty manufacturing industries were calculated for selected years.

Year	c.v.	Year	c.v.
1909	22.0%	1948	24.5%
1914	21.7	1952	28.6
1919	17.6	1956	30.2
1924	19.7		
1930	30.7	1956[a]	28.4
1933	33.3	1966[a]	22.7
1935	32.1		

Source: WCKNSK, p. 470

[a] My additions on the basis of the data used for series 2, Chart III.

These estimates indicate that the interindustry wage differentials in manufacturing during the late 1950s were very much like those during the 1930s. The prewar peak was in 1933 as mentioned in Chapter 1. The coefficient of variation for 1933, according to the Showa Dojin Kai, was 33.3 percent. Since 1956 was not the year when postwar interindustry wage differentials were the widest, one may well suppose from the foregone estimates that at the peak, which was in 1959, the differentials were just as wide as in 1933. But in 1966, the differentials were back to the predepression level, that is, the level of the 1920s. After the extraordinary narrowing during the First World War, the interindustry wage differentials evidently widened (although data are not clear on this point). According to the Showa Dojin Kai's calculations, the 1924 differentials were wider than the 1919 differentials but were still narrower than the 1909 differentials. According to Chapter 1 of this book, the interindustry wage differentials were at the peak of a cycle in 1909, whereas the 1920s were a period of transition from the trough in 1919 to the peak in 1933. Although the postwar differentials were still larger in 1966, when they had so far been the smallest in the whole postwar period, than in 1919, the long-term statistical series indicates that the characteristics of wage differentials during the 1950s were transitory in nature and so not particularly attributable to any radical alteration of the resource-allocative process in the Japanese economy. In other words, the interindustry wage differentials during the 1950s were within the expected variations in the ordinary functioning of the labor market subject to existing factor endowments and the state of the goods market.

In addition to supplying a long-run historical perspective, the Showa Dojin Kai data just quoted also offer a much desired glimpse into what happened to the interindustry wage differentials before 1951, which is lacking in series 2, Chart III. Evidently, the postwar years prior to 1950 were a period of widening for the interindustry wage differentials as may be seen from the comparison of figures for 1948 and 1952 in the set of coefficients of variation quoted above and from considering at the same time what has happened since 1951 according to series 2, Chart III. This pattern of variations in the interindustry wage differentials agrees with that in the intersectoral wage differentials.

Occupational
Wage Differentials

Series 3 on Chart III illustrates the size and transition over time of the average differential of skilled wages over unskilled in construction. This differential has been rather stable fluctuating within narrow limits throughout the postwar period. This near constancy may seem somewhat enigmatic, because one would have expected noticeable undulations over time in this differential as in others. However, it belongs to the same group of market phenomena as the near absence of wage differentials between unskilled construction workers and agricultural day laborers as shown by series 1-d and the near constancy of differential between agricultural wages and the marginal product of labor in agriculture as shown by series 1-e. One plausible explanation is that workers of all grades in the construction industry are drawn from a large, unstructured, freely competitive labor market where relative wages are sensitively adjusted by the forces of supply and demand.[6] This labor market includes no less than two thirds of paid labor, practically all but the small portion of the labor force regularly employed in relatively large firms and a large proportion of farm households.

Agriculture and small-scale industries are particularly close competitors for labor with the construction industry. Pressures such as sudden increases in demand or in supply in any part of this fluid labor market tend to permeate the whole system rather quickly. Casual unskilled workers hired by day in agriculture and construction are almost perfect substitutes. The wage differential between agriculture and construction for these workers, if adjusted for transfer costs involved in traveling to the sites of construction from time to time, would disappear entirely and stay roughly constant over time. This is what series 1-d on Chart III indicates.

The process of skill acquisition is competitive so far as the skills used in construction and small-scale industries are concerned. What is meant by "competitive" in this connection is that there are many opportunities for acquiring these skills, and no one has control over its process. Since living and working on the farm are natural training grounds for the children to acquire rudimentary skills useful in other industries as well, agriculture in this sense can be said to put the floor to the wages for these skills. They include carpentry, masonry, plastering, roofing, furniture making, painting, smithing, gadgetry, and repair works of many kinds, and—nowadays one should add—driving automotive equipment. Children grow up on the farm increasingly familiar with tools, materials, and skills of handling them, all of which can be transferred to nonagricultural occupations. When an economy is endowed with a large and reasonably progressive agricultural sector as in the case of postwar Japan, the likelihood for skilled craftsmen to emerge from family life on the farm is very high. In addition to these widespread chances for learning rudimentary skills, the small social groups formed around master craftsmen and masters themselves in the nonagricultural sector are so numerous that there is no possibility for restrictions on the acquisition and practice of manual skills in this sector. Similar observations apply to small-scale workshops producing parts, tools, pottery, wood carving, metal casting, leather tanning, and sundries of household wares. These shops interact intensively with agriculture and construction in demand for labor. Thus wages for manual skills and common labor are fully subject to the market forces which determine and maintain the appropriate skill differentials. The near constancy of the wage differential by skill on Chart III results from the very high degree of allocative efficiency of Japan's manual labor market.

Two points are worth mentioning in this connection. First, the comparison of the postwar and prewar differentials by skill in the construction industry indicates that the postwar differentials are on the whole more stable over time than the prewar. This is due in part to the greater stability of the Japanese economy after than before the war. The rate of growth has varied widely after the war, but the economy has been growing consistently. This is a great difference compared with Japan's prewar economy. Second, the spread of manual skills is far more extensive and the general level of technical knowledge and proficiency is far higher after than before the war. This is what usually happens as a consequence of economic development. At the same time, the higher technical level of Japanese life and the higher level of education and information have also downgraded the personalized manual skills relative to organized techniques of production in larger firms. By simply being a part of the integrated technology, an unskilled worker in these firms can produce more than an individual worker, however skilled, can produce on his own. For this reason, the wage differentials for manual skills of the type considered here are perhaps less representative of "occupational" wage differentials after than before the war even among the manual workers. "Skills" in large firms are depersonalized and largely functions of the changing technology. Versatility and adaptability are more in demand than accomplished skills in today's large firms. This certainly is not limited to Japan alone. The changing nature of "skill" under new technology has induced economists in other countries in recent years to speak of efficiency differences more in terms of "quality" of labor than in terms of "skill" as such. "Skill" today connotes too much of personalized manual proficiency to be useful for the kind of ability and work habit needed for efficient mass production in modern firms. In other words, a worker is now an amorphous pool of ability from which "skills" for specific tasks may be drawn from time to time according to the exigencies of evolving technology. Differential rewards for different sizes of this "ability pool" are today more important than wage differentials by skill. I shall have more to say on the changing nature of skills and production techniques in Part II of this book.

Geographical
Wage Differentials

Series 4 on Chart III traces the coefficient of average deviation for average nonagricultural wages in forty-five prefectures and Hokkaido. The average of the data is the same as the wage data used for series 1-a, that is, establishments employing thirty or more regular workers, though some allowances for the inclusion of smaller establishments are made for relatively nonindustrialized areas. The downward trend which was already visible during the 1950s took a sharp plunge at the beginning of the 1960s. The abrupt change between 1959 and 1960 arouses some suspicion although there is no doubt that there was a considerable narrowing of geographical wage differentials around 1960 as attested to by government publications (*RH* for 1961 and 1962, for example). Miyohei Shinohara has examined the dispersion of prefectural per capita incomes and obtained roughly the same pattern of variations over time as series 4 on Chart III for the 1950s.[7] His series ends in 1961 and shows an increase from 1959 to 1961. While wages and incomes often diverge in movement over time, it is perhaps useful to keep alive a certain amount of skepticism about the size of change in the interprefectural wage differentials between 1959 and 1960 as depicted on Chart III.

To a surprising extent the course of geographical wage differentials is closely associated, with some lag, with changes in the rate of growth of the postwar Japanese economy. The shrinkage of the differentials between 1950 and 1955 was due in large part to the Korean War boom, while the partial reversal in the trend during the latter half of the 1950s was related to the slowing down of economic growth in the middle 1950s. The unprecedented economic expansion between 1959 and 1961 at annual rates higher than in any other period was associated with the shrinkage of geographical wage differentials during the 1960s. Certainly this is a remarkable degree of sensitivity for any kind of wage differential to attain in relation to economic conditions. That such a degree of sensitivity is observed in geographical wage differentials more clearly than in other differentials may imply an important labor market phenomenon, that is, the greater sensitivity of labor mobility to geographical differences in employment opportunities.[8] A vigorous reshuffling of the labor force over the geographical dimension of the economic system is surely what is expected of an efficient resource-allocative mechanism. The labor market in Japan is doing its job fairly well.

A Statistical Experiment on the Intersectoral Wage Differential

Chapter 3 advanced a set of hypotheses to relate the variations in the intersectoral wage differential over time to changes in the aggregate demand and intersectoral labor transfer. In this section I would like to repeat a statistical experiment similar to that undertaken in Chapter 3. I take the differential between manufacturing and agricultural wages (series 1-c, Chart III) as the dependent variable to be "explained" by variables that indicate the aggregate demand and intersectoral migration of labor. The evolution of the agricultural labor force is charted as series 5 on Chart III. For the purpose of statistical experiment, I have linked the different segments of this series to the center segment running from 1953 to 1961 by additions to the later segment and subtractions from earlier segments. By these adjustments I have obtained a single time series of the agricultural labor force for the whole postwar period.

The net number of workers transferred to nonagricultural sectors is estimated by the same method as explained in Chapter 3. Each segment in series 5 gives rise to the corresponding numbers of transferred workers. These numbers are then expressed as percentages of the total numbers of persons employed in agriculture.[9] The net rates of labor transfer from agriculture during the overlapping years are then averaged and a single time series is obtained for the net rate of labor transfer. Finally, three-year moving averages are applied to show the pattern over time more clearly out of the rather sharply fluctuating annual rates.

The representation of the aggregate demand has posed some difficulties. The method of adjusting for trend has proved useless for the postwar GNP data. If the whole postwar period is viewed as being subject to one linear trend, three periods with reference to this trend are observed in the time series of GNP in constant prices; above trend during the recovery period of 1946 to 1952, below trend during the rest of the 1950s, and above trend again during the 1960s. The intersectoral wage differential increased fast during the recovery period when the aggregate demand was also rising fast. This upsets the hypothesis that when the aggregate demand is strong, the wage differential should narrow. When the differential is lagged as in Chapter 3 behind the trend-adjusted aggregate demand, the moderate narrowing during the 1950s fits beautifully with the trend-adjusted GNP of the recovery period, but the GNP of the 1950s, which was below trend, fits badly with the narrowing of the differential in the 1960s. The series of growth rates in GNP shows no promise whatever because of their sharp short-run changes. A smoothed series suffers from the same consequences as the trend-adjusted series.

After much pondering, an indicator of the differential impact of the aggregate demand on industry and agriculture was tried and has turned out to be rather efficient. This is the index of relative prices defined as the ratio of the index of wholesale prices for all commodities to the index of wholesale prices for farm products. I have cut out the indices prior to 1950 when the extreme food shortage and direct control on food distribution made relative prices meaningless as variables impinging on resource allocation. Even so, the good fit between wage differentials and relative prices may be fortuitous, for the determination of farm product prices in recent years have been more political than economic. At this point, however, one may say that in whatever manner prices are determined, they are bound to have resource-allocative effects so long as the producers are free to adjust all other factors. In recent years farm prices have risen faster than the prices of nonfarm products, which is what is expected to happen to relative prices under prosperity. The actual situation in Japan in this respect is enormously complicated, but the formal resemblance of the behavior of relative prices during the recent period of rapid growth to what is a priori expected makes the use of their index plausible for a proxy for the impact of the aggregate demand.

Some of the better results are as follows:

$$(1) \quad D_t = 227.3 - 0.708 m_{t-4} \qquad\qquad R^2 = 0.4124$$
$$ (30.0) \quad (3.39) \qquad\qquad\qquad t: 1951-1966$$

(2) $D_t = -177.5 + 24.2L_{t-4}$ $\bar{R}^2 = 0.7388$

     (3.22) (7.01) $t: 1949-1966$

(3) $D_t = 23.7 + 1.92P_{t-1}$ $\bar{R}^2 = 0.7887$

     (0.95) (7.55) $t: 1951-1966$

(4) $D_t = 0.495 + 0.64P_t + 10.0L_t$ $\bar{R}^2 = 0.8487$

     (0.02) (1.54) (2.77) $t: 1950-1966$

(5) $D_t = 98.4 + 1.42P_t - 0.622m_t$ $\bar{R}^2 = 0.8743$

     (4.45) (7.27) (3.95) $t: 1950-1965$

(6) $D_t = -53.85 + 16.74L_{t-4} + 0.847G_{t-4} - 24.05\lambda$ $\bar{R}^2 = 0.8487$

     (0.80) (4.28) (1.06) (2.89) $t: 1951-1966$

where D = the intersectoral wage differential (series 1-c, Chart III)

    m = the net rate of labor transfer from agriculture (net out-migrants per thousand of persons employed in agriculture)

    L = agricultural employment in millions of persons (series 5, Chart III)

    P = the ratio of the wholesale price index for all commodities to the wholesale price index for farm products (from the Bank of Japan, *The Hundred-Year Statistics of the Japanese Economy*, p. 77) with 1960 as the base (= 100)

    G = the rate of growth of gross national product in constant prices (*ibid.*, supplemented by data from more recent issues of *KH*)

    λ = a dummy variable (0 before 1959, 1 after 1959).

The t ratios are shown in brackets below the regression coefficients.

A fairly strong relationship obtains between the intersectoral wage differential and the rate of labor transfer from agriculture with a four-year lag (Equation 1). The larger the migration out of agriculture relative to agricultural employment, the narrower the wage differential. The number of persons employed in agriculture as an explanatory variable does better than the rate of labor transfer (Equation 2). The positive relationship between this variable and wage differential indicates that larger agricultural employment is associated with wider intersectoral wage differential. It is the relative prices that go the longest way to explain variations in the intersectoral wage differential (Equation 3). The wage differential falls as agricultural prices rise relative to industrial.

The joint use of the relative prices and labor force variables improves the explanation substantially (Equations 4 and 5). The relative prices and the rate of labor transfer from agriculture have produced the best explanation of all the relationships tried in the course of this statistical experiment. While lags help improve simple correlations, they do not prove to be of much use in multiple regressions. With the relative prices at the level of 1960 (= 100) and with no labor transfer ($m = 0$), Equation 5 would give an intersectoral wage differential equaling 240 percent. This situation roughly obtained in 1953. In 1960, with the same relative prices, a positive labor transfer (46 per thousand of agricultural employment) reduced the differential to 223 percent. (The value estimated from Equation 5 is 212 percent.)

Agricultural prices have risen faster than industrial prices since 1960. The index of relative prices with 1960 = 100 is 60 for 1966. Suppose that the index of relative prices stabilized at 50 after 1970 and that the net rate of labor transfer from agriculture rose to 70 per thousand (the actual rate was 60 per thousand in 1966). Then, from Equation 5, the intersectoral wage differential would come down to 125 percent. This is very close to the "normal" intersectoral wage differential prior to the First World War as examined in Chapter 3. In other words, it is possible that the intersectoral wage differential would be no wider in the 1970s than in the 1900s. This possibility is even more remarkable when one considers the differences in the quality of labor between the sectors today which must have been absent before the First World War. Of course one should always be cautious about extrapolations, but the point is that a considerable narrowing of the intersectoral wage differential is within the range of possibilities for the economic framework of post-Second World War Japan, that is, the flexibility and efficiency of the labor market in today's Japan are just as great as in all other periods of Japanese history.[10]

A few words may be added here on the role of economic growth in relation to the intersectoral wage differential in the light of Equation 6. The GNP growth rates alone show absolutely no correlation with the differential. The best performance of this variable, although still weak, is obtained when used with agricultural employment and a dummy variable as in Equation 6. The positive coefficient of the GNP growth rate in this equation is not inconsistent with the theoretical considerations offered in Chapter 3 under certain conditions. One should not be too much impressed with this relationship, however. A weak relationship of this kind easily turns into an equally weak negative relationship as observed in the course of the present experiment. One hopes that the dummy variable will catch the effects of whatever qualitative differences there were between the period before and that after 1959. The Japanese often refer to the 1960s as the era of rapid growth (*kōdo seichō ki*) or the era of structural transformation (*tenkei ki*). Since rapid growth is an indicator of strong aggregate demand, this dummy variable may well be considered a proxy for the aggregate demand. Fortunately, it is inversely associated with the movement of the intersectoral wage differential over time, in conformity with the theoretical conjecture offered in Chapter 3.

"Unlimited Supplies of Labor" and "Dual Structure" [11]

The sensitive market mechanism which unifies the whole economic system in Japan is incompatible with any notion which seeks Japan's structural characteristics in resource immobility and the absence or weakness of equilibrating forces. I have already commented upon one structural notion, namely, the Lewisian concept of "unlimited supplies of labor." Another, more elusive, structural concept is "dual structure." I have suggested that there has never been a Lewisian period in Japanese development. Another way of saying the same thing is that the Japanese economy was already at a post-Lewisian stage at the beginning of modern Japan. Since the economic system after the "turning point" in the Lewisian theory is neoclassical, my suggestion implies that Japan's neoclassical market mechanism has no place for "dual structure" which arises from structural barriers to resource mobility.

For the sake of logical exercise, let us accept for the moment that the Japanese economy was Lewisian with "unlimited supplies of labor" before the First World War. It has been widely accepted that "dual structure" arose during the interwar period. It seems therefore that just about the time when the "Lewisians" were ready to graduate the Japanese economy from the stage of "unlimited supplies of labor" to a neoclassical stage, the "dualists" interfered to postpone applying the neoclassical framework to Japan. Furthermore, the state of wage differentials during the 1950s, which looked very much like the one that prevailed during the 1930s, elevated the concept of "dual structure" to the position of a theoretical doctrine which to some persons was capable of explaining all the characteristics of Japanese economic process.[12]

What is not clear, however, is how the "dualists" regard the economic characteristics of the period which the "Lewisians" claim as their own, that is, the period before the First World War. This period was evidently nondual. But since "dual" is often synonymous with "unbalanced" and "dual structure" with "disequilibrium," the "nondual" stage of Japanese development preceding the "dual" may be supposed to have been a stage of "balanced" or "equilibrium" growth.[13] If so, the Japanese economy at the "nondual" stage may well have been neoclassical. In other words, what is the stage of "unlimited supplies of labor" to the "Lewisians" is a neoclassical stage to the "dualists," and what is neoclassical to the "Lewisians" is the stage of "dual structure" to the "dualists." This is certainly a great predicament. Although my adherence to the notion of the unity of markets in Japan throughout her modern economic development saves me from the task of reconciling the "Lewisian" and "dualist" views of Japanese development, I cannot go through the writings of Fei and Ranis, the "Lewisians," [14] and those of Ohkawa and Rosovsky, the "dualists," [15] without sensing a crisis of interpretation. Add to this division among the "structuralists" a growing group of "neoclassicists" such as Jorgenson and Patrick.[16] And the students of Japanese economic development are surely assigned a good amount of homework to do.

There is one more aspect of the issue. It is sometimes felt that the *analytical* relevance of the Lewisian theory may be dissociated from its *historical* implications. For one, Charles P. Kindleberger takes this position and considers the theory useful for the analysis of the United States experience, to mention one astounding example among many.[17] If disguised unemployment or slack in manpower is created by whatever forces—war, disaster, depression, immigration, industrial revolution—the subsequent growth can be regarded to be analogous to the Lewisian type of development with "unlimited supplies of labor." Thus some of the European countries after the Second World War have had Lewisian development. From this point of view, postwar Japanese growth is *analytically* also Lewisian, although *historically* doubtful. I cannot take this type of exercise too seriously, for the only methodology involved here is a crude analogy devoid of any possible historical content. If the Lewisian theory is only a "disaggregated" model of economic growth with two sectors, two factors in each sector, and different rates of return to factors between the two sectors, the theory is certainly helpful for the understanding of the resource transfer mechanism and the rate of growth of the aggregate output with an eye on the sectoral contributions to growth. But the analytical usefulness of the "model" to many diverse circumstances is totally different from its historical relevance to the course of development of a given economy.

Conclusion

This chapter offers a bird's-eye-view of wage differentials in postwar Japan. The presentation follows the pattern of Chapter 1. While institutional information on the working of the labor market is the task of Part II, I have given some of it in this chapter. Wage differentials as a whole widened rapidly between 1945 and 1950. After uncertain developments during the 1950s, they have been narrowing rapidly during the 1960s. But even when they were widest some time during the 1950s, postwar wage differentials were no wider than in the 1930s. In the 1960s some differentials like geographical and occupational are even as narrow as they were prior to the First World War.

An experiment on statistical explanations was made on the intersectoral wage differential after the model of Chapter 3. If economic growth and labor transfer from agriculture continue at their present pace, the narrowing of the intersectoral wage differential to the "normal" size that prevailed during the Meiji period is no idle speculation.

The impressive flexibility and sensitivity of the Japanese labor market are grounds for a brief commentary on the logical difficulties involved in structural concepts like "unlimited supplies of labor" and "dual structure." People have so far discussed the structural aspects of Japan's labor economy without the aid of detailed information on what the labor market is supposed to do, namely, equalization of net advantages of different occupations. I have tried to offer some of the necessary information before it is possible to evaluate the institutional aspects of wages, employment, and industrial relations. I now turn to the task of historical interpretations of labor market institutions.

Part II

Institutions in the
Labor Market Process

5

The Labor Market
Origins of
Employer Paternalism

IT IS WIDELY ASSUMED among Western scholars that "employer paternalism" fully explains the fundamentals of the Japanese industrial relations system. Instead of trading work for pay or pay for work, the
worker and the employer are said to reciprocate "loyalty," which implies both the obligations of the inferior to the superior and the responsibilities of the superior to the inferior. Production is a by-product of
the loyal relationships between worker and employer and has nothing
to do with the criteria of economic efficiency. The uniqueness of employer paternalism was described by James Abegglen in 1958 [1] and has
since dominated the Western view of industrial relations in Japan.
Abegglen writes:

> At whatever level of organization in the Japanese factory, the
> worker commits himself on entrance to the company for the re-
> mainder of his working career. The company will not discharge
> him even temporarily except in the most extreme circumstances.
> He will not quit the company for industrial employment else-
> where.[2]

And again,

> The worker, whether laborer or manager, may not at his conven-
> ience leave the company for another position. He is bound, de-
> spite potential economic advantage, to remain in the company's
> employ. The company, for its part, must not dismiss the worker
> to serve its own financial ends. *Loyalty to the group and an inter-
> change of responsibilities—a system of shared obligation—take
> the place of the economic basis of employment of worker by the
> firm* [italics mine].[3]

He observes further that wages bear no resemblance to those in

American firms, which "would be given in relation to the capacity of the individual to contribute to efficient and maximal production." Abegglen characterizes Japanese wages as follows:

> . . . recompense in the Japanese factory is in large part a function of matters that have no direct connection with the factory's productivity goals . . . . It is not at all difficult to find situations where workers doing identical work at an identical pace receive markedly different salaries, or where a skilled workman is paid at a rate below that of a sweeper or a doorman. The position occupied and the amount produced do not determine the reward provided.[4]

Under this situation, marked wage differentials arising from the length of service quite naturally discourage labor mobility. As Abegglen says:

> The importance given to education, age, length of service, and similar factors in the total wage scale means that the worker is heavily penalized for job mobility and strongly rewarded for steady service. Taken together with the factors involved in recruitment, it will be seen that *labor mobility is virtually nonexistent in the Japanese system* [italics mine].[5]

As shown by the above excerpts, the *statement* and *interpretation* of the observed phenomena are inextricably intermixed in Abegglen's book on the Japanese factory organization. The central features of what is called the "Japanese system" of employment relations, which are to be interpreted, include (1) an extremely high degree of employment stability, (2) new hirings limited to new school leavers, and (3) a chaotic wage structure within the enterprise. Abegglen explains these phenomena by the traditional Japanese culture which prizes loyalty more than anything else. In contrast, I suggest that the observed phenomena can be explained primarily by the *transitory economic conditions* during the first ten of the years after the Second World War and secondarily by the long-run trend of economic factors influencing employment, wage structure, and hiring practices during the whole modern period of Japan, especially after the turn of the century.

The fluidity of economic conditions during the postwar period has been described in the preceding chapter. The interplay between the labor market and industrial relations in postwar Japan will be discussed in detail in Chapter 7. In this chapter I propose to look into the historical background of "employer paternalism" in order to show that this phenomenon, popularly attributed to unchanging Japanese traditions, was in fact a new institutional invention in response to the labor market conditions which prevailed during the first cycle of Japan's industrialization and persisted with varying strength throughout the prewar period.

Delving into the history of Japanese industrial relations serves another useful purpose. A deeper understanding of the past of any country and of the historical socio-economic processes through which that country has come to display certain characteristics today contributes toward a proper evaluation of the place of that country in the framework of international comparison made across the world at a given point of time. For example, Clark Kerr and others regard Japan as a country that in large measure fits a "dynastic-elite type" of industrialization rather than the "middle-class type." [6] It will be useful, if possible at all, to examine to what extent the system of industrial relations ("paternalism") deduced from this type of industrialization fits Japanese experience during the relevant period of Japan's industrialization.[7] Unfortunately, these types of industrialization and the corresponding systems of industrial relations are not "testable" propositions, as they are distilled from the contemporary experiences of a variety of countries by a method that is not capable of independent replication. One only hopes that an account of the historical roots of industrial relations in Japan will clarify which type, "dynastic elite" or "middle class," Japanese experience comes closer to.

Just what kind of industrial relations obtained during the first round of Japan's industrialization is a question that entails far more substantive consequences than the typological issues just mentioned. Alexander Gerschenkron advances a set of hypotheses to explain why industrialization in countries which belatedly join the race for industrialization tend to show marked differences vis-à-vis the advanced countries in the rate of growth, choice of industries, and factor proportions.[8] Henry Rosovsky, while ascertaining the existence of Gerschenkron's follower-country characteristics in Japanese industrialization, emphasizes equally important dissimilarities between Japan and the "Gerschenkron model." [9] Rosovsky attributes these dissimilarities to what Gerschenkron's follower-countries lacked, namely, the availability of an adequate labor force. In explaining this crucial difference, Rosovsky draws upon Abegglen's aforementioned work on Japanese factory management and assumes, in much the same way Clark Kerr and others do, that the Japanese employers were able to create a "disciplined and reliable labor force, suitable for factory work" more easily and quickly through their paternalistic labor policy than was the case with Western employers. Thus the question of "employer paternalism" takes on added significance that reaches into the essence of Japanese industrialization.

Reviewing the place of Abegglen's work in Japanese sociology, Ronald Dore correctly suggests the importance of historical studies. "One promising line of inquiry is historical. . . . It appears that some of the industrial features thought to be traditionally Japanese—the lifelong commitment, the seniority wage system, etc.—are in fact fairly recent innovations, supported by traditional values to be sure, but consciously designed for good profit-maximizing reasons." [10] The relationship between the institutional aspects of industrial relations and employers' profit-maximizing behavior is certainly a welcome suggestion. Its importance is heightened when one recalls that the distorted description of the Japanese practice by Abegglen has misled an economist of no less stature than E. H. Phelps-Brown, who reviewing Abegglen's book, was willing to revise his own habit of thinking in so far as Japanese experience was concerned. Phelps-Brown observed: "We are used to thinking of changes in social structure as both prerequisite for the rise of industry and consequent upon it. Here is an illuminating study of how industry can be imported into a social structure without changing it." [11]

In seeking after the origins of Japanese employer paternalism in employers' profit-maximizing behavior, I shall use a method of exposition that may be characterized broadly as "dynamic." The basic idea is to regard the evolution of industrial relations as a series of dynamic interactions of two sets of demand and supply functions (broadly interpreted), one for entrepreneurs, managers, or employers, and another for workers. For example, entrepreneurs having certain characteristics are likely to call forth a type of employment relations befitting their leadership and ambition. Aggressive and adventurous entrepreneurs are often despotic and even cruel in the treatment of their employees, while the succeeding generations of managers who inherit the business empires of the earlier entrepreneurs tend to mold employment relations into a more tolerant type that reflects the changing spirit and techniques of business leadership and organization. Furthermore, the evolution of institutions is cumulative over time. The characteristics of labor market during a given period are partly inherited from the preceding period, while they in turn condition the developments in the labor market in the next period. During each period changes in the labor market processes are added to the customary practices and bequeathed to the next period.

What needs to be done is implicit in S. B. Levine's definition of industrial relations: ". . . the respective roles of management, labor and government in the processes which relate workers to employers, workers to workers, and workers to work." [12] My emphasis will be on the processes which relate workers to employers. Rational explanations of these processes in the context of changing general socio-economic conditions constitute my dynamics of industrial relations. In the following pages I shall first lay out the elements of Japanese "tradition" in the processes of relating workers to employers and then proceed to describe how these traditional elements underwent modifications during the period of transition, and transformation during the ensuing period of industrialization. Although no conscious efforts for methodological comparisons are made, I believe that the type of dynamic considerations I am offering in this part of the book is in sharp contrast to the grand statics of industrial relations such as the work by Kerr and others referred to above. When the static views are fashionable, the dynamic ones may appear to be unnecessarily rebellious and muddled. But the evolution of institutions in the course of economic growth is essentially dynamic.

Elements of Tradition

In feudal Japan the whole nation was divided into fiefs, each of which had a lord (*daimyō*) surrounded by his vassals (*samurai*), reigning over and extracting feudal dues from numerous families of peasants, artisans, and merchants. Although the Shogunate attempted to perpetuate this simple social structure by making all statuses and functions hereditary, the rule of heredity failed in the long run as a social mechanism of allocating human abilities to appropriate functions and positions necessary for the peaceful functioning of society. In addition to discrepancies between the abilities of individuals and their inherited functions which corroded the feudal structure over time, one particular method of political control exercised by the Shogunate was highly effective in undermining the system which it was designed to maintain. This was the famous system of *sankin-kōtai* which required all feudal lords to live in Edo, the Shogun's capital, and to leave their families there as hostages during their visits to their respective fiefs.

The agglomeration of lords and vassals and their families in a metropolis in prolonged leisure raised the standard of living and increased the demand for income. The lords most naturally turned to the peasantry for more dues, but since the peasantry had already been squeezed to the bare minimum of subsistence, additional revenues clearly had to come from net increments in production. Increases in the demand for income called forth a class of *samurai*-managers who devised and undertook various measures to raise the revenues of their lords. Thus the effect of *sankin-kōtai* was the slow but steady transformation of feudal Japan into a system of multilateral interdependencies in which local fief products were exported to urban centers and in which the incomes thus earned were, in turn, spent on goods and services by the lords and vassals moving about for *sankin-kōtai*.[13]

At the level of the commoner also, networks of exchanges and business connections developed within and among urban centers and between cities and villages. The rural-urban economic relationships redirected the activities of the peasantry to production for sale, and the increasing commercialization of agriculture produced a differentiation of the peasantry from a monotonous collectivity of self-sufficient farm households into richer and poorer strata, that is, those in a position to demand labor from outside and those in a position to supply labor for additional income. Thus labor markets emerged in rural Japan and supplanted to some extent the traditional method of supplementing the deficiency of labor supply in the peasant household, namely, mutual help and cooperation that the farm households rendered and received from one another.[14]

In cities two types of employment developed, one in trade and craft which required skill, knowledge, and experience, and another in a variety of undertakings for which unskilled hands sufficed, like construction, civil works, fire and water control, household services, hauling of goods, transportation of persons, and the like. The unskilled labor markets clustered around labor bosses, who were simultaneously information centers, recruiters, and general caretakers. These bosses (*oyabun*) had some permanent underlings (*kobun*) who were subjected to them in a corrupted blend of lord-vassal and parent-child relationships which accorded absolute power to *oyabun* and demanded absolute obedience of *kobun*.[15]

The craft had well-structured master-journeyman-apprentice relationships. A worker would spend his childhood and adolescence with a master, and, upon reaching manhood and acquiring the customary level of skill, become a journeyman, who, after having served the master, would normally set out in independent practice. In the merchant household a young boy under ten years of age would be hired as an apprentice (*detchi*) and promoted to the position of a regular employee (*tedai*) when he was about eighteen. In about twenty years after this promotion, the employee would be promoted to a managerial position (*shihaiyaku*), and, after several years in this capacity, he would set up his own business with the employer's aid of various kinds, such as a gift of capital, the privilege of using the trade-mark, and enrollment in the trade guild. These offshoots of the master-house (*bekke*) were treated like its relatives, and the children of these former employees enjoyed priority in training and employment at the master-house. The employment practice of the merchant household represented, indeed, the highest degree of nepotism and the purest type of lifetime commitment.[16]

To sum up this section, these are the traditional modes of labor utilization that had developed within Japanese feudalism by the middle of the nineteenth century: (1) a small class of *samurai*-bureaucrats with managerial and administrative ability and training; (2) employment in the merchant household characterized by nepotism and lifetime commitment; (3) craft markets composed of essentially independent practitioners, each of whom employed a limited number of journeymen and apprentices; (4) urban unskilled labor markets clustering around labor bosses; and (5) rural unstructured labor markets where employers and workers were in casual contact.

Transition,
1853–1886

The period of transition was triggered by the visits in 1853 of Commodore Perry of the United States, punctuated by the historic Meiji Restoration of 1868, and closed by the end of the monetary disturbances that attended the post-Restoration reforms and civil strife. It was a period of great upsurge in entrepreneurial energy as well as one of spectacular failures of traditional merchant houses.[17] The risks and uncertainties that accompanied the economic dislocations of the period and the characteristics of successful entrepreneurs under these conditions had their peculiar concomitants in the types of relations between employers and workers. Brief sketches of a few leading entrepreneurs during this period will illustrate the socio-economic milieu in which they operated, the tactics by which they rose to their successful positions, and the types of relations they created with their employees in the course of their successes. Stories were similar and no less exciting wherever there were successes, though in different scales, at various levels of society during this period.

Yasuda Zenjiro (1838–1921),[18] a son of a local merchant in Toyama, came to Edo at eighteen and was first employed by a money-changer.[19] After several years of service and having acquired a modest capital, Yasuda set himself up in the trade of money changing. There were then in circulation many kinds of coins which, owing to frequent debasement by the Shogunate, had different values of metal content for the same nominal values, so that discernment of the intrinsic value of these coins required specialized knowledge and training. Yasuda used his intelligence, energy, and experience to the fullest extent and, by active sales and purchases of coins, built up his fortune quickly and steadily. The monetary disturbances during the early Meiji years also helped him expand his business by enabling him to deal in paper money and government securities. The first half of his life culminated in the founding of the Yasuda Bank in 1880.

Minomura Rizaemon (1821–1877), of an obscure origin, drifted to Edo at the age of eighteen and worked first for a dry-fish wholesaler, and then, through a connection of his employer's, he became a servant for a Shogunate treasury official. At the age of twenty-four he married a daughter of an Edo merchant, and, after some years in his father-in-law's employ, he bought himself a money-changing concern. With this new trade he came in contact with the money-changing offices of the House of Mitsui. In those days the Shogunate was in financial distress and was demanding contributions from the merchants. The Mitsui's Edo managers, who were favorably impressed with Minomura and informed of his former connection with a Shogunate treasury official, hoped to stall the Shogunate demand on Mitsui by appointing Minomura to the position of a manager of Mitsui's external affairs. Once in office, Minomura not only measured up to expectations but also went ahead to stake the fortune of the House on the victory of the Imperial Court, the Shogun's political adversary, laying the foundations for later intimate relationships between Mitsui and the Meiji Government.

It is no exaggeration that Minomura and Yasuda were embodiments of profit motive, acquisitive urge, and economic rationality. They were noted for shrewdness in external transactions and single-handed firmness in internal management. Yasuda, as founder of his own business dynasty, always enjoyed unbridled decision-making power, but even Minomura, as a hired manager, clearly demonstrated that economically irrational customs and traditions had no place in his management. Despite objections by the members of the House, Minomura reorganized the House of Mitsui by deleting some of the traditional lines of business and adding new ones according to profitability criteria. He also forced the members of the House to retire into the background and consolidated the power of management in the hands of the hired top executive—himself at the time.[20]

The association of pioneering entrepreneurship with autocratic handling of internal affairs is also illustrated by the practices of Hirose Saihei, executive of the House of Sumitomo, and Iwasaki Yataro, founder of the Mitsubishi Zaibatsu. Hirose (1828–1914), a son of a medical practitioner, began to serve the House of Sumitomo at Osaka at the age of eight in 1836. After having acquired diverse experiences in various Sumitomo offices over many years, he was placed in charge of Sumitomo's Besshi Copper Mines in 1865. When the Shogunate, then the largest single customer for Besshi copper, forced a cut in the price, Hirose correspondingly reduced the compensations to the miners.

Hundreds of miners rioted against this reduction and Hirose, heroically facing the mob, calmed it down with impromptu, false promises for improvements. After the miners returned to their homes, he led the local police under cover of night and arrested the ringleaders of the riot.

Iwasaki Yataro (1834–1885), son of a poor unemployed *samurai* in Tosa, after a series of unfortunate incidents, including a prison term during his early life, "mounted the clouds of success" (as the Japanese would say), when he was appointed to manage the shipping business of the fief in 1867. Later, in 1871, he acquired the shipping property of the fief together with all the debts connected therewith and established Mitsubishi Company, which later became the second largest Zaibatsu. Iwasaki then laid down "Rules of Management," Article I of which declared that the firm was entirely a family enterprise of the Iwasakis and that for this reason there should be no misunderstanding about its president's power over all the affairs of the firm. Commensurate with this absolute power, Article II stipulated that the president of the firm should appropriate all the profits and assume full responsibility for debts and losses. Article III followed up with a stern warning that while wages and salaries could be increased during profitable periods, they could also be cut during adverse periods and that, in cases of prolonged losses, men might be discharged.[21]

As the Mitsubishi Zaibatsu extended its activities into new areas, the Iwasaki spirit magnified its despotic aspect to a bizarre extent that shocked the sternest *samurai* of the early Meiji period. The labor conditions at the Takashima mines, which fell to the Iwasakis from the Meiji Government, reflected the combination of the Iwasaki authoritarianism and the cruelty of the labor boss system (*naya-seido*). The labor bosses recruited workers through various connections (including outright kidnapping), housed them in compounds called *naya*, and supervised them in and outside the workplace with power to administer reward and punishment at will. The Takashima miners were recruited or kidnapped from far and wide and labored under conditions close to outright slavery.[22]

The processes of adjustment of socio-economic disequilibrium during the period of transition produced admixtures of dazzling successes on the one hand and unbearable miseries on the other. Lured by the prospect of success and whipped by the fear of failure, individuals throughout the nation vigorously experimented with their abilities and chances to find appropriate places in the new society. "Suddenly the whole pack of human cards were shuffled," to use an apt simile of Foxwell's,[23] but in the absence of predetermined rules for the new game, each card had to vie with another for its life and value. Soon the cards were to be stamped with proper values and stacked on the table of the nation for many rounds of the game in the future, but in the meantime the race had to go on in all the directions of life and at all the levels of society. With these uncertainties of the age and the expansion of occupational and personal freedoms, the traditional attachments between lords and subjects, masters and apprentices, and merchants and employees loosened considerably.

Industrialization, 1886–1911 [24]

Industrialization, narrowly defined as a rapid spread of factory production, started in Japan in the latter half of the 1880s. While by then the basic institutions requisite for the economic progress of a market economy had been laid, new problems arose from the acute maladjustments in the demand for and supply of labor in rapidly expanding industries. The Japanese employers, workers, public, and government groped for acceptable standards of market behavior in a new environment where no precedents were available for guidance. This groping culminated in the Factory Law of 1911, which opened a new stage of Japanese industrial relations.

As new factories appeared and existing ones expanded, the problem of finding sufficient labor in short order became acute. Although the labor force of the whole nation was sufficient to man the small, though increasing, number of factories, the workers willing to enter industrial employment fell short of needed numbers. In manufacturing establishments using skilled and semiskilled male labor, the standard practice of labor recruitment was to rely upon the craft-masters or factory foremen for finding appropriate workers. For jobs in which unskilled workers sufficed, labor bosses supplied needed workers. All this was of course consistent with the labor market mechanism that had previously developed in Japan. The problem was that this type of labor recruitment and commitment was not in the interest of efficient factory production.

As in many other countries, textile manufacturing was the first industry to adopt extensive factory production in Japan. As recently as 1930, employment in this industry accounted for more than half the entire industrial labor force. The industrialization of textile production started in the 1870s, and by 1890 the local supplies of labor to textile mills had been exhausted. As a result, the shortage of labor at the factory level became keener every year in the expansionary decade of the 1890s, and employers were compelled to spend more and more money for recruiting workers. The processes of recruitment, the methods of retaining the recruited workers, and the state of employer competition for labor in the 1890s were documented in detail in the reports of the Ministry of Agriculture and Commerce in 1903, *Shokkō jijō* (Conditions of Factory Workers).

To tap the labor reserve in the Japanese hinterland, the textile employers contracted labor recruiters. Three components of labor cost then became clear to the employers: (1) the direct wages paid to the worker, (2) the additional nonwage expenses incurred to keep the worker in employment, and (3) the recruitment expenses paid to the recruiter. Since bargaining superiority of the professional recruiters kept recruitment expenses beyond their control, the employers, in their effort to control labor costs, turned to wage cuts and reduction of nonwage expenses directly affecting the welfare of the worker. First, they sought to exact more effort from the workers at a given wage level by lengthening the workday or speeding up machine processes. Second, housing, eating, and recreational facilities were made as economical as possible.

The consequences of the steps taken by the employers were, however, that in addition to ill health and accidents induced by long hours of intensified labor under poor working conditions, the workers' efficiency was reduced because of absenteeism, sabotage, strikes, and, in most cases, desertions. With deterioration of employee morale, the employers turned more and more to coercive measures to increase production. The measures entailed greater expenses for supervision and policing, which offset low wages and cheap facilities. At the same time recruitment expenses increased in the countryside, for the misery of factory life, which became known through rumors, agitation, or from the workers who returned home sick and disabled, raised the phycological cost of transfer from farm to factory. Thus actions taken in the hope of reducing labor costs in the short run proved self-defeating in the long run.

The instability of employment was not limited to the textile industries. All industries suffered from high labor turnover, and the metal and machine industries employing skilled male labor were no exception. Although employment in these industries was small relative to total factory employment, the skills required resulted in a relative scarcity of qualified workers. According to the *Shokkō jijō:*

> It was said that labor piracy was rampant a few years ago. . . . But the examples of labor piracy in these industries are largely due to the voluntary movement of workers and quite different from the case of the textile industries where female operatives were threatened away or kidnapped by factory owners or recruiters. Although labor piracy might be against the interest of the employers in the metal and machinery industries, it did not entail the same hazards to workers as in the textiles.[25]

Much of the labor mobility in the metal trades consisted of voluntary job changes by workers themselves. To quote the *Shokkō jijō* again:

> The metal and machinery workers are less unstable than the textile workers but still show a higher degree of instability than similar workers in the advanced countries. Especially when workers are scarce in busy periods, slight wage differentials are enough to induce workers to move over to other factories, and many workers are literally in a perpetual journey from one place to another.[26]

The insatiable demand for labor in these industries had a pernicious effect on the willingness of the workers to undergo skill training. It is the human weakness that, in the seller's market, the seller's effort to offer high-quality ware melts away. Likewise, in response to the excess demand for labor in the metal trades, many apprentices cut short their terms of apprenticeship and took off into the world as independent journeymen. There were two kinds of apprenticeship. One was the learning of skills under a craftmaster in his workshop. The other was the training within a factory as one of its employees. The period of training ranged from 3 to 5 years. But the intrafactory training, although increasingly practiced, only duplicated the traditional type within the factory: unskilled youngsters were assigned to skilled craftsmen, and the learning process was much the same as in the traditional system, lacking only the personal warmth and mutual obligations which characterized the traditional master-apprenticeship relations. Many of the craftsmen in the factory were craftmasters who were in factory employment temporarily because of the increased demand for their skills and who returned to their own shops when the demand slackened. More often than not, they had brought their own helpers and apprentices.[27]

Within the factory, the skilled workers were likely to neglect the training of the company-hired youngsters or tended to show little positive obligation for their growth and welfare. This behavior was unlike the traditional situation where apprentices lived and worked with their masters. The factory apprentices learned their trades not through training but through "stealing," that is, they observed as best they could how the craftsmen worked while they were themselves doing insignificant tasks in the factory. When these young workers felt that they had seen enough, they would leave for the opportunity to practice the trades. Having acquired a taste for moving for better wages and more satisfactory opportunities, the metal workers spent a good part of their youthful periods as traveling journeymen. They later settled as craftmasters, working on their own account with a few journeymen and apprentices. Thus the metal workers who emerged from factory apprenticeship joined the craft communities, which constituted a good part of the metal and machinery industries.

Employer Organizations against the Labor Market

Learning the rules of the labor market was a painful process for many Japanese employers at the first stage of Japan's industrialization in the midst of an acute labor shortage. Some employers did almost anything to get the factory hands to work for them. One of the things that employers did to avoid the financial effects of the tight labor market was to organize themselves for the restraint of competition for labor among themselves. It is useful to review some examples of these activities because they illustrate that under stress due to the penury of labor some of the Japanese employers behaved in ways quite contrary to what the notion of "employer paternalism" would have led us to believe.

In 1882 the employers of thirteen cotton-spinning factories, which owned 28,000 spindles out of a total of 28,792 in the whole economy, organized a club. It grew into a cartel called *Dainippon boseki rengō kai* (Federation of Japanese Cotton Manufacturers), which by 1889 had thirty member factories, owning 206,000 spindles out of a total of 267,-264. The main purpose of the Federation was to coordinate individual employer actions in both product and factor markets. At the general meeting of 1888 the Federation adopted a constitution in which provisions were made for the regulation of employer competition for labor. These provisions required all employers to make a cross reference of each new hiring and to obtain the consent of the last employer if the worker was experienced. In the course of the prosperous 1890s, employer competition for labor was intensified, and the Federation's regulation of it (at least in documents) became more strict. In addition to reaffirming that no employer should employ a worker without the consent of the worker's last employer, the Federation adopted new provisions requiring the Federation's board of directors or its legal counselors to inspect the lists of employees, accounts of wage payments, and other books of the members of the Federation, and empowering the Federation to arbitrate disputes among employers arising from hiring practices.[28]

Employers in the silk-reeling industry also organized themselves to counter increasing labor costs due to employer competition for labor. Silk reeling required a high manual dexterity attainable by a young girl after about a year of training and experience. For technical and financial reasons, the operation of a silk filature was uneconomical during the winter months, so that the period covered by an employment contract was customarily a year. During each winter, thousands of new contracts were struck between employers and workers through recruiting agents. Each employer would, above all, try to secure all his employees of the previous year, and by the time the girls returned to their homes recruiters were already there waiting for them to draw up new contracts. The bargaining between the whole family of an operative and the recruiter was a long, drawn-out process, subject to constant threats of other recruiters working for other firms. Having no absolute guarantee that workers would return to their former workplace and being under pressure to obtain a larger work force in order to keep pace with the expansion of the whole industry, each employer in addition to trying to get contracts with his former employees also attempted to attract workers away from his competitors. During the winter months, the homes of the experienced or would-be workers were bombarded by the endless visits of many recruiters. In effect, employers, through their recruiters, were merely bidding against one another for a limited supply of suitable workers, while the workers and their families did their best to exploit the market condition for higher wage rates on the job, larger down payments, sizable gifts at the signing of the contract, or like stipulations.

Employer associations in the silk-reeling industry aimed first of all at the reduction of labor costs that would result from consolidation of the chaotic employer competition in recruitment.[29] One of the most successful employer associations in this industry was the *Okaya seishi dōmei* (Okaya Federation of Silk Manufacturers), organized in 1902 in the Prefecture of Nagano and dissolved by the order of the prefectural authority in 1926. The Okaya Federation centralized the procedures of recruiting or contracting for workers and coordinated travel arrangements for the workers reporting to or returning from their work for the affiliated employers. The Federation also adopted a central register of all the workers employed in the factories of the affiliated employers.

The membership of the Okaya Federation, which originally covered silk factories in three villages of the Prefecture of Nagano, in time expanded inside and outside the prefecture. In 1922 the number of operatives registered in the central Okaya office of this federation amounted to more than 40 percent of all operatives in the silk-reeling industry of Japan. In Nagano Prefecture the proportion was more than 50 percent higher than the national average.[30] To some extent, the number of workers registered with the Federation might have overstated the number of workers actually employed in the affiliated factories, for it is conceivable that some workers who once worked in these factories might have been employed in the nonaffiliated factories at another time, with their names remaining in the Federation registers.

In the regulation of employer competition for labor, the Okaya Federation introduced an innovation. Not only did the silk employers agree that no member should seek to draw workers away from another member without the latter's consent, but they also went a few important steps further than this "gentlemen's agreement." In order to stabilize the work force of each member from year to year and to minimize the hazards of competition in connection with annual recontracting, the Federation adopted a rule requiring the members to honor, at the risk of considerable fines, each member's "rights" over workers once they entered his employ. The idea was that in recruiting workers for a new season, each employer would have the exclusive right (among the member employers of the Okaya Federation) to recontract his former employees and that the other members would not approach these workers until they were released from their last season's employer by an appropriate notice to the Federation headquarters. This arrangement was widely condemned as being tantamount to establishing the employer's "property rights" over workers.[31]

The document of the Okaya Federation of Silk Manufacturers that defined the employer's "rights over workers" was the bylaw of the Federation, long restricted to its members only. The constitution of the Federation, which stated the basic objectives of the organization, was published from the outset and did not contain the pernicious arrangements on employment relations. The second chapter of the bylaw is deceptively entitled "Rights of the Worker" (*Shokkō no kenri*). Upon reading the provisions of this chapter, one scarcely gets the impression that the rights of the employer over his employee are being defined rather than the worker's rights in relation to his employer. Suddenly one comes to a strange statement in Article 20 that the affiliated employer should not employ "the workers belonging to the rights of the other affiliaed employers." The document goes on to define the certification, correction, alienation, loss, borrowing, and so on, of the "rights," the penalties for violations, and the procedures for settling disputes involving the "rights" of different employers.[32]

To paraphrase the rather opaque wording of Article 16, Chapter 2, the employer's right to retain the labor service of a worker during a given year arises from the fact that the worker was in his employ for more than thirty days during the preceding year. To the worker, this stipulation means that all the doors of the factories affiliated with the Okaya Federation save those of her last employer are closed to her. On the other hand, Article 32 provides that an employer's rights over a worker would disappear if the employer allowed the employment of the worker to be interrupted for a year, that is, any member employer was free to sign a contract with workers who were not employed by any other member employer during the preceding calendar year.

The critics of the employer's "rights" over workers argued that some workers could not afford to stay home for a year, and therefore returned to the same employers year after year even if they did not like the terms of employment offered by these employers. The bylaw of the Okaya Federation of Silk Manufacturers, sounded, at least at the conceptual level, like the feudal master-servant relationship in which the master exercised unlimited control over the person of his servant. It was the concept, rather than the practice, of the employer's "rights" over workers that drew the sharpest condemnations and the severest criticisms from many quarters of Japanese society before the Federation was abolished by a prefectural decree in 1926.

However, the practical success of activities guided by that concept was by no means clear-cut. On a national scale the multiplicity of employer associations in this industry, though each may have tried to control markets for its members, did not preclude interassociation competition for labor. Presumably, the impact of the Okaya Federation was more pronounced in the prefecture where its head office was located and most effective in the particular villages where the Federation originally arose and where practically all the silk manufacturers belonged to it. But even in this local context, the Federation's success was not absolute. Moreover, the supply side of the labor market developed an extremely interesting and sensible type of organized effort. These associations were composed of operatives in silk factories and their parents, known as Jokō kyōkyū kumiai (Association for the Supply of Female Operatives), and formed in small units in various towns and villages supplying large numbers of girls to silk filatures. Although these associations belonged to the period which is the subject of the next chapter, it is useful to consider here their significance in relation to the silk employers' efforts to restrain the labor market process.

The first association for the supply of workers to silk factories was organized in a district in Nagano Prefecture in 1915 by a schoolmaster who was grieved by the miserable working conditions in silk factories. Similar associations were formed in many prefectures between 1915 and 1925. Each association centralized contracts between employers and workers, requiring all the member workers to refrain from independent transactions with employers. Each also undertook inspection of factories for the purpose of boycotting those having unsatisfactory working conditions and of exposing the unsavory practices of some employers and their agents in recruiting and contracting workers. At the same time the associations set high ethical standards for their members by prohibiting them to take unwarranted advantage of the labor market, which was extremely tight during the First World War, by such dishonest practices as contracting with two or more employers at the same time. (More will be written later on the instances of abuse and dishonesty in the labor market during the First World War.) In addition, the associations occasionally organized lectures and study sessions in the hope of improving the members' knowledge of economic facts and market conditions. The associations' revenues came from commissions received from employers at specified rates for each worker supplied. Although these associations were started as purely private, voluntary organizations, the prefectural and local authorities later (after 1925) transformed them into semi-official organs by appointing the public officials to their directorates. In some cases they were resolved in favor of public labor exchange agencies.[33]

The foregoing accounts of textile employer associations were only some of the more spectacular examples. On smaller scales and in surreptitious ways, there must have been numerous attempts by employers to restrain labor market competition whenever labor shortage arose. In 1911, for example, when the shipbuilding industry experienced a sudden boom, the Mitsubishi Shipbuilding Works at Nagasaki made a pact with the Naval Arsenal at Kure not to bid workers away from each other. The correspondences exchanged between the two shipbuilding concerns then revealed that similar bilateral agreements had already been in practice between Nagasaki or Kure and other shipbuilding works. In the case of the Nagasaki-Kure pact of 1911, the technique of control was similar to, though somewhat more lukewarm than, the practice of the cotton textile employers. The Nagasaki and Kure concerns would inform each other of the names of the workers separated from employment in either concern. Neither party would employ the worker who had worked for the other party unless six months had elapsed since his separation. Each party would deal a strict punishment to the worker discovered to have entered its employ with a false name to escape this six-month limitation between jobs. When one party needed the services of some workers working in the employ of the other party, the two parties should formally negotiate over the transfer of these workers. The wording of the pact was reckless and high-handed, as if the blacklisting, swapping, and punishment of the workers were natural prerogatives of the employer. But the two ship-building concerns neglected carrying out the terms of the pact, ostensibly because the labor shortage eased in the meantime.[34]

One can only speculate on the outcome of the collusive efforts of employer associations for the regulation of labor market competition. To judge by the tone of past and present discussions of these matters by various authors, the cotton textile manufacturers' association does not seem to have succeeded at all in combating employer competition for labor. The silk manufacturers' associations evidently scored a certain measure of success at times but had to contend with an effective countervailing power on the supply side of the market. The shipbuilding works, despite occasional collusions to restrain labor mobility, had already instituted many positive measures of inducement for the stabilization of their respective work forces. Being large and financially powerful, they did not have to fear the repercussions of these measures on the cost of production in general. The large firms in heavy industries intensified their efforts to find solutions to the problem of labor turnover through more constructive approaches, which I shall discuss in Chapter 6.

Learning the Rules of the Market

While some employers were making mistakes in their hiring policies —that is, in the sense that they did not accomplish what they wanted by the method they used—others were learning the rules of the labor market. One of the rules was that one should offer higher wages and better working conditions to induce a larger labor supply and a reduction in labor turnover. Large established firms were naturally in a better position to obey the rules of the labor market than small ones. The fact that these firms were more willing to go along with the labor market was also a reflection of changes taking place in the top management of these firms. The top positions were beginning to be filled by a new generation of executives who were highly educated in modern universities in Japan and abroad and who because of their educational background tended to take a more functional view of human relations than their predecessors.

In large firms a series of innovations took place in the relationships among the owners, directors, and various layers of the managerial staff. The largest and most attractive employer of educated manpower prior to the 1890s was the civil service. Because of the large salary differentials between civil service and private business for comparable positions requiring similar backgrounds of education and experience, employment in private business was unattractive to educated persons. When he entered Mitsui in 1891, Nakamigawa Hikojiro (1854–1901), one of the most highly educated persons of those days, initiated a veritable "salary revolution" by doubling the salaries of the directors by a profit-sharing device (explained below) and raising those of managerial personnel in varying degrees all down the line. The effect of this salary revolution was an influx of educated manpower into Mitsui concerns, demonstrating the obvious truth that the higher the pay, the larger the supply of labor.[35]

After some years passed, tension arose among salaried managers on the question of equitable salary scales. Wide income differentials had developed between the directors (*jyūyaku*) and the executives in charge of departments or branch offices (*buchō* or *shitenchō*). The source of this gap was the distribution of 10 to 29 percent of the net profit to the directors as "bonuses." Although this profit-sharing device, when initiated, was a revolution that transferred some of the profit from business owners to their directors regardless of share holdings, economic growth and expansion of profits subsequently widened the income gap between the profit-sharing directors and the salaried managers. Tension from this disequilibrium of the pay structure was dramatically demonstrated by a protest movement led by Ikeda Shigeaki (1867–1950) during his junior executive days in the Mitsui Bank in the 1900s. (He later became the top executive of the Mitsui Zaibatsu.) As salaried managers in time moved up to assume directorships, the demand from below for greater equality was increasingly realized. For instance, Wada Toyoji (1861–1924), once one of Nakamigawa's lieutenants, as managing director of the Fuji Spinning Company in 1906 reduced the directors' bonuses from the customary 15 percent to 5 percent of the net profit, using the other 10 percent for bonuses, pensions, and other benefits for managers, staff employees, and factory operatives. Other firms adopted similar practices.[36]

The acceptance of the fact of markets was eloquently expressed by Shoda Heigoro (1847–1922), Mitsubishi executive, at a conference of businessmen and government officials held in 1898 for the purpose of deliberating the possibility of factory legislation to prevent actual or probable exploitation of labor in factories.[37] A few direct quotations will show how thoroughly modern Shoda was. In relation to the high turnover rates of factory labor, Shoda said:

> Since it is the nature of man to be tempted by better opportunities, it is impossible to keep workers without adequate provisions. That is, if a worker desires to go to another factory because of better pay there, his present employer should allow him to go. If the employer wanted to keep the worker, he should raise wages so that the worker would see no reason to move. Were I censured for this statement on the ground that the competitive spiraling of wages would damage the profits of factory owners and retard industrial progress, I would rebut by calling attention to the simple logic of demand and supply in the market. Factory operatives, engineers, machinists, and other workers in modern industries are scarce in Japan today, because these occupations unlike the traditional crafts emerged only recently. It is true that their relative scarcity enables them to command relatively higher wages than other types of labor. But this very fact of high wages also induces more workers to flow into these occupations. . . .
>
> Therefore, if the forces of demand and supply worked normally, the increase in their number would in time reduce their wages. But this subsequent decrease in their wages would spell no hardship for them, because workers would move into these occupations only insofar as the advantages there were sufficient to make them willing to move. . . . Thus, in my opinion, it is highly necessary that factory owners should acquiesce in the economic motives of workers in seeking high wages and better occupations . . . ." [38]

The *Shokkō jijō*, a few years later, quite cogently summarized the prevailing sentiment about the forces of the labor market. It stated approvingly: "There is nothing objectionable, if properly conducted, in factory owners paying higher wages to attract workers, or in workers leaving low-wage factories for higher wages elsewhere." [39]

Paradoxical though it may seem, learning the rules of the labor market was the beginning of whatever meaning one now associates with "employer paternalism." If "paternalism" means good wages, generous fringe benefits, job security, and other measures of humane treatment for employees, the controlling factor is its cost. No employer would ordinarily go all the way for such a package of desirable conditions for his employees if he could avoid doing so. But there is a certain state of the labor market which leaves almost no choice to the employer, that is, a labor market characterized by labor shortage and difficulty in holding workers. It is within the rules of the labor market that the employer tries to trade off the cost of labor turnover and that of lost production due to the lack of manpower against the cost of "paternalism," which would call forth more workers with greater willingness to stay on the job. Thus under labor shortage a rational employer with a strong profit motive turns out to be "paternalistic." "Paternalism" in this case is indistinguishable from economic rationality. A modern textbook on wage determination defines "adequate compensation" as the level of pay that "will attract and hold the quantity and quality of labor force required by the organization and motivate the labor force to accomplish the goals of the organization." [40] I shall show how the Japanese employers intelligent enough to learn the facts and rules of the labor market before the First World War became "paternalistic," that is, economically more rational under the prevailing circumstances.

The Emergence of "Paternalism" [41]

There were two related problems that employers in the cotton-spinning industry faced: (1) how to induce a regular flow of work from employees, that is, the problem of absenteeism, and (2) how to fill vacancies and expand the work force, that is, the problem of recruitment. The first problem was subdivided into (a) the problem of day-to-day stability of effective work force and (b) the problem of year-round stability of work force. The following description will show how employers responded rationally and pragmatically to these problems and how employer responses resulted in the improvement of wages and working conditions.

Employer policy to counter day-to-day instability of work force

The ups and downs in absenteeism within each month were found to be related to the method of wage computation prevalent in those days. At a spinning mill in Osaka, for example, the work records were closed on the twentieth day of each month, and the wages earned during the month ending on this date were paid on the fifth day of the next month. The daily attendance records showed that attendance fell drastically after the twentieth day, reached the bottom on the twenty-third, increased irregularly until the fifth day of the following month, then fell drastically again until the ninth day, after which attendance steadily improved until the twentieth day.[42]

According to one explanation,[43] the fact that work on the twentieth day of the month was paid for fifteen days later, while work on the twenty-first was paid for thirty more days later, made the psychological cost of work on the twenty-first day much higher than that of work on the twentieth day. A similar hypothesis was advanced for the drastic increase in absenteeism after the payday of the fifth; with money in pocket there were many desirable alternative ways of using one's time, so that the time spent at work was very painful and the unpaid accretion of wages was of little immediate value to the worker in this situation. After income diminished or disappeared during the few subsequent days, the utility of additional earnings became large enough to balance the pains of work, so that the worker returned to work.

Such an explanation is in no way startling to the behaviorist economist of today, but what is important is that the Japanese employers, without the aid of economics or psychology, explained the fluctuation of absenteeism in this manner as a basis for countermeasures. To explain a problem rationally was in part to solve it. Some firms thus made every day a payday for a certain group of workers, so that, given the rate of absenteeism following payday, there would at least be a stable level of work force day after day.[44] More popular was a variety of bonuses paid on an individual as well as on a group basis.[45] Payments in addition to the regular daily wages were made to individuals or groups of individuals who worked without absence for a whole month.

The bonus sometimes took the form of exemption from boarding charges for workers housed in company dormitories. Another form was a remittance of additional cash directly to the homes of the workers in the hope that parents might become instrumental in encouraging their children to cultivate regular work habits. A group bonus was also widely used. One variety of it was designed to improve the facilities of the dormitory rooms of the commendable groups of workers so that they could share in an increase in comfort as the fruit of group effort.

Of course it cannot be supposed that Japanese employers manipulated only the wage or income incentives to solve the problem of absenteeism. There was a variety of disciplinary measures for the same purpose; for example, the workers who did not report for work were hunted out and subjected to physical torture, and the employer intervened in the worker's personal life outside the workroom by regimenting her private activities solely for the purpose of increasing efficiency at work.[46] Negative wage incentives were also used. For example, unless a certain consecutive number of days was worked, even the wages for work done were confiscated by the employer. The relative weights of all these inducements by positive and negative measures varied from firm to firm. But since in any age the same people can be cheated only once or twice and since nothing travels farther and faster than rumors of scandals, one could assume that competitive strength and survival potential during the early years of Japanese development lay with the firms that relied more on the positive incentive measures than on the negative.

Employer policy to counter seasonal irregularity of work force

In many cotton-spinning mills the difference between the peak turnout (March and April) and the trough (August) of a given regular work force amounted to nearly 30 percent.[47] Given the pattern of seasonal fluctuation of the work force, one of the countermeasures easiest for the firm to use was to employ two sets of work force, so that when one set was falling below the normal level of work requirements, the other set could be called in to fill the gap. Most firms hired temporary workers from the neighboring communities, but some undertook more elaborate measures. One large establishment hired a number of girls twelve to fourteen years of age, housed them in dormitories, taught them factory work part of the time after school, and used them as supplementary workers to fill vacancies due to seasonality or absenteeism. Some other plants established a training course for the wives and daughters of the male salaried employees for similar purposes.[48]

It was widely recognized that the seasonal fluctuations were closely related to labor requirements on farms, since the factory operatives were predominantly from farm households. From the point of view of the farm households, the value of work on the farm during busy periods was much higher than the regular wages at the factory. The essence of countermeasures on the part of the factory, therefore, was to offer such inducements as might make staying on the job more attractive than return to the farm during such periods. A variety of inducements developed that were based on this premise. One was to grant bonuses to those who stayed on their jobs during the months of peak activity on the farm. Another was a profit-sharing plan of one kind or another that was related to length of period of consecutive work. The third was a variety of devices such as company-paid pleasure trips, participation in company-sponsored lotteries, and recreational opportunities granted only to workers remaining on the job during busy seasons on the farm. The fourth type of inducement was the encouragement of savings with the company which, in addition to the ordinary interest earnings, carried additional increments related to length of employment. For example, a worker would be required to save 10 percent of his wages from time to time at the regular rate of interest of 4.5 percent per annum. At the end of the year the worker who had worked regularly during the year would receive an extra payment equal to 35 percent of the sum of the principal saved and interest earned.[49]

The problem of recruitment

In many factories the annual turnover rates exceeded 100 percent of the regular work force, which meant that practically every year a whole work force had to be recruited. As to the manipulation of earnings incentives for employment stabilization, measures were similar to those already mentioned, that is, differential rewards, financial and in kind, for longer-service employees. But these measures were less efficient for long-term employment stabilization than for short-term, for the worker could exert herself under these inducements for a relatively short period but might not keep up that level of effort year after year. In this sense the short-term success of earnings incentives could very well have been a cause of long-term instability of work force in some factories. There was evidence that some firms, which recognized this fact, adopted "leisure bonuses," such as shorter workdays and paid holidays for workers who were overresponsive to short-term pecuniary incentives.[50]

There were three interrelated problem areas of labor administration in the firm that needed to be improved if long-term employment stabilization was to be achieved: (1) the source of labor supply, (2) the relative unattractiveness of work and life in the factory, compared to them away from the factory, and (3) the instrumentality of recruitment that brought demand for and supply of labor together. Because the textile workers were predominantly young girls from rural households located beyond ordinary commuting distance the factory dormitory was indispensable. The girls, who ranged from fourteen to twenty-one years of age (a period between the completion of compulsory primary education and marriage), lived in the dormitory and worked in the factory. From the workers' point of view, the advantages of factory employment had to be judged in terms of the total combination of "life and work" in comparison with another possible combination which they might follow by, for example, staying with their families.

There was no doubt about the decisive superiority of factory employment in one respect, namely, the cash income earned by the worker. But many soon wondered if the cash added to the family income was not earned at the expense of "living." In extreme cases a girl went to the factory at the age of fourteen and returned home at the age of twenty-one, having learned nothing that would contribute toward the further enrichment of life for the subsequent stages of her roles as wife, mother, and member of the community. This realization, aided by a host of other defects of factory employment, frequently led to silent revolts of local communities against the factories, revolts which took the form of total opposition to supplying workers for factory employment. In this way many sources of factory labor "dried up" one after another, and recruitment activity had to be pushed further into new areas, which in turn would dry up within a short period.[51]

Two alternative measures to counter or eliminate the recruitment problem were proposed. On the one hand, it was proposed that the textile factories should shift the source of labor from rural girls to urban male adult workers by raising wages enough to attract the latter. This proposal would eliminate the difficulty of housing workers and the enormous recruitment expenses suffered by factories.[52] The second proposal was that, without materially altering the existing practice of recruitment, the "living" aspect of the factory dormitory should be improved to such an extent that the period of factory employment would cease to be just one big hole in the personal and cultural development of a young girl coming away from her home. The second measure appealed more to the textile employers, and the eventual consequence of employer effort in this direction was the well-known feature of "employer paternalism," intrafactory welfare facilities.

The third problem area of labor administration in the factory had to do with the instrumentality of recruitment. The source of labor and place of employment being far apart, there was a need to bring labor from its source to the place where it would be used. In a highly developed economy with efficient networks of communication and transportation and with travel time and expenses relatively low in terms of income, it is ordinarily the worker who presents himself for labor to an employer. The situation was different in underdeveloped Japan before 1915; communications, transportation, literacy, and market information were all underdeveloped. The task of getting a worker to an employer was then fulfilled by specialized human agents. These were of three kinds: (1) members of the staff who toured the source areas looking for workers for their company, (2) the relatively stable long-service workers who collected recruits from among their relatives and friends or through other connections, and (3) the contractual labor recruiters who dealt with any company.

Whatever the recruitment agent may have been, one grave disadvantage to the employer was the considerable power that the recruiter held over the recruited. For example, the first or second type of recruiter (who was an employee of the firm) sometimes bargained with a potential employer for better employment conditions for himself in return for bringing with him the workers he had recruited for his present employer.[53]

If a firm's own employee fell prey to self-interest in this way under the impact of labor shortage, the contractual recruiter, as an independent businessman, was prone to drive the toughest bargains with the employer that the market would bear. He was a monopolist of labor supply to the firm and a monopsonist in relation to hundreds of farm households in his recruiting preserve. Much of the stability, regularity, and morale of the workers in the factory depended on how the recruiter represented factory work to them back in the villages. In many cases the recruiter drew a rosy picture of wages and working conditions as a recruitment device. On some occasions a recruiter who regretted a deal with one employer caused unrest among the workers he had recruited and pulled them out to "sell" to another employer for higher fees.[54]

However, the defects of the existing recruitment methods suggested their own remedies. Of the three types of recruitment agent, the firm's own employees gave less trouble than independent recruiters. One remedy, then, was to improve direct recruitment and eliminate professional recruiters. The crude form of direct recruitment consisted of sending out some of the low-ranking clerks with simple instructions to bring back some workers within a specified period. Aside from setting some broad limits, mainly financial, within which the recruiter was to operate, the top management of a firm ordinarily paid little attention to the difficulties that the recruiter encountered in his search for workers and the grievances that were likely to arise in consequence. At the same time the feelings of freedom and power that the crude method of recruitment afforded the recruiter for hiring, organizing, and even regimenting a number of workers outside the firm directly conflicted with low job satisfaction in the daily clerical routines where there was little power or responsibility. These conditions sometimes gave rise to schisms of the type mentioned above.

After many years of random recruitment practices by employees, supplemented by the services of professional recruiters, some firms began to set up personnel departments headed by high-ranking employees. Under an ideal type of recruitment, which was approximated in some firms by 1910, the company secured a "recruitment territory" of a size that made it possible for the resident representatives of the firm to maintain direct personal contacts with the families supplying workers to the firm and to acquire intimate, first-hand knowledge of the demographic potential of the area. The firm consciously coordinated its labor requirements within the demographic dynamics of this area, so that as the older workers withdrew from factory employment after several years of service, vacancies were filled by younger ones recruited from the area. When the growth of the firm required more labor than the area could supply, the firm used more capital per worker instead of enlarging the recruitment territory, which might have started "colonial wars" with other firms. Thus the improvement of recruitment procedure accompanied increases in labor productivity. Concomitantly, since the security of the recruitment territory depended on the working and living conditions of employees, the firm made continuous efforts to improve them at a rate that would maintain amicable relations between the workers and their families on the one hand and the firm on the other.[55]

Conclusion

This chapter suggests that the employer labor policy commonly regarded as "paternalistic" resulted from employers' rational responses to the labor market conditions characterized by acute labor shortage and high labor turnover during the first round of Japan's industrialization. However, one should not forget that "employer paternalism" as an alias for an enlightened labor policy on the part of employers was not yet a common characteristic of all the employers of Japan even at the end of the Meiji period after half a century of modern economic development. In hindsight, indeed, one regrets that Japanese employers were not more "paternalistic" during this crucial period of Japanese history. The persistent excess demand for labor or labor shortage during this period was partly employers' own making because of their failure to learn the proper rules of the labor market. Although labor was hard to get and the work force, if built, melted away quickly under the working conditions they offered, many employers were taken in by a perennial illusion that labor was cheap. Perhaps it was the conventional wisdom of the time that labor *should* be cheap. The conventional belief was overcome only with great difficulty, and even then only to a limited extent.[56]

Although this may sound paradoxical, it cannot be denied on logical grounds that employers' belief in low pay had beneficial effects on the income distribution over the whole nation. Since workers willing to work at low wages were found in economically backward regions, employers guided by their belief in low pay pushed the frontier of the labor market farther and farther into Japan's hinterland. In other words, Japan's rural poor had the first share in the fruit of Japan's industrialization. Recall in this connection that the geographical wage differentials narrowed in the 1890s and 1900s. The sons and daughters of the rural poor were not efficient workers and may not have been economical even for their low wages. Employers could have profited more from high-wage workers if their productivity had been proportionately higher. This last possibility would have raised the rate of economic growth, but it was not realized because of employers' belief in low pay. In this way, Japan's earlier industrialization sacrificed the possibility of rapid growth in the interest of equitable distribution of the gains of industrialization. All this was unconscious to be sure, but what would happen to income distribution if growth became a conscious target for management was shown clearly by Japan's interwar experience, which will be discussed in Chapter 6.

One should also mention in this connection that another benefit of low pay from the point of view of wider sharing in the fruit of industrialization was the utilization of the urban poor as a sort of preferred factor of production. That workers should be paid low wages was certainly a sinister belief for anyone to entertain. But Japanese employers were at least honest with themselves and tapped low-wage labor resources before they tried alternative sources. Reflecting anew on the characteristics of Japan's early industrialization, one can no longer doubt that the poor built the industry of modern Japan. The realization of this striking truth in Japanese development is an important by-product of this chapter's search into the origins of "employer paternalism." [57]

6

The Labor Market,
Group Power,
and Public Policy

How THE DYNAMICS of industrial relations works at an advanced stage of economic development may be schematically illustrated by a summary of historical experience in developed countries.[1] In the beginning there was a long period of "free competition," characterized by numerous participants and atomistic decision-making in economic activities and in the labor market. The initial "free" labor market gives way to interactions between power groups like big corporations and industrial associations on the demand side and trade unions on the supply side. The bifurcation of power in the labor market and the disruptive conflicts of interest that occasionally erupt between the power groups induce the State's regulation of industrial relations to ensure the process of reaching just and equitable agreements between them. While the power groups first "balkanize" the labor market and keep improving the terms of employment within their respective "territories," the market forces and competition in the rest of the labor market fail to realize comparable improvements. The State is then compelled to move directly into the labor market by a variety of social legislations to generalize as far as possible the standards and benefits that collective bargaining has brought about in the organized sector and by a variety of policies to maintain full employment. In the meantime the labor movement gains a good deal of political influence and moves into the highest policy-making circles for the system as a whole. With the increase in its political power and the extent of its participation in policy-making, the labor movement becomes a responsible locus of power and designs its collective bargaining strategies with an eye on the equilibrium and equity of the whole resource-allocative process. Once full employment becomes a normal feature of the economy, problems develop concerning a rational and equitable determination of prices, wages, and profits. Policies to resolve these problems put the State deeper into the problems of rational and equitable resource allocations, which end with economic planning and labor market policy. But by this time the State power has come to be shared widely by the groups with vital interest in the economic system. The end product of economic development and social progress is the combination of "participatory democracy" in polity, equality in social relations, and efficiency in resource allocation.[2]

On appropriate occasions in the pages to follow I shall be using the foregoing "model" of historical development as a scale by which to measure Japan's socio-political progress in the context of economic development. Each step in the "model" presents interesting questions. The development of collective bargaining and its impact on the labor market have been at the center of labor history. In Japan trade unions as legally recognized bargaining agents and collective bargaining as a regular process of wage determination belong to the period after the Second World War. Even then, just how collective bargaining impinges on the labor market is a complicated matter, which I shall examine in detail in Chapter 7. In this chapter I shall first describe how the unbridled free labor market worked during the First World War and how public policy helped improve the working of the market during the interwar period. I shall also examine the characteristics of the interwar labor movement and its possible impact on wages and employment. Finally, I shall evaluate long-run trends in labor mobility and industrial relations.

The Labor Market
during the First World War

When the labor shortage was intensified to an unprecedented extent during the First World War, whatever had remained of the organized power of the employers proved powerless in the face of the surging market forces. The war heated the Japanese economy so much that no amount of production seemed sufficient to keep up with the aggregate demand. The Tokyo wholesale price index on the base of 1914 rose to its peak of 338 in March 1920, when the stock and commodity markets collapsed to put an end to six years of extraordinary expansion. The state of the labor market during this period was described in realistic detail in the Annual Reports on Factory Supervision (abbreviated *KKN* from their Japanese title) which began in 1917 following the long-awaited implementation of the Factory Law in the fall of the preceding year. How the Factory Law came into being is the story reserved for the next section of this chapter. The administration of the law produced enormous masses of information on all aspects of factory labor and production processes. The description of the labor market in these reports is particularly illuminating from the point of view of the present issue of "market versus power."

The situation of the labor market during the First World War was a magnified repetition of the experience of the 1890s. Prices and profits soared; employers scrambled for whatever workers they could put to work; the labor recruiters swept the whole country; it was enough for farm families to sulk in order to get higher wages and larger advance payments for their youngsters' labor services; workers easily changed jobs and employers for the slightest differentials of pay; employers raided one another for decoying workers out. With the intensification of the inflation, honesty and integrity in the negotiation and conclusion of employment contracts well-nigh disappeared on both sides of the labor market. Any product sold at profit; any worker found a job at wages he quoted. There was too much of competition everywhere, the excess eventually verging upon delinquency.

The First Annual Report on Factory Supervision was a review of 1916. It noted differences in the strength of demand for labor in different prefectures and pointed out the existence of labor surplus areas and labor deficit areas. "But, since the outbreak of the hostilities," observed the Report, "even the 'labor surplus areas' have already been invaded by labor recruiters and, due in part to the rise of industries and the expansion of by-employments within these areas, there are signs that foretell an exhaustion of labor supply." On the other hand, in the labor-deficit areas, "the employers are suffering from great difficulties in recruiting workers and making tremendous efforts to retain the workers they have already engaged." [3]

In 1917 the labor market tightened further. The Second Annual Report on Factory Supervision observed: ". . . labor shortage was intensified in every industry. There are three reasons for this state of affairs. First, farm incomes have increased greatly and many farm families dislike to send their children to factory employment. Secondly, labor surplus has greatly diminished in areas traditionally rich in labor because many industries are expanding in these areas too. Thirdly, a general feeling of labor scarcity has been created in the labor surplus areas due to reckless competition for labor among labor recruiters who have come from other prefectures." [4] It is remarkable that labor supply dried up and the supply price of labor rose so quickly as described here in only three years after the outbreak of the war. In the labor deficit areas, "the labor shortage is causing labor piracies among employers. Many employers are improving the conditions of employment for self-defence and trying very hard to prevent labor turnover. Some have begun to employ Korean workers." [4] The Report also noted that labor shortage was especially intensified in industries like shipbuilding, machinery manufacturing, silk reeling, cotton spinning, and fabric weaving.

By 1917 the labor market had come dangerously near a breaking point; there were abuses by both workers and employers. Labor piracy between employers was one of the notorious abuses. It worked in this way: "An employer would send his assistant disguised as a worker to another factory in order to tempt the latter's employees away. Or one would bribe a few workers in the employ of another employer and use them for getting other workers out. One would also bribe the parents for advising their children in other factories to quit and come to work in one's factory. The traders who frequent factories and the keepers of tobacco shops or restaurants where workers visit are asked to suggest job changes to the workers they know. Soft speech, cash, gift; just any available means is used for getting workers out of competitors' employ." [5] Dishonest practices were not employers' monopoly. Far more serious was what was called "double contract" (*nijū keiyaku*) engaged in by many workers. It meant the conclusion of contracts with two or more employers at the same time. The incentive for this kind of practice was the customary advance payment of wages and allowances at the time of concluding contracts. As already described in the preceding chapter, there were all kinds of practices for profiteering available to labor recruiters, magnified by several factors during the First World War.

Prosperity continued throughout 1918, although a small jolt was felt consequent upon the armistice in November. An interesting description of labor mobility in Tokyo was recorded in the Annual Report for 1918. "The Factory girls carefully select their employers by the sum of advance payment of wages. Even after they are employed in a given factory, they would find many excuses for moving to other factories in search for higher wages." [6] Jobs were easy to get and easy to change. Money seemed to fly in and fly out with no apparent relationship to work. The labor market with its magical attraction siphoned labor away from the countryside, demoralizing whoever remained behind. Consequently, the Annual Report for 1919 lamented: "The virtue of long and diligent service has been supplanted by a propensity to change jobs. The good custom of rural Japan is exposed to the danger of destruction. Habits of hard work and parsimonious saving are going out of fashion, and wasteful behavior rules the day. Workers simply go out for money without knowing where they are going or what they are going to do." [7] Japan was about to disintegrate when the panic of March 1920 saved her from the throes of destructive prosperity.

Even discounting the moralizing tendencies of public officials, the prosperity during and immediately after the First World War was not an unmixed blessing. The situation looked very much like run-away inflation, which was something that the Japanese had not experienced since the early Meiji inflation was broken by the Matsukata deflation in 1881. Economic policy was nonexistent, and the art of control over money supply and foreign exchange earnings was primitive. Of course Japan was not alone in this respect; throughout the world economic policy was unwise or wrongly applied. But it cannot be denied that wiser public policy could have reduced the impact of the sudden surge in the aggregate demand on the supply potentiality of the Japanese economy. One thing is certain, however: the boom, if demoralizing in certain respects, was a tremendous equalizer of all kinds of differences. It compressed income differences, wage differentials, and regional disparities of all sorts. It also obliterated social distances between classes, between employers and workers, between city and country. It ushered in Japan's first democratic period celebrated to this day as "Taisho demokurasii." [8]

Public Policy
and the Labor Market

So far as the labor market was concerned, there was an apparent preference for a "free labor market" on the part of the Japanese Government
throughout the period before the Second World War. Strictly speaking
it is not possible to prove the existence of this preference, for there
were no official pronouncements to that effect. The preference was
expressed by the government in negative form by abstaining from in-
tervening in the labor market with labor standards which the labor
market, if left to itself, would not have brought about. But this was as
much an expression of policy as any explicit statement, for, as W. W.
Lockwood says, "a full assessment of the role of government in Japanese
economic life would take account of policies of inaction as well as
those of action." [9]

There were broader historical reasons for the choice of modern Japan
to experiment with a "free" labor market.[10] The private enterprise
economy consciously promoted by the Meiji Government was in large
measure a reaction to the failure of earlier attempts to achieve economic
development by an extensive central direction, combined with a
minimum of private initiative, during the last two decades of the
Tokugawa Japan just preceding the emergence of modern Japan. In
fact, many of the public sector enterprises during the early Meiji
period (1868–1888) consisted of public enterprises taken over from the
Tokugawa Government. During the 1880s, however, the Meiji Government sold a majority of the public enterprises to private entrepreneurs. The sale of public enterprises was due to two predominant
considerations: (1) they were operating under losses and (2) they contributed toward the expansion of public spending which had, in turn,
brought about enormous inflation from 1876 to 1881. Although the
actual sale of public enterprises was a protracted process ending in
1888 (long after inflation was reversed into deflation), the *idea* of the
sale germinated in 1880 as one of the measures for controlling inflation.[11] Thus, to some degree, economic liberalism during the three
decades before the First World War in Japan can be said to have

grown out of the failure of economic *dirigisme* during a still earlier period.

The initial set of rules for economic behavior was the Civil Code adopted in 1890 in which employer-employee relationships were regarded essentially as contracts freely concluded between the parties concerned.[12] In anticipation of the worst cases that might arise under the pretext of a contract, like permanently indentured labor or outright slavery dressed up as a voluntary agreement of the worker, the Civil Code prohibited employment contracts that lasted more than five years and, in such cases, explicitly enabled either party to terminate the employment contract unilaterally with a three-month notice. In cases where wages were paid at specified intervals, employment relationships could be terminated on the initiative of either party with the period of notice equal to at least one half of the interval for wage computation and payment. In cases of a legitimate emergency, the employment contract could be dissolved immediately, but the party who abused this right could be sued by the other party for the damages incurred thereby. In such ways the Japanese Government hoped that symmetry and reciprocity would apply to the employment contract as they did to other commercial contracts.

The rules of symmetry and reciprocity in the employment contract were later supplemented by an additional destructive rule (of atomistic competition) implicit in the Public Peace Police Law of 1900. Although this law ostensibly prohibited only the violent uses of organized power in arriving at, or revising, employment contracts and did not explicitly outlaw either trade unionism or even the workers' right to strike, all the ordinary activities of organizing a union or conducting a strike were liable to interpretation as activities prohibited by this law on the ground of being "instigation," "temptation," or "violence." [13] The early growth of the trade union movement was thus confronted with the severest obstacles in the stern suppression of any signs of vigorous group action directed at wresting favorable wages and working conditions from employers.

The Japanese Government's selective decisions on where to act and where not to act indicated a degree of consistency in favor of active preferences for leaving the labor market alone. The first major piece of legislative intervention in the labor market was the Factory Law of

1911. An interesting point about this law in relation to the pattern of the Japanese Government's policy preferences is that the first official overture for having some sort of factory regulations enacted was made at a subministerial level within the Ministry of Agriculture and Commerce well before the promulgation of the Civil Code. Drafts for statutory regulations of employer-employee relations and factory safety were prepared in the early 1880s by the Bureau of Industry (*kōmu-kyoku*). It is therefore of some value to know what tortuous route the idea of factory law had to travel for these thirty-odd years.

The first step in Japanese social legislation in any age is a series of consultations with eminent and learned people of the country. The preparatory work for the factory law started in this way. In the 1880s the Government repeatedly consulted representatives of industry and commerce on the draft statutes of labor. The consensus was hard to obtain, and these early attempts were duly abandoned. Nevertheless, the Bureau of Industry continued to explore new avenues of thought and methods, while accumulating data on the conditions of industry and labor.[14] In 1896 prefectural governors were sounded out as to the desirability of legislation for the "protection and regulation" of factory labor. Of 46 prefectures, 20 turned in their opinions, and 15 of them roughly favored the idea. The Ministry then appointed a council consisting of representatives of industry and of the academic world to discuss economic and industrial problems, including the question of factory legislation. It was called "Superior Council on Agriculture, Commerce and Industry" (*Nōshōkō kōtō kaigi*), and it met three times with an increasing emphasis on the question of factory law. A draft of Factory Law emerged from the conferences of this council. The Cabinet crisis in 1898 destroyed the chances for the draft to reach the floor of the Diet (national legislature).[15]

Since workers were neither "eminent" nor "learned," they were not consulted by the Government on the question of factory legislation. When the Superior Council came into being, metal workers already had their own trade union called *Rōdō kumiai kiseikai* (Society for the Promotion of Trade Unions), claiming a membership of more than 3,000 workers. The Society was wholeheartedly for the intended factory legislation. In order to make its wishes heard, the Society organized a petitioning group to approach the Ministers of State, Bureau chiefs, and the members of the Superior Council. The workers were greatly disappointed and angered when the draft factory law failed to reach the Diet floor and the Peace Police Law, with its notorious provision previously mentioned, came out of it instead.[16]

Adopting a draft factory law, the Third Conference of the Superior Council on Agriculture, Commerce and Industry, held in the fall of 1898, nevertheless found it fit to debate a minority resolution introduced by Shoda Heigoro and his supporters. The minority resolution first pointed out that protection should be generalized to cover all the workers instead of limiting itself to factory employees only, and it urged that such a general coverage being obviously impossible for lack of information on all aspects of labor, the envisaged legislation should be narrowed down to matters of safety within the factory. It singled out the problem of "labor piracy" (*shokkō sōdatsu*) and emphasized that since it was due to a rapid increase in the demand for labor, there was no need to prevent or suppress it by the force of law.[17] The excess demand for labor and labor shortage must have been hurting employers, and yet, interestingly enough, some of them were at least willing to play the game according to the rules of market. This was the conference where Shoda expounded his views on the working of the labor market as previously quoted.

In the meantime the economy expanded, many more problems arose, and the knowledge of life and work within the factory improved. The great benchmark in the improvement of knowledge was the *Shokkō jijō* of 1903, frequently referred to in the preceding chapter. The labor market worked as tolerably as any market would. The terms of employment did seem to respond flexibly to the state of the labor market. But as the masses of data accumulating in the Ministry of Agriculture and Commerce showed, once workers crossed the divide from the market to factory, they were in some cases subjected to conditions of work and accommodation radically different from those they were led to expect when they made the decision to work. Information on what was happening inside the factory was not fully available in the labor market, and the workers were making decisions on the basis of imperfect secondary information. The "free" labor market was far from "perfect" as a "perfect market" is defined in economics. The girls in the textile mills were too young to form independent opinions on the relative advantages of different employment opportunities in the labor market, although cases to the contrary were not absent. The parents and relatives of these workers did their best to assist them as far as possible in the selection of jobs and employers, but they too suffered from imperfect information. Moreover, the great physical distance which often existed between factories and the homes of young workers was a strong incentive for employers to offer one thing at the time of employment contract and to offer another thing at the time of work. There were no objective standards for industrial hygiene and safety except in vague customary notions which employers were free to vary according to their discretion. The labor market did not fully reflect these peculiarities of factory management as sensitively as was desired for an efficient market. By 1910 the "free" labor market for industrial labor had been on its own for at least thirty years, but it was admittedly not a "perfect" market. The time for action, if only to help the labor market function more efficiently, had arrived.

A draft factory law actually reached the Diet floor in 1910, but the Government voluntarily withdrew the bill.[18] Further revisions were made, and copies of a new draft were sent to various ministries, prefectural governments, chambers of commerce and industry, textile manufacturers' associations, other industrial associations, and the Association for Social Policy, an academic organization which had recently come into being. In March 1910 a special commission called *Seisan chōsa kai* (Commission for Inquiry into Production) was appointed by an Imperial Ordinance to examine the draft Factory Law.[19] The draft that emerged from the second meeting of the Commission was approved by the Cabinet Council of Ministers (*kakugi*) and sent to the Diet in 1911. The House of Commons quickly acted upon the bill and within a month passed it on to the House of Peers with certain modifications. The Upper House passed the bill within three weeks.[20] The Factory Law was enacted on March 20, 1911. But as was usually the case with the prewar legislative process in Japan, no date for the implementation of the Factory Law was specified in the law itself, and a few more years were to pass before the administrative arrangements and budgetary appropriations were made for the purpose.

The Factory Law
and Related Measures

The Factory Law proper, a short document of 25 articles, stipulated a minimum set of standards for employment, covering manufacturing establishments employing 15 or more operatives (later amended to cover those employing 10 or more). It prohibited the employment of persons below the age of 12 (Article 2), the use of operatives 15 years old or younger, or of female operatives regardless of age for more than 12 hours a day (Article 3), and night work for minors or women between 10 P.M. and 4 A.M. (Article 4). The law required at least 2 rest days per month for minors and women, at least 4 rest days per month for night-shift workers, and at least a 30-minute rest period per day where a day's work exceeded 10 hours (Article 7). The law prohibited the employment of young workers under 15 years of age on certain dangerous or disagreeable jobs and obligated the factory owner to support disabled workers and their families (Articles 8–15). Factory owners who violated the provisions of the law or who did not cooperate with the factory inspectors were subject to fines (Articles 20 and 21).

For the specification of some vital matters the Factory Law depended on an Imperial Ordinance for the Implementation of the Law, which was finally issued in August 1916 to put the law into effect, beginning in September of that year. At the last moment there was an unexpected foot dragging by the Privy Council whose support was formally necessary for securing the Emperor's signature on the Imperial Ordinance. Ordinarily, the Privy Council would give its support to any action coming up from the Government. This time, however, there were some trifling disagreements, largely emotional in nature, between some of the Elder Statesmen on the Council and the Prime Minister. The Elder Statesmen seized the opportunity to harass the Government for no valid reasons. But the age of the celebrated Taisho Demokurasii had already dawned. The Tokyo Asahi regretted the whole affair in strong language and challenged the intellectual competence of "a bunch of oldsters" (rōjinren) on the Council for further refinements of the measures which had already been thoroughly thought out by the Government and debated in the two Houses of the Diet.[21] The Privy Council reconsidered its position and obtained the Imperial signature on the Ordinance.

The Ordinance elaborated the provisions of the Factory Law. It specified compensations for industrial accident, disablement, sickness, death, and funeral. Benefits were computed as multiples of the daily wage, but there was no definition of what constituted "wage" for the purpose. Matters related to recruitment, hiring, and dismissal were elaborated to some extent. Each factory had to maintain the register of workers employed. Wages were to be paid in legal tender at least once a month. When the employer took charge of workers' deposits, he had to obtain a prior approval from the prefectural governor. No employment contract was allowed which obligated the worker in advance to compensate the employer for a possible breach of the contract or damages on property. For school-age youths employed, the employer had to guarantee continued schooling. Young workers and women employees who were discharged at the employer's discretion were entitled to travel expenses to return to their homes. In addition, certain formalities were prescribed for employing apprentices. Fines were stipulated for violations of the Law and the Ordinance as well as for fraudulent practices in the recruitment of workers either by employer or by recruiter. Additional rules to follow in the implementation of the Factory Law were simultaneously issued as a Ministerial Order of the Ministry of Agriculture and Commerce.

Two exceptions were written into the Factory Law for the duration of 15 years. The first exception had to do with Article 3, which limited a day's work to 12 hours. The Minister of State was allowed to permit the extension of the workday by 2 more hours in certain industries. The other, more important, exception was to Article 4, which prohibited the night work of young workers or women. These exceptions were granted to factories where the production process required continuous work and where workers were organized in two or more shifts. The workers in the night shift, who were more numerous in the textile industries, fluctuated between 15 and 25 percent of all the workers in the factories covered by the Law during the first six years (1916–1922).[22] In the textile industries it was the large concerns that took more advantage of the night shift exception. Smaller ones did not have much night work to do on the whole. The number of workers in factories where the workday was allowed to exceed 12 hours was about one tenth of one percent of all the workers in the covered factories.[23]

Other state actions related to the labor market during the interwar period may now be quickly noted. The Factory Law, together with the Mining Law, was revised in 1926. By this time a few important pieces of legislation had been enacted. The Labor Exchange Law set up labor exchanges in several parts of the country and subsidized job seekers with transportation expenses, keeping an eye on the activities of private labor recruiters at the same time. This took place in 1921. In the following year the Health Insurance Law was enacted, to be implemented in 1927.[24] In 1923 there were laws to define minimum ages for factory workers and seamen. Among the administrative ordinances issued during this period, the most important from the point of view of the labor market were the Ordinance to Regulate Labor Recruitment (1924) and the Rules to Regulate Private Labor Exchange Businesses (1925).

The revisions of the Factory Law and related statutes in 1926 postponed the life of the escape clauses on the use of women for night shifts for three more years (until 1929). An important innovation was made, however; that is, two weeks' advance notice for the termination of employment when initiated by the employer or two weeks' pay in the case of an immediate dismissal. The standards for the benefits payable to the worker or his family were all upgraded substantially. Certain benefits which overlapped with the Health Insurance Scheme were transferred to the jurisdiction of the latter entirely.[25] Modifications of legal provisions continued throughout the interwar period due to the necessity for adjustments with other statutes. In 1931 the Law to Aid Injured Workers was passed to take care of the workers not covered under the Factory Law, the Mining Law, or the Health Insurance Law. These were the workers employed in civil engineering, construction, quarries, transportation, docks, and warehouses. Because of complexity of these industries composed of several subcontracting arrangements, there was a technical difficulty in pinning responsibility on any employer. The State therefore agreed to underwrite benefits paid and placed primary responsibility on the principal contractor for the workers in his employ and those employed by his subcontractors.[26] In 1936 the Law for Funding Retirement Allowances and Payments was enacted, requiring factories and mines employing more

than fifty workers to pay allowances to retiring or dismissed workers.[27] By comparing the provisions in the relevant statutes and the
Factory Law before and after 1926, one can get some notion of the
development of statutory benefits for workers during the interwar
period. Table 15 is obtained from these comparisons.

TABLE 15

LEGAL MINIMUM NONWAGE BENEFITS

BORNE BY EMPLOYERS, 1916–1940

Item	1916–1926	1926–1940
1. Compensation for work injury:		
(i) medical care	facility or cost	facility or cost
(ii) sickness benefit	50% of daily wage up to 3 months, 33% of daily wage thereafter	60% of daily wage up to 180 days, 40% of daily wage thereafter
(iii) disability benefit		
(a) unable to care for self	170 days' wages	540 days' wages
(b) unable to work	150 days' wages	360 days' wages
(c) unable to do previous work	100 days' wages	180 days' wages
(d) temporary, able to return to previous work	30 days' wages	40 days' wages
(iv) death benefit	170 days' wages	360 days' wages
(v) funeral allowance	10 ¥ or more	30 days' wages but not less than 30 ¥
(vi) terminal medical benefit after 3 years of medical care	170 days' wages	540 days' wages
2. Travel expenses for young workers, women, and disabled workers	stipulated	stipulated
3. Dismissal allowance	not stipulated	stipulated
4. Health Insurance premium	not stipulated	equally shared with employee, 3% of pay
5. Retirement allowance	not stipulated	stipulated

Sources: Described in text.

One can see that there was substantial progress in the social provisions of nonwage benefits for workers during the interwar period. In
any age, however, it is only the least efficient employers who stay on or
close to the legal minimum standards for the compensation of workers.
Most of the employers are always ahead of the law, so that it is difficult
to judge to what extent the law actually improves the labor standards
over those determined in the labor market through the interactions of

voluntary responses and bargains by employers and workers. At best, one may say that the law puts in a floor and occasionally prevents some people from slipping farther down. In a "perfect" market system, least efficient employers would be eliminated through sustained losses because no workers would be willing to work for them under the working conditions and safety standards they offered. It is conceivable, however, that the market forces do not weed out "bad" employers as quickly as desired from a social point of view in the world of practice where markets are not "perfect." There are therefore some marginal factories where employment conditions would have been worse had there been no statutory minimum standards enforced.

To view the same thing somewhat differently, the enforceable standards are usually of such nature that only a limited number of firms are significantly affected by them. Otherwise, violations of the prescribed standards are so common that the law might just as well be dead. Perhaps it is useful to emphasize this viewpoint in order to guard oneself against the temptation to infer the prevailing practices to be what was provided for by law. The modest standards that the Factory Law and related measures prescribed during the interwar period were the lowest tolerable standards, and the majority of firms and workers were doing much better than the legal prescriptions.

Something that usually arises early in the history of public intervention in the labor market was conspicuously absent in interwar Japan. That was the legal minimum wage. Not that Japan did not know how wages in other countries were regulated. In 1928 Japan was exposed to the International Labor Organization's Convention on the machinery of minimum wage fixing. Even today, forty-odd years after the Convention, Japan is not a signatory to it. In regard to the ILO Conventions Japan always insisted that the special characteristics of the Japanese industry did not allow her fully to espouse the labor standards of the ILO. Japan's selective responses to the ILO Conventions during the interwar period clearly indicated the areas which fell under the "policy of inaction." [28] The absence of public intervention in wage determination implied that the single most important variable was left to the forces of the labor market and the private institutional responses of workers and employers. In the pages to follow I shall describe workers' organized responses first and then evaluate the character of the labor market during the interwar period.

Trade Unions
and the Labor Market

The trade union movement had its modest start after the Sino-Japanese War, but this early attempt quickly came to an end partly because of the Peace Police Law and partly because leaders and workers lacked experience in effective organization. Toward the close of the Meiji Era a new wave of the labor movement arose with labor-management cooperation and harmony as its organizing principles. The First World War boom and the commensurate socio-economic disturbances turned the growing unions into instruments for the class struggle. The leftist bent of the labor movement during and immediately after the War was largely a product of the ideology and tactics learned from the West, stimulated to a great extent by the success of the Russian Revolution. The panic and subsequent stagnation of the economy sobered the trade unions and made them look for leading concepts more suitable to the situation. On the one hand, workers and peasants came to form a united movement to promote economic well-being through organized pressures on the Government and collective bargaining with employers and landlords. On the other hand, those who disliked the lukewarm practical and functional approach broke away from the ranks of organized labor to form their own radical group in 1925. The formation of this group was auspicious, for the trend was for a more intense politicizing of the masses. The general manhood suffrage was proclaimed in the same year. Proletarian parties arose, and trade unions were soon heavily involved in the political activities of these parties.

The Japanese Government never recognized the labor movement as a legitimate institution. After it became clearly impossible for the Government to cover up the scandals of selecting labor representatives and sending them to the ILO, it finally yielded to the labor movement for the rights of the latter to select its own representatives for the ILO conferences. In 1926 the Government retreated a step farther by abolishing the notorious clause in the Peace Police Law which was used time and again to suppress the labor movement. At the same time the Government enacted the Peace Maintenance Law to suppress communist or communistic movements. Factions of the labor movement combined and split many times under the harassing tactics of the Government, which condoned trade unions for an international reputation and suppressed them for the purposes of domestic peace. The depression of 1929–1931 demoralized the labor movement, and the Manchurian Incident drove a portion of it to be the prey of national socialism and national defense. With the spread of nationalistic trade union centers in 1932, the interwar labor movement of Japan entered its dying stage and clung to life in spasmodic fashion until it put an end to itself by a formal dissolution in 1939. The patriotic movement in industry known as Sampo, which was inaugurated in 1938, took the place of the labor movement, and by a miraculous *coup de théâtre* at the end of the Second World War emerged as a new postwar labor movement. The postwar unionism is the topic of the next chapter. For the present, I shall examine the labor market effects of the interwar unionism.[29]

The extent of unionism

The membership at the end of the First World War was about 100,-000 workers. A great spurt occurred in 1924, adding more than 100,000 workers in one year to the 1923 membership of 125,000. It took the labor movement five more years to acquire another 100,000 and seven more years in addition to take on a further 100,000. In 1936 the trade union membership was at its prewar maximum with 420,600 workers. In 1941 less than 1,000 workers remained in trade unions. In 1945, just before the surrender of Japan, there was no trade union. The rate of unionization, that is, the union membership as a percentage of the total paid labor force in nonagricultural sectors, fluctuated within a modest range. It reached its peak in 1931 at 7.9 percent and declined thereafter. Table 16 shows the rate of unionization by major sector and by major industry. The over-all rate of unionization for this period has been well known in recent writings on Japanese labor, and the absence of union power is usually inferred from the low over-all rate. But when the data are examined industry by industry as in Table 16, some industries appear to have been rather highly organized in the 1930s. It may be supposed that in these industries trade unions may have made some difference to wages and working conditions. But it is not possible to infer anything from the unionization data alone without the knowledge of the behavioral and structural characteristics of trade unionism.

TABLE 16

THE RATE OF UNIONIZATION BY SECTOR AND BY INDUSTRY, 1930–1938

(PERCENT)

Year	All Sectors	Mining	Manufacturing						Gas and Electricity	Transportation and Communication	Day Laborers and Others
			Total	Engineering	Chemicals	Textiles	Food	Miscellaneous			
1930	7.5	2.4	7.9	27.7	7.9	1.7	3.4	15.1	83.2	28.2	2.2
1931	7.9	3.6	7.9	28.1	10.3	1.7	3.4	12.1	85.7	29.8	2.5
1932	7.8	3.3	8.0	23.0	9.3	1.8	3.3	13.8	83.5	29.1	2.7
1933	7.5	2.5	7.8	17.9	9.1	1.7	4.2	13.1	74.6	27.9	2.9
1934	6.7	2.6	7.3	14.6	8.3	1.4	3.8	11.8	58.3	29.7	2.3
1935	6.9	2.1	6.3	15.8	8.2	1.5	3.1	11.2	71.4	32.5	2.2
1936	6.9	1.9	6.3	12.7	6.7	1.7	3.0	11.1	73.1	33.0	2.5
1937	6.2	1.4	5.7	10.2	4.9	.9	2.3	10.0	73.8	32.8	2.1
1938	5.5	.9	4.8	13.2	3.8	1.1	1.9	9.1	59.5	28.2	2.2

Sources: NRUS, Vol. 10, pp. 426–27. Figures for all sectors, mining, manufacturing total, gas and electricity, transportation and communication, day laborers and others in this table are directly quoted from the source. The figures for the subdivisions of manufacturing are calculated by comparing union memberships mentioned for these industries (ibid., pp. 426–27) with the number of persons employed in the same industries found on other pages (ibid., pp. 168–69).

The structure of interwar unionism

During the 1930s, more than 30 percent of the trade union membership belonged to industrial unions. Craft unions and general workers' unions split the rest. The industrial unions had more than 900 members per union, while the other unions claimed considerably less than 200 per union. Interwar unions were less successful in organizing large firms than small and medium firms. Data on the unionization by size of firm are not available in reliable form, but there was an inquiry in 1933 which may be used to infer the strength of unions in large firms. The inquiry covered factories, mines, and other establishments employing 500 or more workers. The extent of unionization in these establishments taken together with the over-all union situation gives some idea of how far unions had penetrated large firms. Table 17 is designed for the purpose of showing this.

TABLE 17

THE RATE OF UNIONIZATION IN FACTORIES
EMPLOYING 500 OR MORE WORKERS IN 1933

Item	Public Enterprise	Private Enterprise	Total
(1) Workers in all the factories	196,534[a] persons	560,532[b] persons	757,066 persons
(2) Workers in factories where unions have entered[c]	65,200 persons	125,170 persons	190,370 persons
(3) Union members[c]	46,100 persons	32,049 persons	78,149 persons
(4) Local rate of unionization = (3)/(2)	70.8%	25.6%	41.0%
(5) Over-all rate of unionization = (3)/(1)	23.5%	5.7%	10.2%

[a] Including office workers, operatives, and miscellaneous workers in all the publicly owned factories. *NRUS*, Vol. 10, pp. 136–39.

[b] Including all workers of the above descriptions in private factories with 500 or more workers. *NRUS*, Vol. 10, pp. 168–69.

[c] Factories only. The source includes mining too. *RUN*, 1933, p. 37.

This table indicates that only 10 percent of workers in large factories belonged to unions in 1933. It implies that an overwhelming number of large establishments were free of trade unions. Public enterprises were better organized than private firms. These large private firms were in fact less well organized than the manufacturing sector as a whole. Furthermore, unions did not succeed in organizing all the workers in the factories which they managed to enter. While 71 percent of workers in public enterprises where unions had entered were captured as union members, only a quarter of the workers in private firms where unions had footholds were union members. All this indicates that the effectiveness of union power must have been limited even in establishments where unions were present.[30]

Collective bargaining

The most important indicator of the weakness of trade unionism in interwar Japan was the near absence of collective bargaining as an established practice. In March 1936 there were 121 collective agreements covering a bare third of the trade union membership. One half of these agreements had been concluded during the three-year period of 1932–1935. Seizing upon these recent events and reflecting upon a long history of unsuccessful history of collective bargaining since the first signs of demand for it arose in the late 1890s, the Japanese Government in the annual report on the labor movement for 1936 expressed a hope that "the age of collective bargaining had finally arrived." [31] The limited scope of the collective agreements extant in 1936 hardly warranted such optimism, but even this kind of modest development was destroyed completely after 1938.

Of the 136,000 workers covered by the collective agreements, 114,000 were seamen and other workers related to the marine transport industry. This left only 22,000 for all other industries, where workers were much more numerous. The collective agreements in these industries covered only 10 percent of unionized workers, who were a small fraction of all workers in these industries. One can hardly imagine that union power expressed through collective bargaining of this kind could have affected the working of the labor market to any great extent. Most of the collective agreements were concluded with small and medium firms, while there were but sixteen agreements concluded with firms with 500 or more workers.[32]

It is appropriate to mention works councils of the interwar period in this connection. The idea came to Japanese industry through an independent ideological channel on the side of employers who wished to prevent unions from organizing their employees. By the end of 1928 there were 171 works councils. In July 1933 there were 196 of them. Three years later, in July 1936, they had increased to 274. A great majority of works councils were created by the initiative of the employers to emphasize labor-management cooperation, or to prevent the entry of trade unions, or to avoid trade disputes. Only 10 works councils in 1933 and 22 in 1936 were set up by collective agreements between employers and unions.[33]

The instability of unions

Although union membership increased up to 1936, the turnover of unions was always considerable. Each year many unions came into being and many others disappeared. For example, between 1927 and 1928, when the number of trade unions was roughly stable, 91 unions disappeared out of the total of 505 in 1927 and 87 unions were newly organized in 1928. The attrition rate was 18 percent. Two thirds of the unions formed in 1923 had disappeared by 1929, giving an average annual attrition rate of 11 percent. The unions formed in the years between 1923 and 1929 were surviving in 1929 at the following rates: 36 percent from 1924, 56 percent from 1925, 66 percent from 1926, 69 percent from 1927, and 91 percent from 1928. The average annual attrition rate from these figures happens to be 11 percent again.[34] Although longitudinal data of this kind are not available for later years, one may well suppose that similar turnover continued until the labor movement was dissolved during the Second World War. In this state of organizational instability, long-term union strategies with lasting effects on the labor market process were hardly possible. Partly for this reason, unions tended to concentrate their efforts on short-run aims through industrial disputes and prospered or perished according to gains or losses from these disputes.

Union participation in industrial disputes

The dispute that the union can help settle in favor of workers is a major step toward organizing these workers or solidifying their loyalty to the union if they are already members. Industrial disputes which involve work stoppages through strikes, slowdowns, or lockouts are especially fertile grounds for cultivating union influence over workers.

Unions began to exploit these opportunities toward the end of the First World War. The disputes, accompanied by work stoppages, increased during the 1920s and, having reached their peak in 1931, tended to decrease during the rest of the 1930s. The participation of the unions in these disputes crossed the 50 percent mark in 1925 and was maintained at a high rate until 1931, when it began to diminish. In 1937 unions were involved in less than 40 percent of disputes accompanied by work stoppages. Evidently, unions became increasingly strike-shy during the 1930s.[35]

The question that needs to be answered is whether unions really helped workers win their disputes over employers. Unfortunately, the available data do not make it possible to make direct comparisons of disputes won with and without the help of unions. There are data which show disputes involving work stoppages classified by type of outcome such as employers' accession to workers' demands, compromise, employers' rejection of workers' demands, and stalemate without settlement.[36] The data run from 1914 to 1937. This period includes the 8-year subperiod of 1925 to 1932 when unions were involved in more than 50 percent of all disputes involving work stoppages. Before 1925 and after 1932 the rate of union participation in disputes was lower than 50 percent. Having this in mind, I have divided the time series of dispute statistics by type of outcome into three parts: (1) prior to 1925, when unions helped workers very little; (2) between 1925 and 1932, when unions helped workers considerably; and (3) after 1932, when unions again stayed away from disputes. Table 18 shows dispute outcomes distributed over three types of outcome for these periods.

The comparison of columns 2 and 3 for the periods 1914–1924 and 1925–1932 might suggest that the increased participation of unions in industrial disputes helped workers win more disputes than would otherwise have been possible. But during the period 1933–1937, when unions tended to stay away from disputes, workers were winning proportionately more of them than during any other period. Interestingly enough, according to columns 4 and 5, employers were less frequently inclined to make compromises and more frequently inclined to reject workers' demands outright when unions were involved in the disputes than when they were not. Column 6 indicates that work stoppages were longer during the period of greater union participation in disputes than during other periods. All this seems to suggest that unions sharpened the

TABLE 18

INDUSTRIAL DISPUTES BY TYPE OF OUTCOME, 1914-1937

(ALL DISPUTES = 100)

Period (1)	Disputes where Unions were Involved (2)	Outcomes of Disputes			Disputes that Lasted More than Ten Days (6)
		Employers' Accession to Workers' Demands (3)[a]	Compromise (4)[b]	Employers' Rejection of Workers' Demands or Stalemate (5)[c]	
1914–1924	36.3%	16.6%	44.7%	38.7%	11.1%[d]
1925–1932	65.4%	25.5%	34.8%	39.7%	36.2%
1933–1937	43.0%	26.2%	43.0%	30.8%	17.0%

Sources: NRUS, Vol. 10, p. 522 for (2) and p. 495 for all other columns.

[a] The product moment correlation coefficient between (2) and (3) on the basis of their annual data is +0.41, significant at 5 percent level.

[b] The product moment correlation with (2) on the basis of annual data is −0.80, significant at 1 percent level.

[c] Correlation with (2) of the type mentioned above is negligible.

[d] Calculated from data for 1922, 1923, and 1924.

issues and intensified confrontation to such an extent that workers and employers were forced to take clearer stands than they would otherwise have taken. Since Japanese life in general has always been characterized with undefined interpersonal relations, the confrontation of adversaries around sharply defined issues may be a sign of modernization. One would regard it as unfortunate that interwar trade unionism in Japan, having shown some promise in this direction, did not last long enough to affect customary practices of defining situations and resolving conflicts.

Summary

By now it is clear that Japanese trade unions during the interwar period did not have permanent instruments within the individual firms effective enough to protect their members from the vagaries of the external labor market or to induce the improvement of wages and working conditions on a long-term basis. But the prevalence of industrial disputes during this period indicates that workers, with or without unions' help, had some notion of minimum tolerable labor standards within the individual firms, however diffuse and uncoordinated the notion may have been, and were able to enforce these basic demands on employers when the latter grossly transgressed workers' customary expectations. The contribution of trade unions was to stand by as a friendly force on the workers' side and lend help to them where desirable or feasible. By this kind of veto power workers and unions were telling employers of the minimum price that had to be paid for employing labor services. Of course employers had an infinite range of action above that minimum, and just where on this range each employer should place his labor policy depended upon his usual economic calculus.

The Labor Market and Employer Responses

To the employer his own profit motive is a strong disciplinary force over a considerable range of his economic decisions. In order to make profits, the employer after having decided what goods to produce must combine factors of production in appropriate proportions. In doing this he is subject to relative factor prices, so that the general socio-economic conditions exert their influence on the entrepreneurial decisions on factor proportions through their impact on factor prices. From the preceding sections of this chapter, one can see that laws, workers, and unions during the interwar period converged upon setting certain minimum standards of employer behavior in relation to the use of labor services.[37] Above these minima each employer was free to choose his own standards for wages and working conditions. He would weigh the quality and productivity of workers he wanted to hire against the cost of conditions he had to offer to attract the right kinds of workers in right numbers. Exceptional employers producing goods of exceptionally high qualities by complex, large-scale technology would go considerably above the social minimum labor standards in search for workers of appropriate training and skill.

Marginal employers scraping a bare subsistence for themselves from whatever opportunities they were able to seize upon would skate on the thin ice of the minimum standards interpreted as stingily as possible, often violating the statutory limits when public power was not watching. However, even the marginal employers of the interwar period with legal minimum standards clearly spelled out for them could not but be more careful about wages and working conditions in their shops than the marginal employers of the Meiji Period. Likewise, the standards of excellence in the quality of products, the technology of production, and the managerial techniques of organization of resources were considerably higher during the interwar period than in the Meiji Era. To a great extent, all this was merely a reflection of the normal upward trends in all aspects of life in the course of socio-economic progress. However, extraordinary conditions of short-run cyclical nature were superimposed on these long-run trends to produce some unusual characteristics of the labor market process during the interwar period.

One of the extraordinary economic conditions during this period was the decline in the labor-absorptive capacity of the nonagricultural sectors. This had many repercussions on the movements over time of wages and working conditions in different sectors and industries. The depression of 1929–1931 was not the only depression prewar Japan had experienced, but its impact was considerably severer in many aspects of the socio-economic process than the impact of any preceding depression. The question now is whether this depression was to any extent due to some fundamental changes in Japan's socio-economic structure that may have occurred during the interwar period. The "structuralists" among the students of Japanese economic history to whom references were made in Part I would certainly answer this question in the affirmative. In them one detects a thought process similar to that of the American "stagnationists," who have overgeneralized about the fundamentals of the American economic system from just one sample, the Great Depression.[38] I have no intention of undertaking international comparisons of motives and methods of "structuralists" of all kinds. The point is simply that a lack of perspective, historical and comparative, often leads to too much emphasis on particular characteristics of a small segment of a historical continuum.

There is another, more meaningful question. No doubt during the interwar period many vital factors of social behavior and economic activity were more clearly defined than before: clearer perception and articulation of group interests, greater sensitivity to labor standards, and more intensive consciousness of life style, human dignity, and political rights. One may therefore ask whether this social force which worked on the upgrading of all kinds of standards may not have been disproportionately stronger in the manufacturing sector and induced an autonomous upward shift in the technological preferences of producers, which in turn resulted in the reduced labor-absorptive capacity of this sector. This is an important, but extremely difficult, question. I am not prepared for a direct assault on this question, but I shall try to extract whatever suggestions bear on this question from the characteristics of the labor market of the interwar period. I shall first examine the state of labor mobility and follow the path of logical analysis toward the examination of employers' labor market strategies in relation to the type of technology that was available to them in production during the period in question.

There are two sets of data on labor mobility for this period. One set refers to changes in the average length of employment over time, and the other to labor turnover rates. Table 19 presents the distribution of workers by length of employment over time. It can be expected that length of employment is inversely associated with labor mobility, that is, a short average period of employment indicates high labor mobility, and a long one, low labor mobility. This is because workers feel less constrained about changing jobs during prosperity when jobs are plentiful than during depression when jobs are scarce. A word of caution may be entered here for the interpretation of Table 19. The figure called "sample" in this table is the basis for the proportionate distribution of workers by length of employment. But the "sample" is not random; it covers a specific part of total factory employment marked off by criteria which were incidental to the purposes of the particular surveys. Therefore the distribution of workers in the "sample" is not representative of all factory workers, in the same sense as a random sample can be. Since the degrees of bias cannot be ascertained, one should attach one's own discount factor to the implications of the table.

According to Table 19, 44 percent of factory workers had been employed for less than a year in 1900, and less than 10 percent for more than five years. The situation was more or less the same during the First World War. But employment in the 1920s and 1930s was considerably more stable than in earlier years. Especially in 1933, when nearly half of the factory workers had been employed in the same factories for more than five years—in remarkable contrast to 1900. Behind this stability in the 1920s was the generally stagnant state of employment, which culminated in the depression of 1929–1931. With the

TABLE 19

DISTRIBUTION OF WORKERS BY LENGTH OF EMPLOYMENT,

SELECTED YEARS, 1900–1957

(PERCENT)

Length of Employment	1900	1918	1924	1933	1939	1957
up to 6 months	20.1	24.6	9.2	9.3	15.2	7.6
6 months to 1 year	24.0	19.4	9.5	9.8	16.2	14.4
1–3 years	33.8	32.6	25.6	19.8	37.0	24.1
3–5	12.3	11.7	17.2	14.4	12.6	17.1
5–10	}9.8	8.0	22.2	22.8	9.7	21.1
10 and more		3.7	16.2	23.8	9.3	15.8
TOTAL	100.0	100.0	100.0	100.0	100.0	100.0
Sample (in 000's of persons)	115[a]	1,371[b]	1,314[c]	1,424[c]	1,234[d]	5,270[e]
Paid employment in manufacturing (in 000's of persons)	649[f]	1,505[f]	1,977[f]	2,133[f]	4,370[f]	5,270

[a] The sample is the basis for the proportionate distribution of workers by length of employment. For 1900 the sample is aggregated from data in the *Shokkō jijō*.

[b] *KKN*, No. 3 (1918), pp. 296–301, covering factories with 15 or more operatives.

[c] *RTJCH*. See Note b to Table 6, *supra*.

[d] Ministry of Welfare, *Rōdōsha chingin chōsa hōkoku* (Report on the Survey of Wages), 1939, covering "experienced" workers in manufacturing establishments with 10 or more operatives.

[e] MITI, *Nihon sangyō no genjō* (The Present Conditions of Japanese Industries), 1959, p. 185, covering manufacturing establishments with one or more regular workers.

[f] *NKTS*, pp. 55–56. Factories with 5 or more operatives.

rapid expansion of employment under the impetus of war requirements in the latter half of the 1930s, labor mobility again increased, as shown by a lower average length of employment for 1939 in Table 19. For purposes of long-run perspective, I have added post-second World War data to the table, although the topic belongs to the next chapter.

Another indicator of labor mobility is the rate of labor turnover. In Table 20 I have shortened the annual data, 1920–1936 and 1949–1966, by averaging them over selected periods. Again, changes in the coverage

TABLE 20

LABOR TURNOVER RATES, MONTHLY AVERAGES, PREWAR AND POSTWAR

(PERCENT)

Year	Hiring (or Accession) Rate	Dismissal (or Separation) Rate
1900[a]	10.1	12.0
1916 and 1917[b]	7.3	5.6
1920–1925[c]	5.6	5.6
1926–1929[c]	4.5	4.3
1930–1933[c]	4.3	4.2
1934–1936[c]	4.7	3.9
1949–1959[d]	2.2	2.1
1960–1966[d]	2.6	2.3

[a] *Shokkō jijō*, Vol. 1, pp. 67–69. Three large cotton textile factories.

[b] *KKN*, No. 2 (1917), pp. 234–35. Prefecture of Kyoto only.

[c] Prime Minister's Office, *Rōdō tōkei yōran* (Handbook of Labor Statistics), 1920–1936. For 1920–25, factories employing 15 or more operatives. For 1926–36, factories employing 50 or more workers.

[d] *RH*, 1949–1966. Manufacturing establishments employing 30 or more regular workers.

of the data made in 1926 prevent long-run generalizations. Although the hiring and dismissal rates were distinctly higher during the period of 1920–1925 than in later years, one cannot tell how much this difference was due to the inclusion of smaller establishments in the data for 1920–1925 and their exclusion from the data for later years. A hiring rate of 4.2 percent balanced by an equal dismissal rate per month means that about half of the labor force changes jobs within a year. This would be considered a rather high rate of labor turnover. (It was just about the average accession or separation rate in the United States during the 1950s, and no one doubts that the U. S. workers are the most mobile in the whole world.) Earlier data on labor turnover are not available on a consecutive basis. The *Shokkō jijō* observed that labor turnover often surpassed 100 percent per year in textile mills. During the boom years of the First World War, factories in Kyoto Prefecture experienced rather high turnover rates, although not as high as in textile mills fifteen years earlier. Although one should not generalize too easily from Table 20, one may nevertheless be allowed to say that labor turnover in the 1920s and 1930s may have been lower even when adjusted for cyclical factors than during the earlier decades. After the Second World War labor turnover decreased enormously. Deferring observations on postwar labor turnover to the next chapter, one may simply conclude that the interwar labor market was considerably fluid according to the data on labor turnover for this period.[39]

The existing data also permit observations on the extent to which workers tended to commit themselves to the same employers during the interwar period. The data from which Table 19 has been drawn show one-year intervals of employment running up to sixteen years. From cross references of these data for different years, it is possible to compute what may be called a "commitment rate," which is by definition equal to 100 percent minus the attrition rate. For example, if 50 out of 100 workers initially employed remain employed in the same factory 10 years later, the "commitment rate" is one half over the 10-year period or 5 percent per annum. Table 21 shows the indices of workers staying with the same employers between 1924 and 1933. Of the workers newly employed in 1924 (Group A), 56.7 percent in 1927, 30.4 percent in 1930, and 19.2 percent in 1933 remained with the employers of 1924. From this it can be inferred that the attrition rate was about 9 percent per annum for the first nine years. As an inspection of each column from top to bottom will show, the tendency to drop out decreases with the length of the period during which the worker stays with the same employer. Of Group A, only 57 percent remained with the same employers three years later, but of Group M, who had already been with their employers for 12 to 13 years by 1924, practically all (96 percent) remained with the same employers three years later.

Table 21 suggests that a hundred-percent commitment rate, that is, "lifetime commitment," was not a general rule in prewar Japan. Nat-

TABLE 21

INDICES OF WORKERS REMAINING WITH INITIAL EMPLOYERS, 1924–1933[a]

Length of Employment (in Years)	Base Year (1924)		Three Years Later (1927)	Six Years Later (1930)	Nine Years Later (1933)
0–1	A	100			
1–2	B	100			
2–3	C	100			
3–4	D	100	A 56.7		
4–5	E	100	B 57.5		
5–6	F	100	C 58.0		
6–7	G	100	D 55.2	A 30.4	
7–8	H	100	E 61.0	B 33.1	
8–9	I	100 (N 100)	F 60.5	C 58.0	
9–10	J	100	G 64.5	D 32.5	A 19.2
10–11	K	100	H 76.2	E 43.5	B 25.1
11–12	L	100 (P 100)	I 59.7	F 37.6	C 19.3
12–13	M	100	J 74.3	G 46.1	D 24.0
13–14	(Q 100)		K 58.3	H 47.5	E 30.0
14–15			L 75.2	I 45.5	F 29.5
15–16			M 96.0	J 66.9	G 41.7
16–20				P 51.0	N 37.5
20–25					Q 51.5

[a] *RTJCH*, for relevant years. The indices are calculated under the assumption that workers employed for less than a year in 1924 would be in the class of those employed for 3 to 4 years in 1927 if they stayed with the same employers, and likewise for all other groups of workers.

urally, some employers looked for measures to achieve labor economy and higher productivity. In the preceding chapter I have described how signs of "employer paternalism" emerged in the textiles in response to the earlier labor shortage. The employer response to the problem of the same nature in the interwar period gave rise to a technique of work-force organization known as *nenkō joretsu* (ranking by years of experience). The ideal type of the *nenkō joretsu* system required that new hiring was limited to young inexperienced workers and that these workers were trained and moved up to fill various grades of skills over time. At the same time this system in its ideal form did not imply lifetime commitment for all the workers. Each worker stayed within the firm only in so far as he had the ability to move to more skilled and responsible positions at such a pace as to maintain his position always ahead of all the workers younger than he. In case a worker's maximum capability was reached at a point short of the highest position on the list of grades and steps scheduled over his working life, he would leave the firm at that point. Thus a certain number of workers were eliminated every year as the original cohort moved up the ladder until only a few remained in the firm's employ till retirement.[40]

This was of course the ideal type which employers would have liked to institute in their respective firms. But the distance between the reality of the work force and the ideal type of *nenkō joretsu* was enormous in the engineering industries of the interwar period. The existing industrial relations inside the firm worked against a quick institution of the *nenkō joretsu* system. In order to bring it about, the firm had first to gain direct control over its work force in all the aspects of recruitment, training, assignment, promotion, dismissal, and retirement. But the formal job structure and informal worker groupings within the factory in the engineering industries were largely based on personal and personalized relations among master craftsmen and between each one of them and his underlings. The situation can be summed up as "*oyakata-kokata* relations." Management's full control over the work force was predicated on securing *Oyakata* craftsmen's loyalty to the firm and winning the struggle with them over the loyalty of the workers, *Kokata*. As mentioned in Chapter 5, metal workers in prewar Japan satisfied their need for identification and belonging not by being employed in any specific firm but by the membership in a broad community of workers practicing the same trades and by being able to move about throughout Japan within this community.[41]

Of course any firm could obtain a loyal, committed work force by training a massive number of young workers without skill and making them fill the required positions after training. In taking this course of action, however, the firm had to be prepared for long years of investment without profits. It was not an economically rational proposition when the firm could start production in short order by hiring a required number of workers with necessary skills from the labor market. Besides, there was no guarantee that the internally trained workers would not change jobs before the investment in their training was recouped. Indeed, many engineering firms with internal training facilities suffered from very high attrition rates among the workers who were trained at their expense. In the Yawata Iron and Steel Works, for example, the regular work force in 1935 stood at 20,000 men. If all of the 6,200 workers who were internally trained from the inception of its training school in 1910 had stayed in Yawata's employ, they would have filled a substantial number of key positions at various levels of skill and responsibility. However, fewer than 800 of these workers were found to be in Yawata's employ in 1935. Under the circumstance, it was not possible to take the first essential step toward instituting the *nenkō joretsu,* that is, limiting new hiring to young unskilled workers. Yawata was forced, therefore, to depend on the labor market for labor supplies to maintain the work force.[42] The story was more or less the same in all other metal works. On the whole, workers of all age groups moved in and out of these firms with considerable ease. Sometimes firms too quickly lost the workers they wanted to keep and were left with the workers whom they would have done without. Occasionally, therefore, firms had to get rid of these inefficient workers by whatever means, pretexts, inducements, or tactics they had available. A high degree of voluntary mobility coexisted with occasional mass discharges made on the initiative of the employers. The economics of the situation was not amenable to a long-term employment planning like the *nenkō joretsu* system, although it cannot be denied that firms did make efforts in that direction as evidenced by their maintenance of training facilities.

The upsurge in the labor movement in the 1920s had an indirect effect on employers' labor policy quite independently of the skill requirements of the *nenkō joretsu* system. In the face of trade unions' challenge, worker loyalty became a great problem for employers. The question of how to keep unions out engaged employers' attention to a great extent. The simplest answer was to pay and treat workers in ways that would defeat the idea that unions were the only agents for improving the lot of the working class. During the 1920s, indeed, there were noticeable efforts among employers to institute a variety of amenities inside the firm and to improve wages and working conditions.[43] Some employers also espoused the idea of works councils in order to demonstrate their good will and to make a friendly gesture to their workers. These voluntary concessions were regarded as superior to having unions as workers' agents. Since the financial capability of each firm must have been the decisive factor in the actual size and extent of concessions of any kind, and since these concessions were geared to the end of keeping unions out, large firms tended to offer more of them and to succeed more in keeping unions out thereby than small and medium-sized firms.

The unions of the interwar period were craft or industrywide unions. Unions of these types had their objective basis in the extensive, informal craft communities and high labor mobility. Therefore, the success of some employers in keeping unions out also implied that they succeeded at the same time in secluding their workers from craft communities and the mobile labor market. In other words, the anti-union employers were buying their master craftsmen to their side and winning the loyalty of the other workers. On the other hand, in order not to create discontent under the changing conditions, employers took care not to disturb the status structure determined by the *oyakata-kokata* relations. The absence of trouble gradually brought about labor-management harmony and in the early 1930s produced a docile work force sold out almost completely to the employers' side.

Again, one should be careful about the interpretation of all this development, which was at best a broad tendency visible but buried under the flux of events in the highly fluid labor market. The victory of larger employers in the struggle with the labor movement over the loyalty of their workers was demonstrated by the data previously considered on the interfirm distribution of union membership; that is, in 1933 the proportion of workers joining the unions was lower in large private firms than in smaller ones. Furthermore, during the depression of 1929–1931 large firms succeeded in cutting their employment proportionately more than smaller ones, without having any more disputes with workers.[44] In the 1930s the industrial disputes were relatively concentrated in smaller firms as indicated by the smaller average number of workers per dispute, despite an increase in the incidence of disputes, than during the 1920s.[45] The relatively generous dismissal allowances that large firms started in the 1920s worked wonders in the 1930s.

With the increasing docility of their workers, large firms began to suspect in the 1930s that they were perhaps paying too much. In the course of recovery after 1931, these firms tested their suspicion by employing "temporary workers" and discovered that large numbers of workers could be hired for much less and for greater discipline than they were able to enforce on workers during the 1920s. The "temporary worker" in question was identical to the regular worker in all aspects of work on the shop floor, but he was formally considered a miscellaneous worker employed for a short fixed term, sometimes on a day-to-day basis, at rates of pay markedly inferior to those of the regular worker. Not only were the "temporary workers" deprived of fringe benefits within the firm, but they were not counted as factory "operatives" protected by the Factory Law and related measures.

The government awoke to the problem of the "temporary workers" and surveyed the state of this particular employment practice in factories employing 100 or more operatives in 1934. A majority of factories did not have "temporary workers" in the sense described above. In factories employing "temporary workers," which were 30 percent of all factories of the stated size group, "temporary workers" were 17 percent of the workers in the "operative" category without counting "laborers." Many of the "laborers" who were not covered by the Factory Law and related measures were in fact operatives who should have been eligible for legal benefits in principle. If a half of the laborers were *de facto* operatives, the proportion of disguised operatives together with the "temporary workers" would rise to 20 percent of all the workers. In the engineering industries the same calculation yielded 26 percent, considerably above the average for all the industries. Remember, however, that we are always talking about those large factories where "temporary workers" were said to be employed.[46]

One of the villains in the "temporary worker" hoax was the Yawata Iron and Steel Works, where nearly 70 percent of its work force of 21,-000 persons were "temporary." In 1935 some of these "temporary" workers were found to have been working for Yawata continuously for 15 years. At a hearing conducted by the Kyochokai, a Yawata manager revealed that his company had always employed "temporary workers." Although their number fluctuated with economic conditions, it rarely fell below 5,000 workers in the worst of depressions.[47] This would amount to a little less than a third of the depression level of the Yawata work force, which was between 16,000 and 17,000 during the interwar period. The Prefecture of Fukuoka where the Yawata Works was located was found to be far ahead of all prefectures in the use of "temporary workers." The prefectural survey of 1934 indicated that in factories with 100 or more operatives where "temporary workers" were employed, nearly 40 percent of the workers were "temporary." In the same survey the engineering firms, of which Yawata was one, were shown to have 54 percent of their workers in the "temporary" status.[48]

The investigations into the problem of "temporary workers" turned up a new type of intermediaries in the labor market. They were called "labor supply agents." They supplied about 15 percent of all the "temporary workers" in the national aggregates referred to above.[49] In the Prefecture of Fukuoka, the agents supplied 84 percent of all the "temporary workers" in the prefecture. The Yawata Iron and Steel Works hired all its "temporary workers" through the "labor supply agents." The use of the labor market intermediaries enabled employers to literally buy work in pure and simple form, leaving all the cumbersome and costly statutory or customary standards for hiring in care of the agents. This was surely an indicator of the enormous power of discrimination that large employers like Yawata were able to impose on the labor market. Furthermore, Yawata was able to designate unilaterally the labor supply agents with whom it was willing to do business.

These official findings on "temporary workers" were necessarily underestimates. No factory management would willingly reveal its unsavory secret to anyone so long as it could conceal it. Temporary workers always existed in Japanese firms as workers going through the test period. They were expected to be discharged or promoted to the ranks of regular workers at the end of the test period. When the test period became unusually long or when management automatically discharged all the temporary workers at the end of the test period, only to rehire them as temporary workers, these workers were already indistinguishable from regular workers. It is wrong, however, to blame only employers in this respect, because when jobs are hard to get, some workers may prefer substandard working conditions to unemployment. In the excess-supply labor market, the market forces press down wages and working conditions. The phenomenon of "temporary workers" in the middle 1930s was a symptom of the prevailing labor market conditions. The curious thing about it is that the burden of the downward adjustment of wages and working conditions was not borne by all the workers equally. But this should not surprise anyone, because the downward rigidity of money wages during depression and the distortions associated with it in the process of resource allocation are universal in all private enterprise economies. If the slack labor market produced "temporary workers," the ensuing tight labor market extinguished them. The sustained economic recovery, which soon developed into a war economy intensified labor shortage, obliterated the power of employers to discriminate some workers against others. The relentless process of adjustment in the market worked its will .

Conclusion

This chapter reviews how the "free" labor market worked under prosperity during the First World War and how legal and institutional forces impinged upon the labor market process during the interwar period. The demand for labor was in excess of its supply during the War period. The labor market was jammed with labor recruiters. Labor turnover was very high. Dishonest practices of all kinds developed on both sides of the market; for example, unruly job changes and willful infringements of employment contracts by workers, false representation of terms of employment and use of force to retain workers on the part of employers. In a sense, there was a need for orderly rules of behavior in the labor market.

During the interwar period the Government undertook to institute some of these rules. The starting point was a rather imperfect Factory Law which took effect in 1916, but it was at least a start. By 1939 the Government had improved the content and administration of the Factory Law and in addition had established employment exchanges, machinery of supervision over private labor recruiters, and limited scales of income and health insurances.

The labor movement was neither strong nor extensive. Trade unions were not recognized in law, but the power of unions displayed through industrial disputes frightened the Government and employers. The Government reconciled itself to workers' right to select their own representatives for international purposes. Employers offered concessions in higher wages and greater fringe benefits to keep unions out of their shops. Large employers scored a tremendous success in this respect. The labor movement itself limped along with its internal problems of factional strife. The depression of the early 1930s weakened the trade unions, and the deepening international crisis in the late 1930s destroyed them.

All this while, the labor market functioned with tolerable flexibility. Despite the generally stagnant economic conditions during this period, labor mobility was at a reasonably high level. "Lifetime commitment" was a far cry from the reality of industrial relations. There was some beginning of the *nenkō joretsu* system of employment, but it was not a general phenomenon. In the 1930s the slack labor market revealed its symptom as "temporary workers," whom the subsequent tight labor market absorbed entirely.

Unionism, Wage Structure, and the Labor Market

DURING THE EARLY YEARS after the Second World War there was a phenomenal surge in the labor movement. The rate of unionization of paid workers, although not constant, has been high throughout the postwar period. From the type and distribution of unionism in postwar Japan, one suspects that collective bargaining may have had its greatest effect on the interfirm wage structure.[1] The question is whether the interfirm wage structure would have been different from what was actually observed had there been no unions in postwar Japan. This is of course a standard question frequently asked in relation to the impact of unionism on wage structure. For example, Reynolds asks: "Does unionism distort the wage structure from its normal pattern, with disruptive effects on relative prices, outputs, and resource allocation?"[2] P. Ford states: "To anyone interested in economic theory, the problem to be solved is how far the wage structure differs from what it would have been in the absence of trade unions; and if it does, what are the economic processes by which the difference has been brought about."[3]

I shall first formulate a working hypothesis which will be useful in defining the nature and scope of the subject of this chapter. Next, the essential characteristics of "enterprise unionism" in postwar Japan will be noted. Then I shall trace the course of the interactions between unionism and market forces and their effects on variations in the interfirm wage structure in postwar Japan. Finally, I shall review recent developments in relations among unions, managements, and the labor market with a particular emphasis on the changing principles and tactics of the labor movement. This chapter also serves as an alternative interpretation of labor-management relations in postwar Japan to that advanced by James Abegglen.

The Hypothesis

From the available studies of relationships between unionism and wage structure in America and Europe[4] a broad hypothesis can be derived which is useful for bringing Japanese unionism and wage structure into the international setting. Simply put, the hypothesis says that the extent of the unions' influence over wage structure can be related to the degree of coverage of a typical wage agreement defined as the proportion that the number of workers bound to such an agreement bears to the whole population of wage and salary earners in a given economy. The degree of coverage ranges from near zero, where all wage agreements are atomistic on the basis of individual bargaining between each worker and each employer, to unity, where all the workers in the economy are bound to one central wage agreement. The apparent precision of the definition is no guarantee of its easy quantification for a nation over time or different nations at a given time. No measurement, therefore, will be attempted here. At present merely "ordinalist" comparisons can be made of the degrees of coverage; that is, it can be said that the degree of coverage is higher in Country A than in Country B, but not *how much* higher. Such "ordinalist" comparisons between countries can be made from the existing body of knowledge on collective bargaining in various countries. What has been learned so far from the American and European experience is that the higher the "degree of coverage," as defined above, the more the relative wages for various occupations, industries, firms, and regions tend to approach the competitive norm of the labor market—uniformity of wages within the same category of work and fair relativity between different categories of work.[5]

The relationship between the "degree of coverage" and the approach of wage structure toward the competitive norm is not linear, however. Wage structure under low coverage unionism might diverge from the competitive norm more than in the absence of any kind of unionism. At this stage a union might look like a labor monopoly of the most reckless and irresponsible kind, demanding more and more for its members at the expense of everybody else. Much of the apprehension that labor unions are distorting the normal market processes of resource allocation stems, in fact, from the behavior of unions in the stage of "minority unionism," as it is called by G. Rehn.[6]

A small union may be able to pursue an egotistic goal of more and better things for its members without caring how its behavior is viewed by the public at large. The union which has grown large by controlling a significant portion of the labor force, however, inevitably feels the repercussions of its action far beyond the narrow confines of collective bargaining and finds it necessary to take these into consideration in managing its affairs and designing its bargaining strategy. The outcome of interactions between union growth and wage structure is summarized by Rehn as follows:

> If unions get both large and strong . . . the moral forces, which they have fostered themselves, prevent the unions from charging as much as the traffic can bear in individual cases. . . . In spite of existing differences (which are not very large) between any union concept of equity or fair relativity and the pure theory concept of equal efficiency wages or equal net advantages, we can therefore conclude that full unionization tends to imply more adjustment than distortion in relation to the productivity criteria of economic theory.[7]

The association of increasing coverage of a typical wage agreement with increasing conformity of the wage structure to the competitive norm is one aspect of the hypothesis that has received considerable attention in recent years. But another aspect, the association of low coverage with the divergence of wage structure from the competitive norm, seems to have gone out of fashion. It is as an instance of this aspect of the hypothesis that Japanese enterprise unionism and its probable impact on the Japanese wage structure can be of interest and significance.

The Nature of Enterprise Unionism

Postwar Japanese unionism owes its designation as "enterprise unionism" to the fact that membership in the typical Japanese labor union is limited to employees of a given enterprise. In 1957 nearly 87 percent of the Japanese unions were enterprise unions, and nearly 80 percent of all organized labor belonged to them.[8] Levine characterizes the Japanese enterprise union as follows:

> In appearance, the enterprise union resembles the local of an industrial union, or an "intermediate" organization like the Ford or General Motors departments of the United Automobile Workers in the United States. However, the similarity ends about there. The essential distinction between the enterprise union and the local industrial union is that the former is a unit in and of itself; it is not merely an administrative component of a national union, nor is it simply an "inside" independent company-wide union.[9]

Each enterprise union independently bargains with management, and there is no coordination of the bargains of various unions and enterprises. It can be expected that the outcome of independent enterprise unions severally pursuing the goal of the highest possible wages in their respective enterprises will be an interfirm wage structure closely corresponding to the interfirm structure of ability to pay. Suppose, for example, that all the enterprises in the economy were organized by enterprise unions and that each enterprise union succeeded in obtaining concessions to the extent that the profit of each enterprise was reduced to a level just sufficient to keep it from going out of business. All elements of rent and quasi-rent that an enterprise could earn as the result of its monopolist or monopsonist power in the product or factor markets, its belonging to a rapidly growing industry, or its unusual technical efficiency would be siphoned into wages and other labor compensation. Insofar as the circumstances giving rise to such rent and quasi-rent varied from firm to firm, the interfirm wage structure would reflect the effects of all the imperfections in the product and factor markets.

In the postwar Japanese labor movement, however, the distribution of union activities by firm has been neither uniform nor random, but heavily concentrated in the large firms, so that ability to pay has been more readily converted to wages in the large firms than in the small. Thus one of the consequences of enterprise unionism and its uneven distribution by size of firm has been a steep wage gradient which rises with the size of firm.

The method and rhetoric of wage bargaining are also conducive to structuring interfirm wage differentials according to the interfirm differences in ability to pay. Japanese wage bargaining has the beauty of simplicity and is mainly concerned with a given percentage increase in the total payroll. As Levine says, "The union simply demands an increment to the total wage bill and proceeds to divide any increase so granted among the various worker groups without further negotiations with management." [10] The rhetoric of both union and management in wage bargains revolves around the firm's ability to pay, each party justifying its demand for higher wages, or refusal to grant wage demands, by its own estimate of ability to pay. No other criteria in Japanese collective bargaining seem to have the same power of persuasion as ability to pay.

The Japanese type of collective bargaining necessarily makes the union so conscious of the business conditions of the firm that the enterprise union is, for all practical purposes, just another management in the firm. If the competitive processes of labor markets work in the direction of determining wage rates for various skills and occupations regardless of employers' abilities to pay, the enterprise union removes its members from the influence of the markets and establishes a kind of workers' commune whose economic well-being is closely tied to the enterprise within which it is organized. Thus enterprise unionism is an exact antithesis of the labor market and is retrogressive in nature, in the sense that it destroys whatever degree of development the Japanese labor market had achieved before its emergence.

Table 22 is a collection of some statistics that illustrate the relationships among unionization, ability to pay, and wages that had evolved in the Japanese manufacturing sector by 1957. It should be noted that in the large firms labor is paid more, is more efficient, and is more highly organized than in the small ones. Although this is consistent with what has been said above on the nature and consequences of enterprise unionism, at the present stage of the argument no basis has been established for judging whether the wage differentials by size of firm shown in Table 22 should be regarded as unusual, or whether in the absence of enterprise unions they would have been just the same as observed here. I shall attempt to resolve this question in two major steps.

First, the data assembled in Table 22 do seem strange in terms of what one would normally expect as concomitants of competitive mar-

TABLE 22

WAGES, FACTOR PRODUCTIVITIES, CAPITAL INTENSITY, AND UNIONIZATION

BY SIZE OF FIRM IN MANUFACTURING, 1957[a]

Size of Firm[b] (Persons)	Wages[c] (¥'000)	Factor Productivities[d] Labor (¥'000)	Factor Productivities[d] Capital (Percent)	Rate of Profit[e] (Percent)	Capital Intensity of Labor[f] (¥'000)	Rate of Unionization[g] (Percent)	Labor Turnover Rate per Month[h] Permanent Regulars (Percent)	Labor Turnover Rate per Month[h] Temporary Regulars (Percent)
TOTAL (OR AVERAGE)	16	43	13.3	8.3	324	39.8	1.8	9.8
1-3	9	13	13.9	4.3	93	3.9	n.a.	n.a.
4-9	10	18	18.6	8.2	97		3.2	14.9
10-19	11	23	25.6	13.3	90		2.5	11.2
20-29	12	26	26.9	14.4	97			
30-49	12	29	28.4	16.7	102	19.1	2.1	9.6
50-99	13	35	25.8	16.2	136			
100-199	14	41	22.1	14.5	186		1.3	8.7
200-299	16	47	20.2	13.3	233	60.4		
300-499	17	58	16.8	11.9	345			
500-999	19	65	14.6	10.3	447	89.2	0.5	7.0
1,000 and over	25	77	10.0	6.8	769			

[a] Except for the degree of unionization, all data are either quoted or computed from *Chūshō kigyō tōkei yōran [A Statistical Handbook of Small and Medium Enterprises]* (Tokyo: Ministry of Finance Printing Office, 1959), p. 38.

[b] Classified by the number of employed persons, including proprietors, family workers, and paid employees.

[c] Average monthly earnings per paid employee.

[d] The net value added divided by the respective factors. Labor refers to all the employed persons in the firm; capital to the value of fixed assets.

[e] The net value added less labor cost (including imputed return to proprietors and family workers at wage rates for paid employees) divided by the value of fixed assets.

[f] The value of fixed assets per employed person.

[g] The number of workers belonging to unions as a percentage of all the wage and salary earners in 1954, *RH* (1956), p. 334. The four size groups are 1–29, 30–99, 100–499, and 500 and over.

[h] A simple average of monthly accession and separation rates for the period from July 1954 to June 1955. Ministry of Labor, *Nihon no rōdō keizai* (Economics of Japanese Labor) (Tokyo, 1957), p. 189. For the definitions of "permanent," "temporary," and "regular" workers, see text.

kets in a free enterprise economy. To put it a little strongly, Table 22 appears to be a description of an enormous disequilibrium in which resource mobility is considerably constrained. Since enterprise unionism is held to be partly responsible for this disequilibrium, it will be desirable to show analytically what difference unions could make in an (hypothetical) economic system which is highly competitive in all respects except in the union-induced imperfections of the labor market.

Second, however divergent from the competitive norm the actual economic events may seem, the situation as pictured by Table 22 may still be just as close to the hypothetical norm as an actual economic system can ever hope to approach, for perfection in the sense of full conformity to pure theory cannot be expected of the actual world of living human beings. Hence it will be desirable to show that the interfirm wage differentials of the order shown in Table 22 are still unusual even in terms of the performance of an actual economic system.

Competition and Union Power

If the product, labor, and capital markets are highly competitive, the rates of return to factors will in the long run tend to be equalized in all the firms regardless of size in the same industry. Hence the differentials of variables by size of firm to the extent shown by Table 22 are probably alien to a competitive economic system. Once enterprise unions arrive on the scene and union power is unevenly distributed by size of firm (as in Table 22), however, it can be shown that this fact alone could (in theory) eventually lead to the emergence of interfirm differentials in wages, productivities, and profits that would not exist in an otherwise competitive economic system.

The chain of reasoning runs along the familiar line of factor substitution in response to changes in relative factor prices.[11] If the unions are strong enough to push wages up in the organized firms and if the employers have no choice but to accommodate union demands, the most obvious step for the employers to take is to increase capital per unit of labor in the hope of raising labor productivity sufficiently to compensate for increased wages. This is consistent with the steep gradients of capital intensity and labor productivity by size of the firm in Table 22.

As more and more capital is applied to a given quantity of labor, the point of diminishing returns to capital is bound to set in sooner or later. According to Table 22, the productivities of labor and capital increase together up to a point beyond which labor productivity continues to increase, but capital productivity steadily decreases. With the diminishing returns to capital, the rate of profit also declines. Insofar as the decline in capital productivity and profit rate is due to the excess of capital relative to labor, it raises a question why the larger firms in Japan have pushed the combination of labor and capital to a level that is decidedly unfavorable to capital and that may even be wasteful in a labor-abundant, capital-scarce economy. It may be an undue exaggeration of union strength, although not unimaginable, that the unions have stampeded the employers into the region of a production function where labor productivity and wages are high, but capital productivity and profit rates are low.

At this point, therefore, one can relax the assumption of the competitive capital market and substitute in its place a more realistic assumption that the large firms enjoy preferential treatment by the financial institutions, public and private, and can obtain capital in greater quantities at lower rates of interest than the small firms.[12] Given the condition that capital costs to large firms are less than to the small, the lower rates of "gross" profit in the large firms, as shown by Table 22, may not necessarily mean lower rates of "net" profit than those in the small. (Defined in the same manner as the rate of gross profit was in Table 22, that is, the share of capital in the net output of the firm after the return to capital evaluated at the borrowing rate of interest, divided by the value of the capital stock.) Moreover, given the monopsonist power that large firms can choose to exercise with varying degrees of emphasis over financial institutions, more capital may be forthcoming to the large firms accordingly as the need for higher capital-intensive processes rises under the pressure of unions for higher wages. Hence, with strong unions in tireless watch over every possible opportunity for increasing the earnings of the firm, the potential gains that the firms could make because of imperfections in markets other than the labor market might find their way into the workers' pockets.

The foregoing comment on data presented in Table 22 is, of course, nothing more than a speculation about the economic mechanism that seems to be consistent with the emergence of wage differentials by size of firm in association with the emergence of enterprise unions. Since there are bound to be some interfirm wage differentials of the kind shown in Table 22 in the actual economic system free of enterprise unionism, it is desirable to show how much of the observed wage differentials would have existed in any event and how much might have been added by the influence of enterprise unionism. This is the second major step in the analysis of the peculiarities of the postwar Japanese wage structure, and it essentially consists in comparison of postwar interfirm wage differentials of the type shown in Table 22 with similar wage differentials for other periods when enterprise unionism was absent in Japan's economy.

A Dramatic but Temporary Impact of Unionism

Table 23 presents wage differentials by size of establishment[13] in Japan for nonunion (prewar) and union (postwar) periods. The two periods covered in Table 23 are so widely spaced that it is doubtful whether their comparison can serve the purpose of detecting the influence of unionism on interfirm wage differentials, but it is of some significance that wage differentials by size of establishment were rather small in the earlier years.[14] Table 23 also shows that the inordinately large wage differentials by size of establishment in the postwar period developed quickly during the brief period of 1945 to 1951. Interestablishment wage differentials widened during this period, in spite of the acute inflation that swept the Japanese economy during much of the same period. The widening of wage differentials during inflation makes this period in Japan one of the rare exceptions to the general rule that wage differentials ordinarily widen during deflation and narrow during inflation.

Table 23 seems to support the hypothesis that postwar enterprise unionism made some contribution to the widening of Japanese interfirm wage differentials. There is at least one piece of evidence, how-

TABLE 23

WAGE DIFFERENTIALS
BY SIZE OF ESTABLISHMENT IN MANUFACTURING,
SELECTED YEARS, 1909–1960
(PERCENT)

Size[a]	1909[b]	1914[b]	1946[e]	1947[e]	1951[d]	1954[d]	1957[d]	1960[d]	1962[d]
4–9	88	71	} 82	} 69	39	43	30	41	50
10–19	} 85	76			44	48	} 39	46	54
20–29					47	49		49	57
30–49	89	79			52	52	} 47	51	61
50–99	91	82	} 95	} 85	58	57		55	63
100–199	} 93	} 83			67	63	55	60	66
200–299			} 99	} 92	} 74	69	} 65	66	71
300–499						78		71	76
500–999	91	86			89	87	76	80	81
1,000 and over	100	100	100	100	100	100	100	100	100

Source: KTH, 1909–1962.
[a] By number of workers, which refers to the number of operatives for 1909–1947 and the number of employed persons for 1951–1962. "Employed persons" include proprietors and family workers as well as paid employees.
[b] Based on average daily wage payments for male workers.
[e] Based on average annual wage payments for clerical and manual workers.
[d] Based on average annual wage payments for regular employees.

ever, that wage differentials by size of firm were once as large as those of the 1950s, but in the absence of strong unionism. Table 24 compares the interfirm wage structures of 1932 and 1957. These are strikingly similar to each other in pattern and magnitude and seem disturbing to the hypothesis that the postwar widening of interfirm wage differentials was due to enterprise unionism. It is useful, therefore, to note the key economic facts of the early 1930s and the late 1940s.

In one important respect economic conditions during the early 1930s and early postwar years were similar in the labor market: the industrial demand for labor was weak relative to the supply of labor during both periods. Slack labor markets are generally conducive to the widening of wage differentials of all kinds. But, in all other respects,

TABLE 24

WAGE DIFFERENTIALS BY SIZE OF FIRM IN MANUFACTURING,
1932 AND 1957

1932[a]			1957[b]		
Size by Capital (¥'ooo)	Number of Workers per Firm[c]	Wage Differentials (Percent)	Size by Number of Workers	Number of Workers per Firm[c]	Wage Differentials (Percent)
1–2	2	38	1–3	1	43
2–5	4	45	4–9	5	48
5–10	7	54	10–19	12	52
10–50	15	68	20–29	22	57
50–100	29	78	30–49	36	57
100–500	68	84	50–99	65	62
500 and over	410	100	100 and over	473	100

[a] Kōgyō Chōsa [Survey of Manufactures]. Arranged and presented by Mataji Umemura in S. Tsuru and K. Ohkawa, eds., Nihon Keizai no Bunseki [Economic Analyses of Japan] (Tokyo: Keiso Shobo, 1957), II, 258.

[b] Ministry of Labor, Nihon no Chingin Kōzō [Japanese Wage Structures] (Tokyo: Rōmu Gyōsei Kenkyūjo, 1960), p. 140.

[c] Manual and clerical employees.

the two periods were different. The 1920s and early 1930s were a period of protracted deflation, while in the postwar period there was an acute inflation. The level of money wages decreased during the 1920s and early 1930s, but increased rapidly after the war.

Interfirm wage differentials widened during the early 1930s, owing to the smaller proportionate decrease in money wages in large firms over those in small, while they widened during the early postwar years, because of the larger proportionate increase in money wages in the large firms. Before the war wages were more rigid both upward and downward in the large firms than they were in the small, resulting in widening the interfirm wage differentials when the level of money wages declined and in narrowing them when it rose. In contrast, during the brief period of several postwar years, money wages exhibited greater upward flexibility in the large than in the small firms, which suggests the emergence of a new force in the labor market that destroyed the ordinary upward rigidity of wages in large, high-wage firms.

There is another vital difference between the early 1930s and the late 1940s. The smaller proportionate decline of money wages in large firms than in the small ones before the war was associated with the larger proportionate decrease in employment in the former than in the latter, as shown by Table 25. This is what one would normally expect from the orthodox shape of the negatively sloped demand schedule for labor. But this orthodox wage-employment relationship was considerably disturbed after the war. There was a brief interlude of disinflation between March 1949 and June 1950, accompanied by an increase in unemployment.[15] During this disinflation wages continued to increase as a whole and increased proportionately more in the large than in the small firms. At the same time, as illustrated in Table 18, employment even increased in the large firms, but decreased in the small.[16] In the light of the prewar wage-employment relationship we should have expected employment in the large firms to fall and to do so proportionately more than in the small firms. The breakdown of the prewar orthodox wage-employment relationship during the early postwar years leads us to suspect that a new factor hitherto unknown in the traditional labor market mechanism of Japan emerged and modified the working of that mechanism for some time after the war.

The considerations above show that, while all the relevant economic conditions during the early 1930s clearly pointed toward a widening of interfirm wage differentials, some conditions during the early postwar years were favorable to a narrowing. It seems that the "balance of power," as it were, was held by enterprise unionism in this postwar vortex of conflicting forces, which showed itself capable of overriding the forces favorable to narrowing the interfirm wage structure. Thus it can be submitted that enterprise unionism accounts for the early part of the evolution of the postwar Japanese interfirm wage structure.[17] But clearly it was an unusual situation; unions, however strong, cannot "have the cake and eat it too." Sooner or later, adjustment has to be made as to how much cake to have and how much to eat, which is what happened in the development of postwar unionism of Japan. Unions would demand wage increases periodically, but would leave management free to do anything with the size and organization of the work force subject to one proviso, that is, that in no circumstances should union members be discharged at management's convenience. This

TABLE 25

WAGE DIFFERENTIALS AND CHANGES IN EMPLOYMENT BY SIZE OF ESTABLISHMENT IN MANUFACTURING, SELECTED PERIODS, 1928–1960

(PERCENT)

Interfirm Wage Differential[a]	1928–1931 Widening	1947–1951 Rapid Widening	1951–1954 Stationary	1954–1957 Moderate Widening	1957–1960 Narrowing	1960–1963 Narrowing	1963–1966 Partly Widening
			RATE OF CHANGE IN EMPLOYMENT				
TOTAL	−14.5	−10.9	+11.8	+28.4	+32.3	+17.5	+7.9
1–4	n.a.	−49.3	+5.2	−3.1	−7.3	+10.8	+5.2
5–29	+2.5	−1.7	+16.6	+21.2	+8.2	+11.2	+11.8
30–99	−6.0	−7.5	+12.1	+35.4	+25.0	+19.3	+9.0
100–499	−5.5	+1.5	+16.2	+34.2	+33.0	+21.5	+8.3
500 and over	−36.5	+7.5	+11.0	+19.1	+34.0	+21.5	+3.1

Sources: KTH, 1928 and 1931; and Bureau of Statistics, Prime Minister's Office, *Census of Establishments*, 1947–1966. Size is by the number of workers employed. The rate of change is over the period indicated.
[a] Tables 23 and 27, and their interpretation in the text.

proved to be a workable arrangement, which resulted in high degrees of stability and regularity in the labor market process during the 1950s.

The Excess-Supply Labor Market and Union-Management Accommodation

Between September 1945 and March 1949, unions expanded rapidly. Between March 1949 and June 1951, they contracted markedly. Closely related to the transition of unionism is that of general economic conditions, which consisted of three phases: the inflationary period of 1945 to 1949, the disinflation of March 1949 to June 1950, and the Korean War boom of mid-1950 to mid-1951.[18] In the early postwar years the Occupation authorities lent support to the unions as a part of their program to reform and democratize Japan. For the first time in Japanese history workers were free to organize with official encouragement, while employers were subjected to many measures of reform which did away with their customary privileges.[19] In the immediate postwar years the employers were stunned by the welter of drastic changes in employment relations and passively yielded to union demands on many occasions. Where the employers did not yield the workers simply took over the enterprises and operated them as they saw fit.[20] Thus the gains of various worker groups were directly related to the degree of aggressiveness, which, in turn, depended upon the numbers united for common action.

The heyday of union expansion was short-lived, however. With changes in Occupation policy from reform and democracy to recovery and "Cold War," the restrictions on the scope of union activities increased, and radical leaders were hunted out and "purged." [21] While the unions lost favor in high official quarters, the employers recovered their confidence and power, resisting the unions with increasing strength. Along came the disinflationary policy, which slowed down the rates of increase in prices and money wages, and brought about some unemployment. In the face of increasing employer resistance and unemployment, the unions were not always successful in protecting their members against the loss of jobs. After March 1949 the number of unions dissolved each month was larger than the number organized, while surviving unions stopped growing or lost members.[22]

Union power, which was strong enough to make heavy inroads on managerial prerogatives in the early postwar years, was subsequently contained by outlawing workers' undue invasions of property rights, on the one hand, and, on the other, by conceding to the unions some participation in production and distribution decision-making through such devices as labor-management joint councils. As time passed, however, the functions of the joint councils shifted from matters predominantly related to production decisions to matters related to grievances. In 1949, 72 percent of the unions which had joint councils concerned themselves with production decisions in one way or another, but in 1957 only 45 percent did so. In 1949, only 31 percent of the unions with these councils used them as organs for processing grievances, but in 1957, 87 percent did so.[23] These changes at least indicate the retreat of the union from an active part in the affairs of the firm, and the disciplining and replacement of the somewhat unruly union behavior of earlier days by manners more appropriate to the division of labor and responsibility between union and management in a market economy.

The 1949–1950 deflation was also instrumental in introducing an important structural change in enterprise unionism which weakened the power of unions to affect the wage level of the firm. The enterprise union as a rule included in its membership all the employees of an enterprise except for the managerial personnel, but the 1949–1950 deflation made it clear that it was not always practicable for the union to protect its members against the loss of jobs. The realization of this fact led to a union policy that limited membership to a size at which the absolute security of uninterrupted employment would be possible at all times. Any worker employed to be a permanent regular employee automatically became a union member. In exchange for this kind of union shop for regular workers, management acquired unrestrained freedom in hiring and firing "temporary workers" in response to changes in the business conditions of the firm and in paying whatever was necessary to obtain their services. The Japanese firms already had an experience in this kind of arrangement during the 1930s. Indeed, the early 1930s and the early 1950s were similar in one respect, that is, the excess-supply labor market. How similar market conditions give rise to similar institutional solutions is striking indeed.

In this connection it should be noted that "permanent" and "temporary" workers in the Japanese official statistics after the War tend to understate the extent of "temporary" workers. A firm's work force is first classified into "casual" and "regular" workers. The "casual" worker is employed on a day-to-day basis or for less than thirty consecutive days. The "temporary regular" worker is employed for more than thirty consecutive days but with a specific term of contract. The "permanent regular" worker is one with an indefinite term of employment. According to the Census of Establishments of 1954, the "casuals" were 6.5 percent of the "regulars" in manufacturing. According to the monthly labor surveys of manufacturing establishments with thirty or more "regular" workers made by the Ministry of Labor, the "temporary regulars" were 7.4 percent in 1956 and 7.7 percent in 1959.[24] The proportions of "temporary regulars" to all "regulars" were higher in industries like primary metals (9.8 percent), machinery (11.0 percent), electric equipment (14.1 percent), and transportation equipment (10.6 percent). The "casuals" and "temporary regulars" together may have accounted for more than a fifth of all workers in these industries in 1959.

But these were official statistics. There is reason to believe that the official definitions of "temporary" and "permanent" workers vastly understate the proportions of workers who in the custom of each firm are hired as "temporary" subject to inferior wages and working conditions, and without being entitled to intrafirm welfare facilities. An independent research suggests that in the transport machinery industry the ratio of "temporary" to total employment rose from 25 percent in March 1960 to 31 percent in March 1961 and that, in all manufacturing, the increase in this one-year period was from 17 to 19 percent.[25] For the same period the Ministry of Labor statistics reported 11.5 percent in December 1960 and 12.1 percent in December 1961 for the transport equipment industry, while the figures for all of manufacturing were 8.3 and 7.9 percent respectively.[26]

Despite a high degree of flexibility in the work force management through the use of temporary workers, the interfirm wage differentials were still too great to be a stable pattern of resource allocation among firms. With the deepening of interfirm disequilibrium in the middle 1950s, pressure for return to equilibrium came from various sources. The large, high-wage firms were surrounded by pools of potential workers who, though ordinarily engaged in less remunerative activities for the want of better, would be glad to move in, once job openings appeared in the large firms. The small, low-wage firms found it increasingly difficult to retain their workers. Thus the instability of employment was inversely associated with the levels of wages in different firms, as illustrated by labor turnover rates that were higher in the smaller firms than in the larger. (See the last columns of Table 22.) In addition, the inordinately high wages enjoyed by the permanent employees of the large firms have, in fact, raised the cost of obtaining permanent jobs in these firms, thus reducing the net advantages of these jobs. The worker who wants such a job might tip the persons in decision-making positions (like union leaders or personnel managers) so that he can secure one when an opening appears. One author has mentioned that such tips per job in a certain large steel mill amount to 100,000 *yen*[27] (which is equivalent to four months' pay in the average firm of the largest size group in Table 22).

The interfirm profit structure was also in disequilibrium during the 1950s (shown in Table 22). Since the large, high-wage firms were not necessarily enjoying high profit rates on capital, this influenced the direction of capital flow in favor of more profitable smaller firms, raising the demand for factors in these firms proportionately more than in the large firms. Some of the manufacturing firms even shifted parts of their productive activities to smaller firms through subcontracting relations to siphon out some of the profits smaller firms were capable of making. Tokutaro Yamanaka observes: "The power of unions has grown to such an extent that it is hardly possible to make wage cuts. . . . In striking contrast, there has been hardly any progress in the unionization of workers of small-medium industries. This explains why more and more large industries have come to find it profitable to subcontract work to small-medium firms. By establishing such relationships, the large industries can take advantage of the 'cheap labor' of small businesses. . . ."[28]

The mutual accommodation of unions, managements, and the labor market is nowhere more marked than in the wage-employment relationship between different size groups of firms. Table 25 compares the behavior of interfirm wage differentials with the relative changes in employment in various size groups of firms. Given the wide disparity of wages between large and small firms at the beginning of the 1950s, the smaller firms had acquired a comparative advantage of labor cost relative to the larger ones. Thus, from 1951 to 1954, employment tended to increase in the smaller firms relative to the larger ones. The strength of demand for labor in the smaller firms tended to arrest the lagging of wages behind the larger firms. With the passage of time, however, the stabilization of wage increases in the larger firms increasingly tended to enable these firms to employ more labor. Finally, during recent years (after 1957) the prosperous economic conditions and the stability of wages in the larger firms relative to those in the smaller ones have resulted in considerable increases in employment of labor by the larger firms. The compression of the wage differential between high-wage and low-wage groups of workers during prosperity associated with the relative increase in the employment of the former group was frequently found in the century-long history of modern Japan, as explored in the first two chapters of this book. Despite its high degree of resistance owing to its institutional (as against economic) origin, the interfirm wage structure of Japan after the Second World War cannot nonetheless escape the influences of the equilibrating forces of the market economy. The "karma" is working its will.

The Intrafirm Wage Structure

Another consequence of the mutual accommodation of labor and management in the postwar labor market was the emergence of an intrafirm wage structure which showed a steep rise in wages corresponding to the age of the worker. When the average earnings for different age groups were compared around 1955, for example, the older workers' earnings were considerably higher than those of the younger ones in almost all skill categories. The range of apparently age-related increments in pay in each skill category was so wide that the earnings of a janitor after many years of service could be higher than, say, those of a young starting engineer. Abegglen suggests that "a prime factor in the Japanese payment system is the employee's age." (See Chapter 5 above.) Why does age alone make so much difference in a worker's earnings? One might be tempted to answer that it is because age itself is something highly valued in the traditional culture of the Orient. Upon a closer look, however, the situation is completely different.

It must be emphasized above all that the nature of seemingly age-related pay in postwar years is entirely different from what is often called *nenkō joretsu chingin* described in Chapter 6. The intrafirm wage structure under the *nenkō joretsu* system of recruitment, training, and promotion corresponds to the degree of proficiency in each skill category and to the hierarchy of skills under a specific kind of technology which requires a worker to stay within the same firm in order to become more skilled. It is implied that the skills acquired by a worker in a given firm are largely nontransferable to other firms. Although firms do not have to fear that experienced workers would leave them for such reasons as dissatisfaction with wages under this set-up, they have to offer adequate incentives through wage increases appropriate to the degree of ability, patience, and effort needed in learning and improving skills. At the same time workers are screened more severely as they move upward, resulting in fierce competition for promotion among workers of similar seniority. The concept of *nenkō joretsu* is therefore antithetical to the postwar notion of "lifetime commitment," which implies that a worker stays in the employ of a firm regardless of his merits and achievements (*kō* of *nenkō*).

It is much more natural to suppose, than to resort to cultural traditions, that the postwar age-related wage system as well as the absolute job security for permanent workers was brought about upon trade unions' insistence. Once established, the age-related pay system within the firm was maintained through subsequent wage increases obtained by the enterprise union supported by the firm's hiring policy. By the end of the Second World War the level of wages had sunk very low, and wage differentials of all kinds had nearly disappeared. Workers in the larger enterprises took to unionism in this milieu, and it was necessary for them to be bound by exceptional solidarity in order to survive these difficult years. Solidarity above all required equality of status of all the fighting members and an equitable distribution of gains made by collective efforts. Workers of all descriptions, male and female, young and old, skilled and unskilled, white-collar and blue-collar, contributed their utmost efforts and sacrifices toward the common goal of survival. A high degree of intraunion democracy was thereby achieved; each contributed according to his ability and strength, and each shared in the gains according to his needs.[29] The age-related pay structure was born of the trade unions' homespun notion of equity, democracy, and solidarity. It was derived from the concept of "living wage."

The need for survival brought about the concept of "living wage" evidently as an emergency concept until the restoration of normal socio-economic conditions. The "living wage" principle was given the first explicit formulation by the Electric Industry Workers' Union in the fall of 1946. It has left its indelible mark as *"Densan-gata"* wage system in the history of Japanese wage determination.[30] Workers hailed the Electricity Formula (my own translation of the *"Densan-gata chingin"*) as a great innovation in the interest of the working class and socialism. Employers denounced it as a worst form of egalitarianism (*aku-byōdō*). The Electricity Formula was revolutionary in that it abolished pay differentials and differences in wage payment methods by education, status, and sex. The total pay was the sum of two components: (a) the "living wage" and (b) additions for skill, work, and length of service. The "living wage" in turn consisted of three elements: (1) the basic wage roughly geared to the physical strength and mental agility of the worker so that it was scaled up to reach its maximum for the age bracket of 26 to 35 years and scaled down thereafter, (2) allowances for the number of dependents, and (3) cost-of-living differentials by geographical area. The proportion of the living wage component was more than 70 percent at first but had decreased to 60 percent by 1955. The average earnings of a worker when the Formula was adopted were calculated to reach their maximum at 45 years of age. This pioneer wage system was adopted in many other industries and firms under the pressure of trade unions. The collective agreements which established these intrafirm wage systems for the first time in these firms have since been honored as The Original Agreements (*genshi kyōtei*).

For the whole manufacturing sector, the pay gradient by age became steeper on the whole until 1958. This was due to the interaction of two forces; the annual wage increases won by the union members who were by definition already in the firm and the excess-supply conditions of the labor market which pressed down the starting (hiring) wages of young workers. Although the wages of the new recruits were fixed as low as the market would bear, the workers after joining the firm and the union shared in the subsequent rounds of wage increases. But significant differentials were already made between new recruits and established workers, and these were maintained through the years. So long as the excess supply of labor persisted, the starting wages increased far less rapidly than the average wages of the established workers who continued to win wage increases through collective bargaining. Low starting wages and subsequent wage increments on that base, repeated over many years, had produced an impressive gradient of wages by length of service in the firm by the middle of the 1950s. It was at this point that people began to speak of the peculiarity of the intrafirm wage structure in which age did seem to be most prominent among the correlates of individual earnings. A little amount of historical perspective and analytical imagination would have saved many of them from entertaining a patently false proposition that the observed peculiarity of the age-earnings correlation was a specialty limited to Japan.

While the organized workers in the large firms succeeded in securing job stability and wage increases, the workers in small and medium firms lacking the strength of organization were fully exposed to the working of the labor market characterized by the excess supply of labor. It has been shown that between firms, wages rise, while labor turnover falls, as the size of establishment increases. In smaller firms older workers were not necessarily longer-service employees, so that the pay gradient by age was considerably flatter in these firms than in larger ones even in the middle of the 1950s. In smaller firms age was even a negative factor after a point. In 1958 the average earnings of male production workers were the highest for the age bracket of 35 to 40 in establishments employing fewer than 100 workers, while they were the highest for the age bracket of 50 to 60 in establishments employing 1,000 or more workers.[31] Besides, the average pay level was higher in larger than in smaller firms. From the point of view of the worker who was fortunate enough to pass the tight hiring standards of a large, high-wage firm, it would have been an extremely foolish action for him to leave his job in the labor market context of the 1950s. Thus, if the workers of these firms were considered in isolation, they appeared to be permanently committed to their current employers.

But the unions had left the employers with a lot of room for their maneuver. In search of greater flexibility of production and labor cost, the large firms during the 1950s made use of subcontractors and a class of workers known as *shagaikō* (extra workers), in addition to temporary and casual workers. The "extras" were brought into the parent firms by the subcontractors who worked on portions of the production process. The core of permanent employees within a given firm was thus surrounded by rings of temporary, casual, and extra workers inside it and by bands of subcontractors and their workers outside it. In the early 1960s it was found that 30 percent of total employment in the engineering and chemical industries was in the "nonpermanent" category.[32]

In addition to the limitation of the "permanent" work force to a necessary minimum, the firm made its cost as flexible as was compatible with changes in the state of business. This was effected by the method of wage payments, which divided the total pay into two broad components, one of which was regularly paid and somewhat rigid, and the other was paid as a bonus or allowance adjustable to the state of business. Thus, contrary to an expected consequence of lifetime commitment—that labor is a fixed cost "not susceptible to adjustment as conditions require" (Abegglen)—it seems that Japanese firms have on the whole maintained labor and wages as variable as conditions and economic calculus require.[33] One would indeed suspect that by acceding to the unions' demand for job security, the employers might have obtained a greater degree of flexibility in production plans and work force management than possible otherwise.

Continuity and Change
in Industrial Relations

The organizational unit, principle, and strategy of postwar unionism are totally different from the general characteristics of trade unions of the interwar period described in the preceding chapter. One should not readily suppose that the interwar trade unionism revived when the repression of the labor movement was over with the end of the War. Many of those who had experience in the interwar labor movement survived the War and took prominent positions in the postwar movement. But the sheer scale of the postwar unionism indicates that there was a far greater crop of new leaders who were entirely the products of the time than the number of surviving prewar leaders.[34] Since trade unions were dismantled after 1938, Japanese workers must have been almost total strangers to the labor movement at the end of the War. That they managed to organize themselves into viable unions as quickly and effectively as we have observed is certainly an enigma.

The key to this puzzle is that the basic unit of organization in the postwar unionism was the plant. The postwar enterprise unionism was a direct outgrowth of the industrial relations set-up that was forcibly promoted by the Government as a measure to align industry to the requirements of the War.[35] The industrial structure was radically re-organized to channel a maximum flow of resources into the expansion of strategic production. Human resources were mobilized and organized in ways appropriate to ensure the continuity of production in high gear. Steps were taken to minimize work stoppages and slowdowns through industrial disputes and time losses through voluntary labor mobility which was in fact considerable throughout the war period because of the labor shortage. But since inflation was a real menace and consumer goods were scarce, monetary incentives to high worker morale and efficiency were unthinkable. How would the country at war make people work more for less pay? Under the circumstance the only available avenue to the commitment of workers to production and work place had to be noneconomic. Workers were given a maximum of moral boost through privileges as members of the enterprise community sharing as equally as possible in what meager facilities and resources there were for making daily living at least tolerable. From the com-pany president down to the floor sweeper, everyone was a full-fledged member of the community and encouraged to transcend the petty formalities in status, ability, and responsibilities in order to achieve unreserved cooperation for the interest of the country at war which needed more and more production. Such was the "Sampo" movement, a patriotic movement with emphasis on production for the country, not for economic gains.

The status differences of all sorts among workers, white-collar or blue-collar, skilled or unskilled, young or old, male or female, new or estabished, were consciously demolished in the course of the Sampo movement. Everyone was ensured an honorable place and perfect security within the enterprise community. Where there were industrial disputes, they were primarily for enforcing the principle of equality on snobbish supervisors. If there was a necessity for wage increases, they were first for correcting unjustified differentials and then for equal raises for all. The enterprises also looked after the families of those who were called to the colors. The workers of all descriptions thus lived through the years of bad luck commiserating in agony and despair under the losing war and intensified air raids. When the War was over, hardships remained. Indeed, survival seemed more difficult than ever in the shambles of economy and society. Workers were angry and frustrated; all they got for all those years of self-denial was the protracted prospect of starvation. The need for community and solidarity was greater under these circumstances. Workers, already organized on the basis of the enterprise, drew up a new name for their collective efforts and employed new tactics and rhetoric to ensure survival. The result was enterprise unionism.

In hindsight it is sensible to treat as a historical unit, as Magota has so ably demonstrated, the Sampo period of 1939 to 1945 and the rise and wane of the postwar unionism between 1945 and 1951. It is not an exaggeration to say that the interwar period of industrial and craft unionism was succeeded by an age of enterprise unions. The interwar unionism had a history of 20 years. By 1960 enterprise unionism had had a history of similar length including the Sampo years. Would it not therefore be in line with history to suspect that there must have been something new in the offing on the Japanese trade union scene in the closing years of enterprise unionism in the late 1950s? Indeed, there were signs of significantly new developments in the structure, principle, and strategy of Japanese trade unions at about this time. The event of great significance was the appearance in 1956 of a supraenterprise arrangement for collective bargaining called *Shuntō Kyōtō Kaigi* (Joint Action Committee for the Spring Offensive). Industry-wide national federations of enterprise unions had long existed. They also belonged to one or the other of major national trade union centers. It was two of these national centers, *Sōhyō* (General Council of Trade Unions) and another grouping which was to be known as *Churitsurōren* (Federation of Independent Unions), that organized the Joint Action Committee for the planning, direction, and coordination of collective bargaining activities of affiliated enterprise unions. Formerly, the enterprise union was the sole master of the situation. The organized workers who were directed by the Joint Action Committee were but 830,000 persons in 1956 but quickly increased to 4 millions by 1961. In 1963 they surpassed 5 millions and, in 1967, were pressing toward the 6-million mark.[36] In addition to the direct influence of the joint action on affiliated unions, the collective bargaining tactics of the Committee exert moral, often perceptible, influences on other unions and federations.[37]

Shunto Unionism
and Wage Structure

Before the impact of Shunto unionism on wages and employment is examined, it will be useful to give a short illustration of how the Spring Offensive works in Japanese industrial relations. Early every spring the Joint Action Committee designates a federation as a "top batter" for initiating the negotiations for pay increases. The federation in turn selects one of its enterprise unions for starting the move. This is followed by the scheduled entries of other unions into the wage struggle. It is hoped that the terms fetched by the "top batter" are favorable enough to spur the other unions for emulation. Before 1960 the agreements reached in earlier months of the calendar year were quite common. Since 1960 they have tended to be concentrated in April and May. Under the Shunto unionism, pay increases demanded are quoted in the absolute amounts of *yen,* which is in contrast to the earlier practice in terms of percentages. The distribution of wage increases is also subject to further negotiations between union and management. Under Shunto unionism the proportion of flat wage increase to everyone, regardless of age, skill, or position, in the total wage gains per capita is large and increasing. This contributes toward greater equalization of intrafirm personal wage differentials. The negotiated pay increases since 1960 have fluctuated between 45 and 75 percent of the demands. The number of demands and offers tossed back and forth between union and management until the agreement is secured varies widely from case to case. In 1967 the "one-shot" agreements (reached upon the first reply by management to the union's first demand) accounted for less than 20 percent of all agreements reached in that year. Nearly 40 percent were reached after six to ten rounds of negotiations, 35 percent after eleven to twenty rounds, and only 6 percent after twenty-one or more rounds. Sometimes negotiations break down and strikes are called. In 1967 unions that struck tended to obtain larger pay increases than those that did not. Firms which responded with smaller amounts at the first reply tended to be struck more frequently than those which responded more generously.[38]

The Spring Labor Offensive is a colorful annual event with many fascinating aspects for the theories of bargaining and conflict resolution. But what is important to the central theme of this chapter is how gains won through the Spring Offensive affect the interfirm pay structure and interpersonal pay differentials. It has been ascertained that the coefficients of interfirm dispersion of negotiated wage gains among large firms as well as among unionized small and medium firms have been declining in recent years.[39] (The coefficient of dispersion used in this connection is the ratio of the interquartile range to the median.) This is compatible with the logic of interunion coordination of wage demands and struggle schedules. Since the firms and unions are spread over many different industries, the decline in the interfirm wage dispersion just noted should also show up as a decline in the interindustry wage differentials. As previously shown (Chapter 4), this is also compatible with recent changes in the interindustry wage differentials.

The selection of the pace-setter ("top batter") is a delicate art. Since trade union leaders have not yet revealed how they do it, one can only guess about it through demonstrated evidence with the help of common sense. It can easily be imagined that the industry selected should not be out of line with all other industries either upward or downward in its ability to pay, profitability, or size of business turnover. The trade union federation in turn must be the one which enjoys prestige and influence in the labor movement. To decide on this kind of industry-federation set is the first step in the strategy of the Spring Offensive. *Ex post,* the wage gains negotiated by the pace-setter usually turn out to be just about the average gains that have been realized by the participants in the struggle. In looking over the experience of the past eight years from 1960 to 1967, one feels that the selection of the pace-setter has generally followed a wise course in the sense that it has brought about the feeling of achievement in many federations and unions because they have been able to do just as well as, or sometimes better than, the prestigious pace-setters. This can be illustrated by the comparison of the pace-setters' gains and the average gains of all the trade union federations participating in the Spring Offensive. There are four federations which served as the pace-setter at least once during the period of 1960–1967. Table 26 shows the gains of these federations[40] and the average gains of all the nineteen major union federations for the period of 1960–1967. It may be noted that the pace-setters' gains

TABLE 26

WAGE GAINS BY THE PACE-SETTER

AND AVERAGE WAGE GAINS OF ALL THE FEDERATIONS

PARTICIPATING IN THE SPRING OFFENSIVE

(YEN)

Year	Average[a]	Synthetic Chemicals	Iron and Steel	Private Railroads	Public Enterprises
1960	1,792	2,073	1,840*	1,662	1,798
1961	2,984	3,478	3,200	3,049	3,260*
1962	2,507	2,605	2,634*	2,400	2,343
1963	2,248	2,257	1,492	2,228*	2,480
1964	3,300	3,737	3,160*	3,336	3,205
1965	3,015	3,526	2,440	3,035*	3,038
1966	3,280	3,772*	2,480	3,536	3,425
1967	4,221	4,553	4,286*	4,336	4,360

Source: EPA, Bukka antei to shotoku seisaku (Price Stabilization and Incomes Policy) (Tokyo, 1968), p. 236. The asterisk indicates the year when the given union federation served as the pace-setter. The figures are increments per month.

a For 19 major federations.

are very close to, or slightly ahead of, the average wage gains (with exceptions in 1963 and 1964). To say the same thing differently, the average wage gains of all the union federations tend to press close to the pace set by the pace-setter.

The Steel Workers' Federation is evidently the favorite choice of the Japanese labor movement as a pace-setter; it served four times in this capacity during the eight-year period of 1960–1967. One notes, however, that the Joint Action Committee did not use this federation as a pace-setter when it actually did rather poorly as in 1963, 1965, and 1966. These were difficult years for the Japanese steel industry so that the wage pace for the whole Spring Offensive could not have been set by this industry. Perhaps it may be hypothesized that any one of the four trade union federations in Table 26 could have been an acceptable candidate for the position of a pace-setter in any year when its actual gains did not deviate from the average gains by more than the pace-setter's gains in the same direction. One then gets the number of years when a federation served or could have served as the pace-setter: Synthetic Chemical Workers, 2; Steel Workers, 5; Private Railroad Workers, 4; and Public Enterprise Workers, 4. The Synthetic Chemical Workers' Federation is somewhat too strong to be the pace-setter, for the other unions would feel bad if they fell behind the pace set by such a strong federation. The Public Enterprise Workers are under different legal constraints and cannot easily be called upon for the job. This narrows the choices to Steel Workers and Private Railroad Workers. These are strong federations. In addition, they are moderate and responsible.[41]

The ability of the Joint Action Committee to select a representative union federation for taking the risk of the first test in the Spring Offensive reflects the deep-rooted desire of the labor movement to stabilize wage increases from year to year. The wage gains in most of the trade union federations follow more closely the wage gains of the pace-setter over time than any other economic or social factors. The EPA study, from which Table 26 has been adapted, shows that changes in the wage pace explain a considerable proportion of changes in the wage gains of most of the federations and that the volume of business turnover per worker in each industry or an indicator of general economic conditions like the rate of unemployment does not help improve the explanation.[42] The stabilization of wage gains is difficult in an unstable economy like Japan's where the rate of growth fluctuates widely by more than 10 percentage points every three or four years. This implies that in exchange for wage increases when growth slows down, unions implicitly agree not to demand too much when growth picks up. Unions' demands and gains therefore tend to be insensitive to cyclical fluctuations, rigid not only downward but upward also. Indeed, in recent years the annual rates of increase in productivity per unit of labor fluctuated widely from minus 2 percent in the fourth quarter of 1962 to plus 18 percent a year later, down again to 2 percent in the third quarter of 1965 and back again to 19 percent a year later. The rate of increase in wages had a smaller amplitude ranging from 6 to 14 percent per annum, higher during the deceleration of growth and lower during the acceleration of growth than the rates of change in labor productivity.[43]

TABLE 27
UNIONIZATION, WAGE DIFFERENTIALS, AVERAGE WAGE INCREASE, NEGOTIATED WAGE INCREASE BY SIZE OF FIRM OR ESTABLISHMENT
(PERCENT)

Year	1,000 or more	500–999	300–499	100–299	30–99	5–29
A. THE RATE OF UNIONIZATION (PRIVATE MANUFACTURING FIRMS ONLY)[a]						
1956	81.3		42.6		21.4	2.5
1960	70.6		40.7		9.7	2.1
1963	69.0		42.9		12.4	1.9
1966	78.7		35.8		11.4	2.1
B. WAGE DIFFERENTIALS[b]						
1950	100.0		83.1		67.3	n.a.
1958	100.0		69.7		54.7	43.6
1965	100.0		80.9		71.0	63.2
1966	100.0		80.9		69.8	61.6
1967	100.0		79.6		67.7	60.0
C. THE RATE OF INCREASE IN AVERAGE WAGES[c]						
1962	6.0		10.0		15.2	22.9
1963	9.2		10.9		13.0	11.6
1964	10.2		11.1		10.0	14.1
1965	7.5		9.6		9.3	12.5
1966	12.4		11.9		10.4	9.7
1967	13.8		13.2		12.0	11.0
D. THE RATE OF INCREASE IN NEGOTIATED WAGES[d]						
1962	10.7			14.2		
1963	9.1			11.9		
1964	12.4			13.6		
1965	10.3			12.1		
1966	10.4	11.5	11.3	11.2	11.0	11.0
1967	12.1	13.8	13.5	13.4	12.7	12.4
E. REPEAT[e]						
1966	11.0		11.2		11.0	11.0
1967	13.0		13.4		12.7	12.4

The coordination of wage demands implies a desire to correct un-justified wage differentials within and between unions. Each enterprise union could ignore the wage differentials between large and small firms so long as it acted alone.[44] But the unions taking a joint action in the Spring Offensive could no longer ignore the situation. Besides, the scheduled bargaining makes unions particularly susceptible to the dem-onstration effect of the pace-setter's wage gains. One therefore feels that the *modus operandi* of the Shunto unionism is in favor of reducing wage differentials between large and small firms and between industries within the organized sector as well as wage differentials within the firm by status, age, sex, or education.

Table 27 puts together some information relevant to interfirm wage structure by size of firm. The overall rate of unionization after a sharp drop in the early 1950s continued to decline throughout the rest of the decade. In the 1960s there was a reversal in the trend. Among large firms the rate of unionization decreased in the 1950s and increased in the 1960s. Among the small and medium firms the variability over time precludes generalizations about the rate of unionization. The higher rate of unionization among large firms than among small and medium firms implies that the weight of negotiated wage increases is larger in the average wage increases of the former size class of firm than in that of the latter. Table 27 indicates that wage differentials by size of es-tablishment increased between 1950 and 1958, decreased up to 1965, and increased again. The sources of these wage data are different from the sources of data for previous observations (Table 23). But the size and movement of differentials over time are identical in both tables.

It has been argued that while the enterprise unionism is a force for widening wage differentials by size of firm, the Shunto unionism is for narrowing them. The Shunto began in 1956, while wage differentials by size of establishment narrowed after 1958. It is highly tempting to suspect that the Shunto may have had something to do with the narrow-ing of these differentials. But this could hardly be entertained. Al-

---

[a] For 1956 and 1960, *RH* (1961), p. 255. For 1963 and 1966, *RH* (1967), p. 205. Union members as a percentage of all the paid workers in firms belonging to the relevant size classes.

[b] *RH*, for various years; especially, *RH* (1968), p. 244.

[c] Data same as under (b) above.

[d] *CH* (1968), pp. 60–61.

[e] Consolidation by simple averages.

though the unions engaged in joint spring offensives were increasing during this period, the universalistic motivations of the participating unions were not strong; nor was the coverage of joint Shunto action extensive before 1963. The workers participating in the spring offensives through the Joint Committee exceeded 50 percent of the total trade union membership in 1963. In 1967 the joint action covered 55 percent of organized labor, to which 10 percent may be added in order to give the full proportion of unionized workers participating in the spring offensives.[45] In a substantive sense, although not in the formal sense because the enterprise union still remains as the contracting agent, one may say that the central variable in the hypothesis which guides this chapter, namely, the coverage of wage agreements, has been expanding and that the hypothesis predicts a narrowing of all kinds of wage differentials, interfirm wage differentials above all.

Nevertheless, a more plausible explanation for the narrowing of wage differentials by size of firm between 1958 and 1965 is the change in the supply-demand relationship in the labor market.[46] Large firms with wages and working conditions far superior to the prevailing standards did not need to worry about their ability to recruit the right kinds of workers in right numbers. But the medium-sized and small firms quickly felt the impact of depleting labor surplus in the course of postwar economic growth and, however grudgingly, were forced to raise wages if workers were to be hired at all. The trade unions in small and medium-sized firms used the market conditions to improve their status, to which I shall return shortly.

Table 27 can be used for making two kinds of comparison: (1) rates of change in average wages with rates of increase in negotiated wages and (2) differences in the negotiated wage increases by size of firm. "Average wages" are the averages over all the firms, union and nonunion, so that by comparing them with the negotiated wages one can get some notion of union-induced differences in the evolution of wage structure. Among the firms with 500 or more workers, the negotiated wage increases were on the whole larger before but smaller after 1965 than the average wage increases. Since nearly 80 percent of those firms are unionized, one can well imagine that wages increased considerably more slowly in nonunion firms before 1965 (with the exception of 1963) than is indicated by figures in Section C of Table 27. From the differences in the rate of increase in Sections C and D for large firms, there has been a kind of balance between union and nonunion firms since 1965. It is interesting to note that even during such years as 1962 to 1965, when the differentials of "average wages" by size of firm were narrowing (Sections B and C), large unionized firms with 500 or more workers were raising wages faster than medium-sized and small firms except for the smallest ones. (Compare relevant columns of Sections C and D.) Although it was in 1965 that wage differentials by size of firm began to widen again, forces for this development were already at work before 1965. Since the rate of unionization is low among medium-sized and small firms, the average wage increases can be considered to be largely due to the market forces. In other words, trade unions in large firms were already abreast of the tightening labor market in the early 1960s. This certainly reflects a renewed vigor of trade unions in that period, which is supported by the increase in the rate of unionization between 1963 and 1966, as shown in Section A of Table 27. This is rather disturbing, for wage differentials by size of firm, even when they were narrowest as in 1965, were not narrow enough to warrant a talk of wage equalization.

Fortunately, there are trade unions in small and medium-sized firms too. Aided by the tightening labor market, trade unions in these firms did much better than those in larger firms in winning wage increases. This can be seen from Section D of Table 27. Trade unions did better than the market too, that is, negotiated wages increased faster than wages in general in small and medium-sized firms. The enterprise unions in small and medium-sized firms are affiliates of a given industry's national federation of trade unions which is a constituent of the Joint Action Committee for the Spring Offensive. At the same time these smaller unions form their own regional federations across industrial lines for the purpose of coordinating wage struggles in these regions. Thus the aggressiveness and effectiveness of smaller unions may deviate from norms set by the national federations or by the Joint Action Committee.[47] Indeed, a moderation of large unions and a greater struggle effectiveness of smaller unions seem to be among the necessary conditions for narrowing wage differentials by size of firm. Whether this type of strategy can be worked out consciously within the framework of the Shunto unionism remains to be seen. It is at least not incompatible with the logic of Shunto unionism.

It is too early to hail Shunto unionism as a real force in the interest of social justice. The widening of wage differentials by size of firm since 1965 still suggests the collective egoism of each of the enterprise unions discussed in connection with earlier postwar years. On the other hand, the economic conditions in 1965 were not favorable to the narrowing of wage differentials. Since the extraordinary boom of 1958 to 1961 the Japanese economy has experienced two recessions, in 1962 and 1965. It is interesting to recall in this connection that Table 25 shows relative contraction of employment in larger firms where wages began to increase relatively faster in recent years (last column). The "karma" of the Japanese economy reappeared.

From the discussion of enterprise unionism and Shunto unionism, one may conclude tentatively that unions in the Japanese economic context can raise wages in firms where they are organized more than is expected to result from the market forces alone. However, the impact on wage structure is different for the two types of unionism. Enterprise unionism, pure and simple, widens wage differentials between large and small firms. Shunto unionism, which may be regarded as an interim arrangement for a full-fledged industry-wide unionism to come, at least shows some promise for narrowing the differentials. The initiative for unionization under enterprise unionism must come from the workers of each enterprise. This has resulted in the skewed distribution of unions biased in favor of large firms. An industry-wide union does not have to be inhibited by this rule of organization drive. The organizers in principle can invade any nonunion firms and start organizing their employees. The unionization of small and medium-sized firms depends eventually on the help that established unions can give to their workers through this kind of technical assistance. Whether Shunto unionism will actually grow into industrial unionism and become an equalizing agent in the labor market is the question one must defer to the future.[48]

Wage Determination and the Labor Market

The extent and distribution of unionism in Japan suggest that unions initiate wage increases for about a third of the paid labor force. Wage increases for the other two thirds are necessarily initiated by the market forces as interpreted by their employers. In the Japanese setting the breakdown of paid sector by union and nonunion characteristics is roughly synonymous with the dichotomy between large and small firms. In 1964, when firms were asked how wage increases were initiated, almost all the firms employing 5,000 or more workers answered that unions initiated the move, while employers with 30 to 100 workers said that it was they who took the initiative.[49]

Why do employers raise wages in the absence of the trade union pressure? Among the answers employers gave to this question, there are some that essentially imply that the demand curve for labor shifted to the right. These are the answers phrased in some such manner: "because productivity, efficiency, sales or profits increased." But answers of this nature in this particular inquiry were but 7.3 percent of all answers obtained. Another a priori answer is that employers are forced to raise wages because the supply curve shifted upward and to the left. In practice the answers which essentially amount to this theoretical position are phrased in this way: "the general level of wages has risen," "other employers in the industry are raising wages," "for the necessity of keeping the workers," "the area wage level has risen," or "starting wages have risen." These answers, taken together, accounted for 69.1 percent of all obtained from small employers in 1964. The remaining 23.6 percent are accounted for by an answer: "with consideration for employees' living conditions under rising prices." One should not be too readily tempted to attribute this type of answer to the famous, but illusory, "paternalism" of employers. To rationalize wage increases by price increases is a favorite pretext also used by workers, union or nonunion. What it implies to the employer is the same thing as saying that it is difficult to keep employees by letting the real wages fall. From the meanings of these practical statements in terms of theory and considering the scales of business of the respondents against the tightening labor market of the 1960s, one is led to conclude that the supply side of the labor market exerted a far greater pressure on employers' wage determination than their own reasons on the demand side.[50]

A tabulation of answers from all the firms, union and nonunion, about reasons for wage increases is worth pondering for its illuminating lessons on interscale differences in employer behavior. Table 28 is adapted from Tadao Ishizaki's work. I have classified the answers under three heads: (1) demand factors, (2) supply factors, and (3) power factors. The demand factors are weak in firms of all scales, although somewhat stronger in the smallest firms with 30 to 99 workers. The supply factors have the greatest weight for all the firms among the reasons for wage increases, while smaller firms tend to be more influenced by these factors than larger ones. Power factors account for nearly one half of the reasons for wage increases in larger firms. In firms with less than 100 workers the power factors are the least important. The inclusion of wage increases in the same industry as a power factor is acceptable for larger firms in the light of the characteristics of the Spring Offensive but may be subject to debate in the case of smaller firms. This would make the power factors weaker and the supply factors stronger for smaller firms than are shown by figures in Table 28. Wage increases in the same area mean little to larger firms but are a fairly strong factor for wage increases in smaller firms.

It may be noted that demand factors are not strong in a class of any size. This may appear rather strange in a rapidly growing economy like Japan's where the expanding product market must always be enlarging the market prospects of most of the firms. Nor can the particular time of the survey, 1964, be used as an explanation for this situation. The year was a prosperous one. Furthermore, the EPA survey undertaken in 1962 also gave similar results to those presented in Table 28. This seems to suggest that however aggressive they may be in the product market, employers tend to drag their feet in the labor market. But then it must be recognized that any buyer in any market would behave in this manner in any case.

It is not tenable to differentiate too sharply between the power and market forces on the supply side. The individual worker is on the whole a reasonably good calculator of the relative gains from the market and by his membership in the union. If the market consistently offers better wages than the union can deliver, the labor movement must eventually crumble. On the other hand, if the union consistently does better than the market, the production of the unionized firm may eventually be diverted to nonunion firms (as, for example, attested by the experience of the 1950s in Japan). The most tenable long-run relationship between union and market is therefore that the union behaves *as though* it were an organ of an efficient labor market. The actual labor market is grossly imperfect anyway, so that the prices of labor indicated in the imperfect market may distort the technological responses of the firm

TABLE 28

REASONS FOR WAGE INCREASES,

MANAGEMENTS' ANSWERS, 1964

(PERCENT)

Item	30–99	100–999	1,000–4,999	5,000+	Average
Demand factor	*24.0*	*17.3*	*16.5*	*18.7*	*18.8*
Business prospect	24.0	17.3	16.5	18.7	18.8
Supply factors	*60.0*	*49.2*	*32.1*	*28.3*	*44.4*
Wage increases in the same area	12.3	16.7	8.2	0.6	11.1
To retain work force	27.7	19.7	13.0	14.3	19.2
To raise workers' living standards	13.6	4.6	6.8	5.5	7.4
Increases in starting wages	6.4	8.2	4.1	7.9	6.7
Power factors	*15.5*	*32.9*	*48.9*	*49.3*	*35.3*
"Shunto" rates	3.6	12.0	18.2	16.5	12.3
Wage increases in same industry	9.2	13.3	20.9	25.1	16.0
To avoid conflicts with workers	2.7	7.6	9.8	7.7	7.0
Other factors	*0.7*	*0.7*	*2.5*	*3.7*	*1.5*

Source: Adapted from Tadao Ishizaki, *Tenkeiki no rōdō keizai* (Labor Economy in the Period of Structural Transformation) (Tokyo: Toyo keizai, 1967), p. 158. The source Ishizaki has used is EPA, *Rōdōryoku ryūdō to chingin kettei jijō chōsa hōkoku* (Report on Labor Force Mobility and Wage Determination).

in combining the factors of production. By its strategic position with a better access to what is afloat in the labor market the union can in principle be a social instrument for transmitting information of all kinds on the quality and quantity of labor supplies more quickly than when the employer can obtain it by acting alone. A part of the gains that the union makes is in substance a reward for the contribution toward greater efficiency of the economic system.

This does not imply that the trade union should proclaim itself to be a labor market agent and behave accordingly. Whatever the rhetoric, if the wage gains won by the union are determined at such a level and distributed throughout the system in such a way as to meet the criteria of an efficient labor market, the union is in substance acting as an agent for bringing the actually imperfect labor market closer to a desired market mechanism. In the logic of the market economy, a change in wages is a signal for changes in technology, productivity, product quality and so on. The initiative held by the union in wage adjustments implies an initiative for changing the quality and performance of the whole economic system. If the whole labor movement is capable of concerted action, it is exercising a tremendous power over the economic system that no power group has ever found it possible to acquire. In the actual case, however, the Shunto unionism of Japan is very remote indeed from that assumed totality of power.

Conclusion

Today trade unions have a direct voice in the determination of wages, amenities, and working conditions of a third of Japan's paid labor force. These are enterprise unions, however. Each union claims its jurisdiction over all the employees of an enterprise. If each union presses the exercise of its bargaining power to the limits of its firm's ability to pay, the interfirm wage differentials will be closely correlated with the interfirm differentials in profitability and market power. Since unions are more extensively and strongly entrenched in large firms, the logic of enterprise unionism works for the widening of wage differentials between these and smaller firms. This is what happened during the first ten years of the postwar period.

But firms have managed to limit the power and privilege of the unions to "permanent" employees obtaining in return the full liberty to hire young workers and temporary workers at the market rates of pay or to let a considerable part of production out to subcontractors. Small and medium-sized firms have been largely subject to the labor market forces. With their lower wages, they have suffered from high labor turnover. When economic growth had absorbed much of the slack in labor supplies, the market pressure forced small and medium-sized firms to raise wages relative to large firms. As living conditions continued to improve, the labor movement itself mellowed.

In recent years there has developed what I call Shunto unionism, which may well be a beginning of industrial unionism beyond the confines of individual enterprises. Under Shunto unionism, wages among organized firms and among union members tend to be equalized but wage differentials between union and nonunion firms or workers may well tend to widen. With the evolution of Shunto unionism into industrial unionism, if it should occur at all, the Japanese labor movement would be accomplishing a much-needed step toward a more mature and responsible trade unionism. In the first place the behavior of a responsible trade unionism tends to conform to the criteria of rational resource allocation by equalizing the net advantages of different occupations at least within the organized sector. In the second place the central leadership of such a unionism would be in the position to trade off a part of its power over wages for a share in the policy-making power for the whole nation. Indeed, this is how powerful industrial unions in advanced capitalist systems have learned to take part in the formulation and implementation of national economic policy. To what extent is Japan ready for this new stage of industrial relations?

8   Labor, Management, and Participatory Democracy

IN THE LAST HUNDRED YEARS the Japanese economy and society have changed greatly. A hundred years ago the labor market allocated less than 10 percent of Japan's human resources to productive activities. Today it clears more than 60 percent. In the meantime the labor force itself has more than tripled. A hundred years ago there was no labor movement. Today trade unions are firmly established as institutional constituents of modern Japan and command the allegiance of a third of all paid workers. Indirectly, the labor movement has a great potential power over the whole process of production and resource allocation. The fragmentation of the labor movement into enterprise unions prevents it from exercising the degree of influence over the economy that may be inferred from the sheer weight of the union membership in the labor force. But it may be expected that the fragments will eventually be consolidated and that the power of the labor movement will become more effective. There are already signs of a new development in this direction.

It has been some time since the political economy in the West became a participatory democracy in which national socio-economic policy is formulated and implemented with the active participation of the occupational and interest groups likely to be affected by public policy. Especially, national economic planning as a fundamental framework of national economic policy loses much of its effectiveness unless participation and cooperation are secured from one of the influential interest groups, the labor movement.[1] As the Japanese economy approaches an advanced status, it is essential to bring economic power and political responsibility into line in the interest of economic efficiency and political stability. The extent to which the labor movement participates in the formulation and implementation of the national economic plan may be regarded as one of the yardsticks by which to judge the degree of society's progress toward participatory democracy. This chapter describes the Japanese economic planning process and explores the power relations between labor and management at the highest level of policy making with a view to evaluating how far Japan has grown toward participatory democracy.[2]

Economic Planning
in a Democracy

The purpose of a national economic plan is to coordinate or harmonize the economic activities of different sections of society in the interest of optimal economic growth and structural balance. But the coordination does not benefit everyone equally. Some are bound to gain more than others. How to compensate the welfare losses of some persons that have been caused by public policy is one of the greatest problems of a democracy.[3] The socio-political process in a democracy allows the losers to seek their compensation or to work for the elimination of the policy from which they suffer.

In a capitalist but democratic society there are three questions which arise in relation to planning and range from its fundamental issues to its practical consequences. The first question is whether planning is needed at all in such a society. The second is the choice of the objectives and targets of the plan. And the third is the question of the extent to which the government commits its power and resources to the implementation of the plan. Unless the first question is answered in the affirmative the other two are superfluous. But, given the characteristics of a democracy as a political system that is peculiarly susceptible to pressures of all kinds at all stages of its socio-political process, an affirmative answer to the first question does not guarantee that a plan will in fact emerge with clear and meaningful objectives and targets. Moreover, even if a plan has been formulated, there are pressures on the implementing government that may force it to reconsider its commitment to various measures of implementation. Thus it is extremely difficult to judge with any degree of certainty whether a given capitalist but democratic society does or does not plan effectively.

At the beginning of the postwar period Japan answered the first question in the affirmative. But planning still remains optional on the part of the Government. The initiative for planning rests with the Prime Minister. If a plan is desired, he refers the matter to an advisory body, the Economic Council (Keizai Shingikai). The Council collaborates with the Over-all Planning Bureau of the Economic Planning Agency (Keizai Kikaku Chō) in preparing a draft plan, which upon completion is submitted to the Prime Minister by the President of the Council. The Prime Minister then presents the draft plan to the Council of Ministers (Kakugi). When adopted by the Council of Ministers, the draft becomes an official plan and is subsequently published by the Economic Planning Agency. The Japanese plan is not formally presented to the Diet, but it is as much an object of attention for the Diet members as any official action of the Cabinet. It is often subject to intensive discussion in connection with other related items on the agenda that are formally presented to the Diet. Although the discussion in the Diet does not entail any modification of the plan, it may bring to the Cabinet's notice some aspects of the public reaction to the plan which perhaps had not been fully expressed through the Economic Council.

The Economic Council

The Economic Council consists of not more than thirty titular members appointed by the Prime Minister from among eminent persons in the private sector or persons engaged in nongovernmental public functions (universities, advisory councils attached to other ministries, etc.). The term of office of a titular member is two years and renewable. He does not serve full time. In addition the Prime Minister can appoint a number of "provisional" members for a specific project like the formulation of a plan, and a number of experts to facilitate investigations of technical matters by the Council. The New Long-Range Economic Plan (1958–1962) had 7 provisional members and more than 200 experts, and the National Income Doubling Plan (1961–1970) had 18 provisional members and nearly 200 experts. The Medium-Term Economic Plan (1965–1968) was the work of the Planning Committee of the Council but still required 30 titular members of the Council, 143 provisional members and 17 experts.[4]

For its deliberations on an economic plan, the Council elects a president from among its titular members; it works through committees whose chairmen are nominated by the president. In administrative matters it is serviced by the secretariat of the Director-General of the Economic Planning Agency. In addition, the Council receives assistance from the Government at two levels: "experts" recruited from among high-ranking civil servants and "secretaries" who are officials of lower rank.

Working arrangements within the Council have changed over the years.[5] At the time of the New Long-Range Economic Plan, it set up a General Committee and eight specialized committees, concerned with industry; energy; agriculture, forestry, and fishery; construction and transportation; employment; internal affairs; foreign trade; and finance and banking. The thirty-six titular and provisional members of the Council were deployed among the nine committees and formed the core of the deliberative activities of each. The General Committee had a special status: it consisted of titular and provisional members of the Council and the eight chairmen of the specialized committees. After a few months of deliberation the specialized committees submitted their reports to the President of the Council, who then referred them to the General Committee. Its draft of the plan, with the specialized reports appended, was then submitted to the Prime Minister.

The Council was differently organized for work on the National Income Doubling Plan (1961–1970). Perhaps this reflected the basic policy orientation of the forthcoming plan. The Council was divided into a General Policy Committee and three other committees concerned with the public sector, the private sector, and quantitative measurement. The Public Sector Committee was in turn composed of ten subcommittees and the Private Sector Committee of seven subcommittees. This plan was particularly careful about defining the relative spheres of action for government and private interests.

As has been seen, the general committee for each of these two plans ranked above the other committees within the Council. For the preparation of the Medium-Term Economic Plan this organizational characteristic was carried to its logical conclusion: the activities of the Council were organized into a hierarchy with a Planning Committee at its apex. The Planning Committee was assisted by two subcommittees on policy and measurement and coordinated the activities of eight branches of the Council. This set-up was repeated at the time of the Economic and Social Development Plan.

The Economic Council is an advisory organ of the Prime Minister, but it is also an "auxiliary organ" (*fuzoku kikan*) of the Economic Planning Agency. As such, it is one of four advisory councils controlled by the Agency. One might ask whether the Council can assert its own views and make them prevail over the Agency's concerning the orientation of economic plans or economic policy in general. The preparation of long-term economic plans and general economic policies is laid down by law as one of the functions of the Agency. On the other hand, legislation also calls upon the Council to examine economic policy questions and to advise the Prime Minister accordingly. Although the question of the relative powers of the Agency and the Council is in doubt, it is generally recognized that the Council works fairly independently of the Agency. With the scrapping of the Medium-Term Economic Plan and the appointment of Kazutaka Kikawada to the head of the Council in 1966, a new relationship between the Council and the Agency emerged. Kikawada actively sought after leadership in the formulation of the plan frame and objectives. Even a reshuffling of technical personnel within the Agency that occurred in 1966 is said to have been a part of this changing relationship. Under Kikawada's leadership the Council produced a five-year plan called "Economic and Social Development Plan" for the period of 1967–1972. A new, although still moderate, emphasis was placed on the "social" aspect of the plan.

The Economic Planning Agency

The technical work associated with economic planning is in the hands of the Economic Planning Agency. A young organization, the Agency has not been able to fill the key posts by promotion from the ranks. Many officials have been transferred from other ministries or from the academic world. Interchanges between the Agency's research institute and universities are particularly frequent. One half of the senior research officers of the institute usually come from universities on fixed-term appointments.[6] From a legal point of view the Agency has great potential influence within the power structure of the Japanese Government. Its Director-General ranks as a Minister of State. When he considers it necessary for the formulation and promotion of long-term economic plans he is empowered by law to request the heads of other executive agencies and ministries to supply him with necessary data, together with other relevant information. In cases of urgency in the interest of planning he can even make recommendations to other executive agencies and ministries concerning the formulation and implementation of their respective plans in a manner that would mean close integration into the over-all plan prepared by his Agency.[7]

Nevertheless, the EPA as an organization within the State Administration of Japan cannot claim the powers and privileges of a ministry. The highest level of the State Administration consists of the Prime Minister's Office and various Ministries. Within, or associated with, one or the other of these top-level offices are the "Agencies" (chō) and "Commissions" (iinkai). The EPA is but one of many agencies of this nature associated with the Prime Minister's Office.[8] While the law defines one of the functions of the EPA as the "initiation and formulation" of over-all and basic economic policies that cut across the competences of two or more executive organs, the same paragraph adds that matters which are the primary responsibilities of these latter organs do not fall under this provision.[9] It can be inferred from this that the EPA is expected not to intrude with its advice on the economic preserves of the established Ministries.

Speaking of the weakness of the Economic Planning Agency vis-à-vis other Ministries, Shigeto Tsuru observes: "In practically no administrative matters can the Economic Planning Agency exercise an independent initiative or power of coordination. It is like an assembly plant which has to make a façade of coordinated harmony out of parts supplied by others beyond its control." [10] This weakness can prove fatal at the stage of the adoption and implementation of a plan as will be illustrated later in this chapter.

There are conflicts of values behind the somewhat lukewarm nature of planning in a capitalist but democratic society like Japan on more fundamental issues than the relative power position of the planning agency in the structure of the administration. Saburo Okita, who directed the EPA's Over-all Planning Bureau for a long time, observes:

An economic plan aims at suggesting indicators of long-term economic policy. It is natural that different interests and outlooks give rise to controversies of all kinds. Although a plan should serve as a guide-post in carrying out economic policy it is not likely to be effective if it points to an image of society radically different from the existing economic relations. On account of these considerations a plan tends to end up as a consolidation of the majority opinions about the future.[11]

On another occasion, Okita characterized the plan as an "equitable distribution of dissatisfaction" for the reason that the plan by nature could not satisfy everyone.[12]

Forces Impinging upon Plan Orientation

The Government

The most important single participant in Japanese planning is the Prime Minister, who can choose either to have or not to have an economic plan as part of his Government's socio-economic policy. Before 1956 Japan had no national economic plans which committed the Government in the name of the Council of Ministers, although there were many studies and documents entitled "economic plan." These were prepared by the predecessors of the EPA: the Economic Stabilization Board (1947–1952) and Economic Council Board (1952–1955). Table 29 lists the major plan documents of this period together with the national economic plans of more recent years.[13] As this table shows, each Prime Minister adopted at least one economic plan during his term of office. But with the sole exception of Premier Yoshida, none stayed in office long enough to see his plan through from start to finish and each has been loath to carry out his predecessor's plan. Premier Sato is evidently on his way to proving that he is another exception. He cast away the Medium-Term Economic Plan which he inherited from his predecessor, but the plan he ordered, the Economic and Social Development Plan, also became obsolete by 1969.

Economic circumstances, especially conditions external to the Japanese economy, have been responsible for the quick obsolescence of Japanese plans. There have been three stages of interaction between economic conditions and planning in postwar Japan. First there was a group of reconstruction plans, illustrated by the first two in Table 29. Second, there were plans whose purpose was to build a viable economy in the absence of assistance from abroad (the United States, items 3–6 in Table 29). There were then plans that emphasized economic growth, the most famous of which was the National Income Doubling Plan. The latest plan adopted by the Sato Government lays stress on the "social" aspects of economic "development." This reflects a new attitude of the Government toward public policy and a new view of economy and society that has come to be shared by many scholars and administrators associated with the groundwork of public policy making. In a word, the ambition of the latest plan is to redress the imbalances between economic growth and its social consequences (like sprawling urbanization, housing shortage, and the squalor of the public sector in general) that arose during the last ten years of rapid growth. I shall return to this particular issue later.

Thus one can see that Japanese economic planning started as a search for guidelines in the reconstruction effort following the devastation of the country by the Second World War and, passing through the stage of equipping the economy for viability and rapid growth, has entered the stage of balanced economic and social development. These stages of planning coincide broadly with the actual stages of postwar Japanese socio-economic development.[14]

Interest groups

The members and experts of the Economic Council are appointed on the basis of their individual qualifications and do not formally represent the interests of the economic activity they follow or of the professional organizations to which they belong. All of them are in principle expected to represent the general public interest. It can be assumed, however, that in practice the participants in the formulation of a plan never succeed in transcending the interests of their professions and organizations. Table 30 shows the occupational and organizational background of the members and experts of the Council on recent plans. While it should always be remembered that social groups as such are not directly represented in the Council, this table is useful as an indication of the types of people who are considered worthy of advising the Prime Minister.

Among the titular and provisional members the predominant occupational background is business; that of trade unionism is conspicuously absent. There are a few trade unionists among the experts of the Council. A good number of university professors also participates as experts. But the role of experts in relation to the basic orientation of

TABLE 29

MAJOR ECONOMIC PLANS IN JAPAN

| Title | Government | Planning Agency | Period of Preparation | | | Plan Period (Fiscal Years)[d] |
			Started[a]	Completed[b]	Adopted[c]	
1. Draft Plan for Economic Reconstruction	Katayama, Ashida	Economic Stabilization Board (E.S.B.)	July 1947	May 1948	n.a.	1948–1951
2. Economic Reconstruction Plan	Ashida, Yoshida	E.S.B. and Commission for Economic Rehabilitation Planning	June 1948	May 1949	n.a.	1949–1953
3. Economic Self-Support Plan	Yoshida	E.S.B. and Commission for Economic Independence	July 1950	Jan. 1951	n.a.	1951–1953
4. Economic Table for 1957 and "Okano Scheme"	Yoshida	Economic Council Board	Not definable	Feb. 1953	n.a.	1953–1957
5. Scheme for Over-all Development	Yoshida	Economic Council Board	Not definable	Sep. 1954	n.a.	1955–1965

	Prime Minister	Economic Council (E.C.) and Economic Planning Agency (E.P.A.)	[a]	[b]	[c]	[d]
6. Five-Year Plan for Economic Self-Support	Hatoyama		Jan. 1955	Jan. 1956	Jan. 1956	1956–1960
7. New Long-Range Economic Plan	Kishi	E.C. and E.P.A.	Aug. 1957	Nov. 1957	Dec. 1957	1958–1962
8. National Income Doubling Plan	Kishi, Ikeda	E.C. and E.P.A.	Nov. 1959	Nov. 1960	Dec. 1960	1961–1970
9. Medium-Term Economic Plan	Ikeda, Sato	E.C. and E.P.A.	Jan. 1964	Nov. 1964	Jan. 1965	1965–1968
10. Economic and Social Development Plan	Sato	E.C. and E.P.A.	May 1966	Feb. 1967	March 1967	1967–1972

[a] For Nos. 6–9, the date when the Prime Minister asked the advice of the Economic Council. For Nos. 1–3, the dates when the respective planning agencies were established.

[b] For Nos. 6–9, the date when the Economic Council reported to the Prime Minister; for earlier years, either the date of submission of a draft plan to the Prime Minister or, during the Yoshida period, the date of announcement by the planning agency of a new scheme.

[c] By the Council of Ministers ("n.a." means not adopted).

[d] The fiscal year runs from April of the calendar year from which the fiscal year derives its designation to the end of March in the next calendar year.

the plan is extremely limited. Tadao Uchida of the University of Tokyo, who has been closely associated with the econometric work of recent plans, observes that all the committees and subcommittees of the Council at the time of the National Income Doubling Plan had to base their work on a predecided rate of growth and that there was no room for new suggestions from below concerning alternative growth rates accompanied by different estimates of the structural evolution of the Japanese economy. He feels that the growth potential of the econ-

TABLE 30

OCCUPATIONAL AND ORGANIZATIONAL BACKGROUNDS
OF MEMBERS AND EXPERTS OF THE ECONOMIC COUNCIL
IN RECENT PLANS

Background of Members and Experts	New Long-Range Economic Plan			National Income Doubling Plan			Medium-Term Economic Plan	
	To-tal	Titular and Pro-visional Members	Ex-perts	To-tal	Titular and Pro-visional Members	Ex-perts	Planning Com-mittee Only	Titular Mem-bers
ALL GROUPS	187	36	151	179	51	128	157	29
Business	117	30	87	85	36	49	68	21
Banking, credit and insurance	29	7	22	15	7	8	23	8
Corporations	47	17	30	36	17	19	25	12
Trade associations	41	6	35	34	12	22	16	1
Associations for agriculture, forestry and fishery	8	1	7	1	1	0	4	1
Labor (trade unions)	4	0	4	1	0	1	4	0
Public interest	58	5	53	92	14	78	83	7
Academic	29	2	27	49	6	43	47	2
Journalism	5	0	5	9	0	9	10	1
Research institutes	12	0	12	20	3	17	18	3
Other[a]	12	3	9	14	5	9	8	1

Sources: Economic Planning Agency: New Long-Range Economic Plan of Japan (1958–1962), pp. 177–194; Kokumin shotoku baizō keikaku (National Income Doubling Plan), pp. 243–46; Chūki keizai keikaku (Medium-Term Economic Plan), pp. 377–80. The table shows the net number of persons serving on the Council as members or experts, sometimes on more than one committee or subcommittee.

[a] Advisory councils, independent commissions, semi-official funds, etc.

omy was incorrectly estimated in this plan and that this was due to the poor management and coordination of activities within the Council at the time of its orientation.[15]

On the other hand, the business world was very well satisfied with the way the National Income Doubling Plan was prepared and with the basic philosophy that guided the work of the Council. At that time there was a keen consciousness of the problem of defining the proper scope of activities for the public and private sectors. The Government spared no pains to emphasize that it would do everything to build up the right kind of climate for private enterprise and to refrain from interventions in the private sector. This basic posture generated considerable enthusiasm for the plan among Japanese businessmen. Takayuki Yamamoto, then Vice-President of the Fuji Steel Company, who participated as an expert in the formulation of the National Income Doubling Plan, wrote:

> It is generally recognized as being untrue to say that the National Income Doubling Plan was formulated by the Government alone. It was a joint product of the Government and the private sector. If we include all who helped the experts of various committees of the Council, the number of people who had some contribution to make towards the plan must have easily exceeded one thousand.[16]

He goes on to declare that it is the "duty" of Japanese businessmen to cooperate with a plan formulated in this manner.

No trade union leaders have been appointed to the Economic Council as its titular members. Trade union participation was particularly low when the National Income Doubling Plan was drawn up (Table 30). At the time of the Medium-Term Economic Plan many people remarked that there were two important developments from the point of view of popular participation in planning: the presence of trade union leaders in the Planning Committee of the Council and the participation of the Sōhyō (General Council of Trade Unions). However, the latter point was new only in relation to the National Income Doubling Plan, for there had been experts from the Sōhyō at the time of the New Long-Range Plan.

The representation of the general public interest in the Economic Council is meager and is mostly carried out by university professors, especially academic economists. But as a long-term plan has to take into account changes in the socio-economic structure, technology, and the general life style, economists themselves feel that experts in the social sciences may be able to contribute as much toward a full appreciation of these changes as economists.[17]

The low trade union participation and the narrow representation of the general public interest in the Economic Council have had their expected consequences: excessive emphasis on the sectors of the economy dominated by big corporations at the expense of other sectors and neglect of the social aspects of national life such as income distribution, social security,[18] employment policy, consumer prices, education, and the regional balance of economic activities. The predominant feeling of the Council at the time of the National Income Doubling Plan was that rapid economic growth would eventually resolve these problems of structure and welfare.

Forces Impinging upon Plan Implementation

A good plan must offer information on at least two crucial matters, either explicitly or by clear implication. First, it must offer a reasonably detailed picture of what would be the normal functioning of the economy in the absence of the plan, currently and in the future.[19] This requires a thorough understanding of the economic system and a fairly correct appreciation of its responses to predictable changes in economic circumstances. Second, a good plan must offer a consistent set of targets which are significantly different from what would be the result of the trend of normal activities without the plan, and which cannot be attained unless efforts are made to implement the necessary measures.[20]

Japanese economic plans have been notoriously defective on both accounts mentioned. Economic planning has so far been little more than a learning process. What one has had to learn is the true potential of the Japanese economy.[21] All the plans have so far been overfulfilled by big margins. This has been accompanied by an escalation of the planned growth rates. In the Five-Year Plan for Economic Self-Support the planned annual rate of growth was 5.5 percent. In the New Long-Range Economic Plan it was 6.5 percent, in the National Income Doubling Plan 7.2 percent, in the Medium-Term Economic Plan 8.1

percent, and in the Economic and Social Development Plan 8.3 percent. All this while the Japanese economy has grown on the average at the annual rate of slightly more than 10 percent. The overfulfillment of economic plans in the 1950s was well within the frontier of technical and economic possibilities. The rapid growth after 1958, which in part coincided with the National Income Doubling Plan, pushed the Japanese economy closer to the frontier of these possibilities; for example, consumer prices rose rapidly, population became excessively concentrated in a narrow stretch of the high-income, highly industrialized areas between Tokyo–Yokohama and Kobe–Osaka, the balance of payments turned adverse, bottlenecks developed in sectors such as transportation, water supply, housing, and education, and private industry itself in a few years ended up with excess capacity, though temporarily.[22]

The private sector

The apparent overfulfillment of the National Income Doubling Plan during its early years gave rise to various conjectures on the impact of the plan on business behavior. This impact may take the form of an information effect, that is, the Government's commitment to the plan targets reduces uncertainties about the future and thus stimulates investment. Perhaps one should call it "misinformation effect"; there was no commitment on the part of the Government in Japanese planning. In the case of the National Income Doubling Plan, there may have been a certain amount of misunderstanding of the nature of the plan on the part of the private industrialists. Allen points out that "They regarded the targets as minima in some sense guaranteed by the government" and that "each entrepreneur in the highly competitive Japanese economy sought to ensure that his own business obtained a disproportionate advantage from the prosperity to come." [23] The point is that there was no such guarantee. The economic plan may also have a market effect, that is, the publication of data on various industries and sectors in the plan may make firms conscious of their respective shares in the relevant markets and stimulate them to activities to expand their shares.[24]

There is no doubt that the information and market effects of a plan are quite possible in theory. But are they as strong in practice as are supposed in theory? A recent inquiry by questionnaires into the determination of investment decisions has thrown some light on the relationship between the national economic plans and private investment decisions. More than 60 percent of the firms which replied to the questionnaires in March 1965 did not take the National Income Doubling Plan into account in making their investment decisions. The predominant reason for not having done so was that they had their own long-term investment plans independently of the national economic plan. Less than 40 percent of the firms replied that they paid some attention to the National Income Doubling Plan in making their investment decisions. Two thirds of these firms did so because they had no other data to turn to. Replies to the same questions concerning the Medium-Term Economic Plan followed the same pattern.[25]

Thus it appears that the dynamic quality of Japanese business is much more a fundamental characteristic of the national economy than it is due to artificial stimuli such as are supplied by an economic plan. Japanese business displays a very high degree of competitiveness and independence in the pursuit of market opportunities. This may perhaps be contrary to the image of the Japanese economy and society held by many people outside Japan. A recent study points out that there is a mistaken feeling abroad that the Japanese economy is highly concentrated and organized, although the fact is that Japan suffers from excessive competition among enterprises.[26]

The public sector

The vigor of competition in the private sector has been an awkward problem for the public sector. If public expenditures expand in pace with revenues, which increase as a function of the private sector, economic activities are stimulated further, intensifying bottlenecks in resources. On the other hand, if the Government does not claim its share in the available resources for investment in social overhead capital (SOC) from a long-range point of view, the avaricious and excessively competitive private sector will use up all the resources in directly profitable activities (DPA).[27] In other countries the private sector, if left alone without occasional shots in the arm by public expenditure, tends to grow less fast than at a desired rate. In these economies the government and private sector would happily pool their efforts for a fuller utilization of slack in resources. In Japan, however, in order to get hold of resources for its own use, the Government may have to restrain the activities of the private sector which if left alone would press against the very limits of available resources. This point has received very little attention in the Japanese planning circles so that the SOC-GNP ratio was allowed to fall consistently between the early 1950s and the early 1960s.[28]

Thus one of the great problems in Japanese economic planning is to redress the imbalances between the private and public sectors. Foreign visitors notice examples of these imbalances everywhere in Japan. Saburo Okita notes as an observation by a student from an Asian country a peculiar contrast between ultramodern private firms and weed-covered national museums in Tokyo.[29]

The National Income Doubling Plan ran into difficulties because this basic dilemma was not taken seriously; that is, it is reckless to try to increase the Government's capital formation when the private sector is running at the top gear fast enough to heat the economy considerably by itself. It is also a poor policy from a counter-cyclical point of view; that is, the public expenditure moves in the same direction as the private, resulting in the accentuation of "the boom and bust." On the other hand, since the private sector in Japan tends to be overheated much of the time, if the government sits tight in order not to add more heat to the economy, investment in SOC falls farther behind private capital formation. The basic trouble is that the potential of the private economy has never been correctly appreciated in Japan.[30] To sum up Japan's dilemma: (1) growth is desirable and the private sector is quite capable of delivering it; (2) investment in SOC is desirable and only the Government can do it; (3) stable growth is desirable and only the compensatory efforts of the private and public sectors can achieve it. A full release of the private sector's potential plus the Government's vigorous SOC formation would be destabilizing. A full use of the private sector potential with the Government's compensatory inaction or negative activity in the sense of accumulating surpluses may increase the chances for stable growth but will surely starve the public sector.

Economic planning in Japan has never been considered an instrument of stable growth. The rates of growth in the last fifteen years have ranged from a low of 3 percent to a high of 16 percent per annum, averaging out at about 10 percent. Suppose that 8 percent per annum was the highest rate of growth that could have been sustained without fluctuations in growth. Suppose further that the future situation is pretty much the same. The hard question is whether stable growth at 8 percent is better than fluctuating growth which averages out at 10 percent. The difference of 2 percentage points in the compound rate of growth is substantial in terms of output foregone over a long period. Whether the benefits of stable growth are great enough to justify this price is the question that must be considered seriously if economic planning should serve as an instrument of stable growth. When the economy is growing at 15 percent per annum, it seems difficult for anyone to believe that there is a need for curbing the economic activities in order to avoid the growth rates sinking below 5 percent in the near future. The pleasure of *present* growth usually outweighs the fear of *future* stagnation. When stagnation actually hits, the primary concern is to get out of it as soon as possible. Here again one has no time to think of measures that would contribute to stable growth under the circumstance. It seems therefore that action for stable growth is paralyzed by the high rate of discount that one applies to the future incomes. One senses this type of impatience among Japanese economists and officials.

The role of the Government is bound to increase in the coming years, not only because there is an autonomous rise in the demand for government services but because the private sector may no longer be able to maintain the level of capital formation that has characterized Japan's economic growth in the last twenty years. In other words, after the prolonged spell of vigorous growth and investment in DPA it is perhaps fair to suspect that private capital formation will sooner or later reach a saturation point in reference to private profitability. Over the last three business cycles the peak in the annual rate of increase in private capital formation has become lower from cycle to cycle.[31] It is ironical that economic planning should demonstrate its power and significance when the private sector has run out of steam, but one wonders if this has not been roughly the kind of economic background that has made planning acceptable and effective in advanced capitalist countries.

At present, there are other factors within the Japanese Government that obstruct effective implementation of an economic policy based on long-term considerations. For example, there is the rivalry among the executive agencies of the Government in safeguarding their prerogatives.[32] In the annual struggle for appropriations the long-term economic plan is of no use to various executive ministries because the plan's macro-economic logic of consistency and feasibility usually cuts down their specific plans in the name of coordination.

A practical illustration of the relationship between the plan and the budget is provided by the draft Medium-Term Economic Plan. The plan was transmitted by the Economic Council to the Prime Minister on November 17, 1964 but had not yet been adopted by the Government when the budget question arose in December.[33] On December 18, 1964, the Ministry of Finance's policies for the budget and for treasury loans and investments, which were formulated on the basis of the draft plan, came before the Council of Ministers. As soon as these policies were announced, complaints arose from various other ministries which were unhappy about the austerity of the proposals and immediately started to maneuver to reinstate their original claims in the budget estimates. When negotiations were opened for readjustments of budget items, many new projects and plans which were termed "urgent" and "indispensable" were presented to the Ministry of Finance by various ministries in order to justify their demands for larger appropriations. These projects and plans had not been envisaged in the economic plan. However, all the claims for readjustments were eventually accepted by the Ministry of Finance at the level of Minister-to-Minister negotiations.

Despite these compromises, which virtually wiped out the draft Medium-Term Economic Plan, the Plan was adopted by the Council of Ministers on January 22, 1965. Two weeks afterwards, in the course of the debate on the draft budget on February 1, 1965, the opposition party in the House of Representatives asked if the Government was determined to honor its commitment to the price stabilization target recommended by the Plan. In his reply the Prime Minister suggested that the Government had no wish to be bound by the figures in the Plan. On May 7, 1965 the Prime Minister addressed the youth sections of the Liberal-Democratic Party and disclosed that he had asked the Director-General of the EPA to revise the Plan. In relation to this casual disposal of the Medium-Term Economic Plan it is well to remember that nearly 200 persons directly related to the Economic Council and countless others indirectly involved in the process worked for ten months to produce the Plan.

The latest Economic and Social Development Plan, under the strong leadership of the new head of the Economic Council, Kazutaka Kika-

wada, and with the full backing of the business community, was differently oriented. The Plan was unusually terse and forceful in expression. The proclaimed supremacy of "policy" over "measurement" and
the mass withdrawal of support by the economics profession heightened
a sense of crisis. This atmosphere made various government bureaus
feel that they could no longer disregard the force of the plan this time
and activated their participation in the plan formulation unusually.
The representatives from different ministries came to the Economic
Council as if they were coming to a budget meeting. They haggled over
small details in the hope of getting a favorable place in the plan frame
for their respective ministries.[34]

In the Economic and Social Development Plan, the Economic Council openly declares itself to be a supervisor over the implementation of
the Plan. In Chapter 6 titled "Implementation of the Plan" it regrets
that in the past the Government did not fully practice what it preached
in plans and that the private sector showed little understanding of
the requirements of the plan. One of the courses of action advocated
in this chapter states that the Government requests the Economic Council to continue the examination of the forces in socio-economic development and to formulate necessary policy measures for the purpose of
securing the development of economy and society in the right direction.[35] In interpreting the Plan, the EPA officials condemn the past attitude that favored the highest possible rate of growth each year and
makes an ambitious statement:

> Economic growth at about 8% per annum adopted in this plan
> has been arrived at through a consolidation of many alternative
> possibilities. Should a rate of growth in the order of 14% per
> annum be reached in the fiscal year of 1967, it cannot be wel-
> comed on grounds that the higher the rate of growth, the more
> desirable it is. Even if the balance of payments were in the black
> and consumer prices stayed stable (though unlikely to come about
> in reality), one should still consider it desirable in the long-run to
> maintain an optimum rate of growth.[36]

This is certainly a striking statement in view of Japanese experience
in much of the postwar period. It suggests a trade-off of a margin of
growth for stability. The fiscal year of 1967 (April 1967 to March 1968)
is now past. At the beginning people expected a "stable" rate of growth

of GNP at 9 to 10 percent in real terms. At the end of the year it was found that growth had been in the order of 13 percent accompanied by an adverse balance of payments and a 4 percent increase in the index of consumer prices.[37] Growth continued throughout 1968, and some people in December 1968 began to speak of revising the Plan. The EPA started work on a new plan in July 1969.

In sum, one may be permitted to characterize Japanese economic plans as optional on the part of the Government in relation to formulation and adoption, indicative for the public sector in relation to implementation, and at best informative for the private sector on the general state of the economy. Even this modest appraisal may sound too favorable, for some Japanese scholars informally mentioned to me that Japanese plans were decorative for the Prime Minister, powerless vis-à-vis the bureaucracy, and misleading to the private sector.

Business and Labor in Relation to Planning

Business

Business exerts constant pressure on the Government through its four major social organizations.[38] They are (1) Keidanren (Federation of Economic Organizations), (2) Nisshō (Chamber of Commerce and Industry), (3) Nikkeiren (Federation of Employers' Associations), and (4) Keizai Dōyūkai (Committee for Economic Development).[39]

Keidanren is recognized as Japan's most influential business association. It is made up of more than 100 financial, industrial, and trading associations and more than 800 leading firms. Its constitution declares that the organization will present appeals and resolutions to the Diet and the Government when the importance of economic policies on the agenda calls for such action, and that it will cooperate with the Government in the implementation of desirable economic measures. Keidanren strives to present a unified front of leading Japanese businesses. Its annual meetings are attended by the Prime Minister and other ministers in charge of economic matters. Its top leaders are titular members of the Economic Council, and a few of its officers are experts for the Council. Its former President, Ichiro Ishikawa, for example, has served for a long time as the President of the Economic Council. Moreover, many of the corporations and banks that send their officers to the Economic Council are affiliates of Keidanren.

The Chamber of Commerce and Industry (Nisshō for short) comes after Keidanren in the hierarchy of influence over the economic policy of the Government. Nisshō comprises more than 400 chambers of commerce and industry all over Japan that have a considerable number of small and medium enterprises as members. A former Director-General of the EPA, Aiichiro Fujiyama, was once president of this organization. Its annual meetings also are attended by the Prime Minister and ministers charged with economic affairs. Its leaders are titular members of the Economic Council.

A colorful actor for the business community of Japan is the Federation of Employers' Associations (Nikkeiren). Formed in the turbulent era of the fierce labor offensive shortly after the Second World War the Federation of Employers' Associations was once known as the "general headquarters" of the employers' counteroffensive against labor. With the passage of time, the employers' policy toward unions has changed from defensive aggressiveness to rational labor-management cooperation in the interest of increasing productivity, decreasing costs, and improving worker morale. Nikkeiren is made up of about 100 regional and industrial employer associations. Some of its officers are active participants in the work of the Economic Council.

Keizai Dōyūkai is best known as the Japanese counterpart of the American Committee for Economic Development (CED).[40] It is an organization of about 1,000 younger industrialists and bankers, who are members in their individual capacity. This characteristic of its membership enables Dōyūkai to experiment with ideas and proposals that are not necessarily bound by the interests of Japanese business but intended as steps toward a certain desirable type of society in which the place of business is also assured. It was formed in 1946 and emerged in a few years as a successful defender of Japanese capitalism. In order to secure the place for business in postwar Japan when its prestige was very low, Dōyūkai launched a radical revolution in Japanese business philosophy. At that time, the whole country was against "capitalism" and a social revolution to do away with it looked imminent. Dōyūkai struck back by saying that there were no "capitalists" in Japan and that there were only "managers" who were members of the working class, like any other worker. It offered a new image of business enterprises as organizations carrying out the decisions taken by a conference of managers, workers, and shareholders. Subsequent events showed, however, that Japanese capitalists did not have to retreat quite so far as Dōyūkai had proposed. Today Japanese business enjoys great prestige both at home and abroad.

Of course the Dōyūkai ideology has undergone changes over the years. Today it is built on the theme of business vigilantism; that is, government interference with the freedom of private enterprise is rejected and in return business is urged to regulate and discipline itself in the public interest. Dōyūkai believes that Japanese business is afflicted with too much competition, which gives rise to violent economic fluctuations. Any socio-economic instability strengthens the excuse for more public intervention. Therefore Dōyūkai wishes to turn excessive competition into "harmonious competition" in the interest of both economic efficiency and general stability.[41]

This ideology does not mean political apathy, however. Freedom from government intervention requires active participation in the public policy-making process in order to keep the Government in check and to secure a proper scope of activities for private business. In other words, freedom from government is identical with freedom to govern. Dōyūkai is as active as ever in Japanese politics. Dōyūkai's Kikawada now heads the Economic Council and has created a kind of coup d'état in the relationship between business on the one hand and government and academic community on the other. Dōyūkai somehow managed to set the notion of "stable growth" against "rapid growth," which it downgraded as inimical to public interest. Kikawada as head of the Economic Council further complicated the issue by dichotomizing "policy" against "measurement" and antagonizing the economics profession. Many econometricians left the Council in anger, and the Economic and Social Development Plan found only a cool reception at the hands of economists.[42]

The findings of an inquiry by questionnaires into Japanese business ideology undertaken by the Japan Economic Research Center suggest that the feeling and thinking of the Dōyūkai type are widespread in the Japanese business community.[43] On the government-business relationship, nearly 60 percent of the firms who answered the questionnaires rejected the view that the Government should intervene in private business, while 30 percent thought that the Government could do so if the general public demanded it. The suggestion that the Government should actively guide private business received support from but one percent of the respondents. On the other hand, in relation to the desirability and scope of managers taking part in social activities in addition to business, only 7 percent supported the view that managers' sole business was management; 25 percent thought that they should participate in the trade associations of their respective industries; 17 percent would permit them to participate in the general affairs of the business community as a whole; and finally, 38 percent went further by welcoming the participation of business in the Government's advisory organs.

These replies indicate that, although the Japanese business community dislikes government intervention in its affairs, it desires to intervene in government through trade associations and advisory councils. In reality, the relationship between business and the Government is extremely close. The strong ties between them are deeply rooted in the common educational background of their respective leaders. In addition, many business and political leaders are bound together through family and matrimonial ties.[44] There are also functional reasons for the closeness of business-government relations. There are two channels by which people rise to positions of influence in the Government. One is through getting elected to political office with the support of the majority party; the other is upward movement through the internal hierarchy of the State Administration. On the other hand, high-ranking Japanese bureaucrats retire from the civil service in their early fifties, although they have more than ten years of active life ahead of them. They either find managerial positions in private firms or semi-official corporations, or launch themselves into politics.[45]

In Japanese history the concentration of wealth, power, and prestige in the business élite is a relatively recent phenomenon. Before the Second World War, business had wealth, but political power belonged to the State Administration and social prestige to the nobility. The three élite groups enjoying respectively wealth, power, and prestige were held together in workable relationships by the transcendental supremacy of the Imperial Throne, which was the source of legitimacy for everything Japanese. The postwar reform reduced the Throne to a mere "symbol of the nation," did away with the nobility, and turned the State Administration into public service. Power and prestige lost by these groups found their way in large part to business. Thus, after a century of modern economic development, Japan has become a typical bourgeois society.

With Dōyūkai moving into the center of economic policy for the Sato Government, the business community has completed its long-awaited objective of taking over the Government. When one recalls that Dōyū-kai was once overwhelmed by the labor movement immediately after the War, its rise to the supreme position in Japanese economic policy in a little more than 20 years since cannot but evoke certain apprehension about the concentration of power, economic, political, and social. For some time now one has heard talk of "business omnipotence" (*keizai bannō shugi*). Take this together with the Sato Government's apparent stability and good luck which have enabled Premier Sato to entertain hopes for "permanent power" (*eikyū seiken*) whatever that means. The perfect teamwork of business and government with increasing monopoly of power, wealth, and prestige may be harmful to the long-run interest of the nation. Indeed, Saburo Okita, foremost leader in Japanese economic planning, sounds an alarm about the danger of the current social trends in Japan. Okita observes:

> . . . the tendency for the rigidity of the ruling groups of Japan is a problem. . . . In prewar Japan, this tendency occurred and the optimistic and open society of the Meiji Era weakened. This created dissatisfaction with the rulers and induced the feeling of social hopelessness, resulting in a polarization of society into the left and the military. The confusion and the breakdown of the old order after the War gave the people a sense of liberation and put them on an equal footing for competition. As if a stagnant pool of water were thoroughly stirred, the mass energy of postwar Japan was stirred up. . . . This atmosphere gave birth to a Sony, a Honda, a National. But 20 years after the War, social order has become stiffer and the ruling groups have begun to solidify and perpetuate themselves.[46]

Labor

Immediately after the War the labor movement had a clear initiative in social reform. What has become of it today? The sad truth is that given the indomitable business-government coalition, the labor movement relies on protest as practically the sole effective method of workers' participation in public policy. One may suppose that the frequency and intensity of protest are essentially proportional to the degree of inequality in the distribution of power and the lack of genuine opportunities for dialogue among various social groups. Since participation in public policy by protest is less desirable than participation by dialogue, a wider sharing of power and more frequent personal contacts among social groups seem desirable.

From the workers' point of view there are two levels where an increased share of power in decision-making is desired, the enterprise and the Government. The factors that immediately affect the welfare of the worker, such as wages and working conditions, are largely determined at the enterprise level. The preceding chapter showed that trade unions had achieved a substantial degree of effectiveness at the enterprise level for promoting and securing workers' increasing well-being. At the level of general public policy, however, the picture is radically different, that is, workers are kept at a distance as a separate class.

Today about 60 percent of Japanese trade unionists belong to one or the other of the two national centers, the General Council of Trade Unions (Sōhyō) and the Confederation of Labor (Dōmei). Japanese trade unions formed Sōhyō in 1950 in an effort to consolidate the trade union movement in the midst of the crushing blows that were being dealt it by the recession of 1949 and the ideological stiffening of the Allied Occupation Forces. In a few years Sōhyō swung to the left and lost some of its original affiliates. This was followed by the formation of a more moderate center, the Japan Trade Union Congress (Zenrō), in 1954. In 1964 Zenrō was dissolved and absorbed into a new Confederation of Labor (Dōmei). In 1967 the national centers of organized labor had the following membership distribution (in thousands of persons): [47]

Total	10,566
Sōhyō	4,208
Dōmei	1,038
Chūritsu-rōren (Federation of Independent Unions)	70
Other independent national unions	3,588

Sōhyō works closely with the Socialist Party. Its ideology denies the possibility of genuine cooperation with the Government in the present stage of Japan's socio-political development, which Sōhyō defines as "monopoly capitalism." But the socialists' chances of taking over public power are so slight that Sōhyō has to work toward desirable social policies through a government of "monopoly capitalists." Sōhyō thus faces a dilemma in putting its theories into practice. Ideologically, it rejects the existing society, and so, by implication, it also rejects any cooperation with the present-day government. But since the kind of society it desires is not forthcoming in any foreseeable future, in practice it has to put up with the existing government, working with it if necessary. Thus Sōhyō's ideology makes it extremely difficult for it to justify its practical actions, which unavoidably have to be based on acceptance of the existing socio-political reality.[48]

The ideologically moderate Dōmei, which supports the Democratic Socialist Party, accepts the facts of life as a point of departure and values any progress that can be made in the democratization of capitalism. Sōhyō rejects planning in capitalism as deceptive or meaningless. But Dōmei at least studies its implications in relation to matters of interest to the workers, such as prospective increase in wages.[49] Despite Dōmei's best efforts, however, it cannot be denied that the workers on the whole are not enthusiastic about economic planning as it is practiced in Japan today. This is due in part to the character of the plan itself, which is highly aggregative in approach and at the same time highly restricted in scope. Its emphasis is on production and resource allocation on the basis of national aggregates of quantitative data. The matters that are of great significance to workers are dealt with outside the planning system by policies having to do with wages, prices, employment, working conditions, social insurance, and welfare. Many of these are the concern of the Ministry of Labor, or the Ministry of Welfare, where the tripartite representation of workers, employers, and the general public is a firmly established principle. In the Ministry of Labor there are two important commissions constituted on a tripartite basis: the Central Labor Relations Commission and the Public Enterprises Labor Relations Commission. They are serviced by their own sizable secretariats. In addition, there are many advisory councils also constituted on a tripartite basis. For example, in 1965, of all the fourteen advisory councils attached to the Ministry of Labor, eleven were constituted on a tripartite basis. The other three councils were entrusted with noncontroversial technical matters and accordingly filled by specialists qualified for them. The total membership of the tripartite councils was distributed as follows: 91 for public interest, 64 for employers, and 60 for workers.[50] Even so, the workers cannot be wholly sure about which side these Ministries are with. Takeshi Ishida points out that the Ministry of Labor is almost a captive of Nikkeiren.[51]

Recent events are arousing workers' interest in economic policy and economic planning. With the opening of the Japanese economy to foreign capital, Japanese firms have for some time been engaged in activities to strengthen their international competitive capacity. This has brought about a movement for industrial reorganization (*sangyō saihensei*) with a primary emphasis on economies of scale. To Japanese firms, industrial reorganization is almost synonymous with merger. The merger of firms implies a merger of enterprise unions. But the interpersonal and organizational problems that arise in this case are no less complicated or difficult than their counterparts for managements. Each enterprise union has built up its own tradition, organizational uniqueness, and ideological preferences. In addition, a merger of firms sometimes accompanies a plan to reduce the work force for the purpose of raising labor productivity. But nothing angers the union more than unemployment. When the unions of firms considering a merger belong to different national centers as in the case of one belonging to Sōhyō and another to Dōmei, the diseconomies in the utilization of the strife-ridden work force after the merger may be so great that technical gains are wiped out. On the whole, the presumption is that enterprise unions desire to be consulted beforehand about the necessity and procedure for merger in order to effect their own reorganization with less difficulties. Unfortunately, managements have rarely thought of the problem as anything that concerns the unions. The merger is complicated enough as it is even in the absence of trade unions.

The unions' desire to be consulted about the merger of firms is a desire for greater participation in the affairs of the firm. It is also a desire for participation in the formulation of the industrial policy that determines the scope and arrangement of mergers. This means that the unions have got to participate in policy making in the Ministry of International Trade and Industry (MITI), which is perhaps one of the most impregnable branches of the Government to trade unions. Indeed, the opening of Japan to foreign capital is a great policy issue, which many Japanese liken to the opening of Japan to the West that took place more than one hundred years ago. Public interest is likely to be greatly affected by the manner of administrative guidance for the industrial reorganization, and there is no valid reason to exclude the labor movement from the conference designed to ascertain the nature of the public interest and formulate policies to best serve it. The labor movement today has a large clientele to look after.[52]

Dōmei and Chūritsu-rōren are especially keen about getting a place in the public organs. The EPA and MITI at least pay lip service to the desirability of labor's participation in the proceedings of their advisory councils. But Kiyoshi Ebata, principal editorialist for the *Asahi,* doubts the sincerity of the Government in this matter. He observes:

> . . . Although the MITI and EPA have declared in favor of trade unions' participation, there are doubts as to how far they really pay attention to trade unions. Indeed, the bureaucrats do not seem to be broad-minded enough to listen to the voices of workers on policy matters. To be sure, unions may fall short of the required ability or expertise about these matters. But the villain of the piece is likely to be the snobbish world-view of the policy-makers. At the same time, the bureaucrats are too close to the firms or business community in general.[53]

Ebata further sounds an alarm about the consequences of the alienation of the labor movement from policy-making.

> One can hardly be responsible for something in which one does not take part. Trade unions have been pushed out of policy making processes. This would force them to behave as if they were outsiders to the whole regime. It does not stand to reason to expect social responsibility or activity for strengthening the existing social order from trade unions so long as they are left out of policy making.[54]

Such is the way in which Japanese society and polity still treat the labor movement. That the labor movement is legal is one thing; whether it is also legitimate within the system of values in today's Japan is evidently quite another. The Japanese government has consistently demonstrated its ability to stall on labor policy for an incredible length of time throughout the modern history of Japan. Now the Government is dragging its feet on the issue of trade union participation in the formulation of public policy vital to the interest of organized labor. The estrangement of the labor movement from economic planning as considered previously is just one small part of the general disinclination of the Government to admit workers into the last preserve of honor, power, and prestige. This point may be illustrated by recent evidence on the Government's active "inaction" in relation to labor policy. The case in point is the question of industrial relations in the public sector.

As early as in 1953, Japan noticed that certain provisions in the existing laws for the regulation of public sector trade unionism were in conflict with the International Labor Convention No. 87 of 1948 on the freedom of association and the right to organize.[55] In the meantime, the public sector unions felt increasingly constrained in their union activities because of the existing legal framework. In 1958 Sōhyō complained to the ILO about the Japanese Government's infringements on workers' right to organize. But the Government continuously failed to ratify the Convention. Finally, the case was referred to the ILO's Fact-Finding and Conciliation Commission on Freedom of Association in 1964. After a year's study, the Commission produced a substantial report in 1965.[56] Satisfied with the preliminary proposals of the Commission made in February 1965, the Government put through the ratification procedure and completed it by the time the report of the Fact-Finding Commission was made public in August 1965.

The prolonged delay in the ratification of the Convention was bad enough, but the ratification as such did not change the industrial relations in the public sector to any great extent. Aside from minimal statutory changes, the major cure for the problems of public sector trade unionism was envisaged to be an increase in mutual confidence between public sector workers and the Government as the employer. For this purpose, the ILO Commission recommended a "policy of high-level exchanges of views at appropriate intervals between responsible representatives of government and labor." [57] Acting upon the preliminary proposals of the Commission in February 1965, the Government initiated meetings of the Prime Minister and other responsible ministers with trade union representatives. The Government also established a tripartite advisory council on the public service personnel system. The ILO Commission's report entered approving remarks on these visible efforts of the Government. Urging the need for a general labor policy applicable to all levels of the public sector and recalling its recommendation of high-level conferences, the report further suggests as follows:

It [the Government] must also develop at all levels the habits of mutual consultation which the regular meetings between the Government and the labor organization initiated by the Prime Minister are designed to foster. There must clearly be a central focal point at which the general labor policy for public employees is defined in an authoritative manner. The newly established Advisory Council on the Public Service Personnel System will presumably provide the required focal point.[58]

By a series of frantic activities between January and August 1965, the Japanese Government succeeded in obtaining mildly favorable comments in the Report of the ILO Commission. But what has happened since August 1965 is not at all encouraging. Between May 1965 and January 1966 there were four "regular meetings" between the Government and the labor movement with an almost perfect regularity of three-month intervals. Then the regularity began to break down. The next meeting (perhaps the 5th in the series) took place in October 1966. Since then, the high-level exchanges of views have been sporadic, hardly deserving public attention as "regular," or as the Japanese once preferred to call, "periodic," meetings.[59]

A more formal institution, the Advisory Council on the Public Personnel System, with eight public members and six representatives each from labor and the employer met more frequently than the Prime Minister's regular conferences with the leaders of the labor movement. By March 1966 there had been eight sessions of the Council. There was another meeting in June 1966 and then a long lapse of over sixteen months. The Council met on October 2, 1967, a day before the terms of office of the incumbents expired. The chairman of the Council selected from among the public members hesitated to serve in that capacity again. The Council was paralyzed because of its inability to find its chairman. In June 1968 labor leaders voiced a strong dissatisfaction with the protracted suspension of the Council activities.[60] In July 1968 the Government secured the consent of the chairman of the Council, complying at the same time with his wishes to retain all the previous public members. In its September 1968 issue the *Japan Labor Bulletin* observed that "thus, after a standstill of more than two years, the Advisory Council is now ready to resume its deliberations upon 'basic matters concerning industrial relations among the staffs of public service and public industrial corporations.' " [61] The new Council sat for the first time in October 1968, and there were a few more sessions of the Council before the end of 1968.[62]

No amount of reported evidence is sufficient to impute any clear pattern of intentions to the Government vis-à-vis the labor movement. But if one recalls that the "habit of mutual consultation" exists between business and the Government on all socio-economic problems, the extreme difficulty that, as reviewed in part above, besets the labor movement when it wants to make its voice heard directly by the representatives of the Government takes on an air of scandalous nepotism by the political standards of participatory democracies of the West. Of course one should not be too impatient about the lag of social change behind economic development. With the history of modern Japan going into its second century, the labor movement will no doubt find its way to power and prestige in relation to the formulation and implementation of economic policy in general and social policy in particular.

Conclusion

This chapter is an exercise in the measurement of Japan's distance to a participatory democracy through the examination of the participants in the formulation and implementation of economic plans. The Japanese planning system consists of the Economic Council, which is a consultative organ of the Prime Minister, and the Economic Planning Agency, which is a part of the State Administration. At present the membership in the Economic Council is a kind of honorary distinction in recognition of personal qualities and achievement. That the councilors are largely businessmen indicates how highly the Japanese Government regards a distinguished business career. Success in business is an acceptable qualification for advising the Prime Minister on long-term economic policy. The absence of trade union leaders in the Council is the other side of the coin.

The social inferiority of the labor movement to business is brought into sharp relief when their relative prestige and influence are analyzed. The leaders of the working class are kept at a safe distance from the crucial center of public policy-making. Consequently, they tend to conceive of themselves mainly as a force of protest against the existing socio-political system which makes decisions without consultation with them. Trade unions have already established themselves as "wage-makers" in individual enterprises. How soon they will find themselves among the "policy-makers" for Japan is the question only the future can answer.

Conclusion   The Labor Market, Individual Freedom, and Organized Effort

THIS BOOK HAS REVIEWED the working of the labor market and the interactions of the labor market and institutional factors in the course of Japan's economic development in the last hundred years. It can be concluded that the labor market has always exhibited a surprising degree of efficiency in the allocation of human resources and the adjustment of relative wages. The significance of the labor market in Japan's developmental process may be better appreciated when it is placed in a broader historical context.

The Meiji Restoration of 1868 was not a bourgeois revolution in the sense that a highly developed, politically articulate business community, with the support of workers and farmers, wrested power from the hands of feudal barons and landlords. But it was at least a revolution in favor of markets, for it dismantled the barriers carefully erected and maintained by the Tokugawa Shogunate against the emergence and growth of a market economy in Japan. In the context of the socio-political doctrine of the Tokugawa regime, the profit motive was a vice and the conduct following its advice a crime. But no sooner had the designs of the Tokugawa polity been completed than the market forces began to creep into the seams of economy and society. During the long period of peace over 200 years, it became increasingly difficult to control the popular tastes and preferences or to prosecute the most glaring violations of the official injunctions against the pursuit of economic gains.

Even the Tokugawa rulers, feudal lords, and their vassals, who should have known how much the strength of the system depended upon their scrupulous observance of economic austerity, surrendered themselves to the temptation of pleasure and comfort. Before long, they were literally an army of conspicuous consumers rather than an army of warriors. The generation and expansion of demand for good life in this powerful sector of the Tokugawa society had far-reaching consequences on the structure and utilization of economic resources as well as on the ability of the producers to meet the demand. The feudal élite capable of controlling one half of the nation's agricultural produce turned much of its purchasing power into demand for goods and services of craftsmen, merchants, carriers, entertainers, and, even, scholars. The desire of the feudal élite for increased revenue in some cases resulted in more vicious exploitations of the peasantry, but the long-run solution was recognized to be the expansion of agricultural production. In this way the feudal rulers themselves were the first to undermine the spirit of feudalism. The lowly commoners, who had nothing to lose from the crumbling of feudalism, followed their instinct for a good life and thereby subverted the system surreptitiously but irreversibly. By the middle of the nineteenth century feudalism was no longer a tenable social order.

To be sure, the Meiji leaders, not being of the masses themselves, were not particularly interested in the wishes and interests of the common folk. But they were at least wise enough to recognize the irresistible strength of economic incentives and the usefulness of the market mechanism. The dynamic qualities of a market economy were demonstrated to them through the superiority of the Western nations in wealth and power. Thus the obstacles to a market economy were removed one after another in rapid succession. The feudal principle of birth as an ascriptive basis for occupation was swept away in favor of free enterprise, freedom of choice, mobility of all kinds, and popular education. The direct taxing power of the feudal élite over the peasantry was bought off by bonds, pensions, and diplomacy. Feudal fiefs were abolished and consolidated into larger administrative units. Property rights were fully established and private contracts were duly honored in the court of law. Foreign capital, enterprise, and commodity made their way freely into Japan, while the Japanese were free to travel abroad or to send things away from Japan according to their wishes and judgments. No doubt there were many social and political shortcomings in the Meiji reforms, but this brief list of reforms relevant to economic performance is enough to show that there was indeed a great revolution of markets.

The subsequent development of Japan was the fulfillment of this initial revolution of markets. It is in the context of Japan's development as a dynamic market economy that the labor market can claim its historic importance. At the time of the Meiji Restoration the labor market was undoubtedly the least developed of all the markets. A great bulk of Japan's production was done by self-employed labor. This was an extremely fortunate starting point for the labor market, however. During the Tokugawa period a high degree of economic rationality with all the analytical requisites of choice, accumulation, and entrepreneurship was engendered within the individual households as units of production. The lively household enterprises as pre-existing and preferred employment opportunities rigorously disciplined the nascent labor market. No one was forthcoming for paid work unless opportunities for paid work were not as agreeable as staying within the household enterprises. A strikingly sensitive matrix of interdependences was built into the Japanese economy at the beginning of Japan's development. It was an almost ideal neoclassical framework.

In due course of time paid employment expanded relative to self-employment. The efficiency of the labor market came to depend more and more on its own self-discipline. But the market is only a short-hand expression for the interactions of decisions and activities of countless individuals. Economic development expands job opportunities, fosters freedom of choice, refines economic rationality, and generates an increasing amount of information relevant to economic decisions. One is not amiss in supposing that after a century of modern economic growth, individual workers of Japan today are more rational, informed, and calculating about employment opportunities as well as being more confident in taking decisions on their own. The freedom of informed and responsible individuals is the ultimate power that disciplines the labor market to be efficient. But one should not forget that interdependence is a two-way traffic. If individuals bear their power on the market, the market also teaches precious lessons to individuals. Indeed, these lessons are vital for reconciling requirements of social order with the dynamic forces of production. E. H. Phelps-Brown observes:

> . . . these same market forces, for all the harshness with which they impinge on some men at times, have a humane function to fulfill. In fact they serve to combine two freedoms which might seem irreconcilable; freedom to spend, within one's means, as one thinks best, and freedom to engage in what work one prefers,

within the range of jobs accessible. How is production to meet the needs of consumers, when it is carried on by men who are free to consult their own wishes about what work they shall do? It is through the play of supply and demand in the product and factor markets that the two freedoms are reconciled.[1]

Indeed, the optimization in the individual mind finds its magnified image in the reconciliation of change and order in the economy and society.

The individual freedom is also the ultimate repository of disciplinary power for any organized effort involving several individuals. The trade unions today are "wage makers" for about a third of the paid labor force, which in turn is approaching two thirds of the total labor force. But the strength of trade unions as organizations is not necessarily a cause for alarm in relation to the efficiency of resource allocation. It is true that there was a brief period after the Second World War when unions did seem to be able to distort the structure of employment and wages in reference to what would have resulted from the market forces alone. But, eventually, the viability of the labor movement depended on the consistency of its purposes and activities with its constituents' aspirations and the opportunities available outside of it for individual exploitation. In final analysis, what is important is not the labor market or labor movement as *an institution* but the resource allocation as *a process*. The labor market has never been a sole allocator of human resources. In olden days it functioned under the watchful eyes of the self-employed sector, attaining a high degree of efficiency for that reason. Today the labor market and the labor movement are in principle reinforcements in the interest of efficient allocation and utilization of human resources. It is the free individual who holds the balance and causes the two to act as such reinforcements. The individual weighs the relative advantages of his individual participation in the labor market and of his group effort within the labor movement. One may well suppose that Japan in her second century of modern development will show her ingenuity in reconciling the goals of organized effort and the dignity and freedom of the individual.

Notes

Introduction

1. M. W. Reder, *Labor in a Growing Economy* (New York: John Wiley, 1957), p. 321.

2. E. H. Phelps-Brown, *The Economics of Labor* (New Haven: Yale University Press, 1962), p. 10.

3. Bert F. Hoselitz, "The Development of a Labor Market in the Process of Economic Growth," *The Transactions of the Fifth World Congress of Sociology*, Vol. II (Louvain, Belgium: Imprimerie Nauwelaerts, 1962), pp. 55–71.

4. Observations on the early Japanese labor market are taken from my "The Labour Market in Japanese Development," *BJIR*, Vol. II (July 1964), pp. 209–27.

5. Even today, Japan retains much of this character of labor force utilization. See R. P. Dore, "Mobility, Equality and Individuation in Modern Japan," *ASCMJ*, Chapter IV.

6. See Robert A. Scalapino, "Japan," in Walter Galenson (ed.), *Labor and Economic Development* (New York: John Wiley, 1959), Chapter 3.

7. See, for example, John C. H. Fei and Gustav Ranis, "Innovation, Capital Accumulation, and Economic Development," *AER*, Vol. LIII (June 1963), pp. 283–313.

8. James I. Nakamura, *Agricultural Production and the Economic Development of Japan 1873–1922* (Princeton, N.J.: Princeton University Press, 1966).

9. *Ibid.*, p. 121.

10. *Ibid.*, p. 135.

11. Henry Rosovsky, "Rumbles in the Ricefields: Prof. Nakamura vs. the Official Statistics," *JAS*, Vol. XVII (February 1968). For my own view of the Nakamura volume, see *AER*, Vol. LVII (September 1967).

12. *ELTES*, Vol. 9, p. 36.

13. *Ibid.*, p. 5.

14. Yuichi Shionoya, "Nihon kōgyō seisan shisū 1874-1940" (The Index of Japanese Industrial Production, 1874–1940), *Keizaigaku zenshū* (Compendium on Economics) (Tokyo: Chikuma shōbō, 1966), Vol. 13, Annex.

15. *Ibid.*, p. 15.

16. *Ibid.*, pp. 22–23.

17. Charles P. Kindleberger, *Economic Development,* 2nd ed. (New York: McGraw-Hill, 1965), pp. 163–64.

18. "The Tokugawa Heritage," *SEEJ,* p. 40. Crawcour puts the figures the other way around, empasizing the proportion of agricultural production self-consumed.

19. "Economic Development with Unlimited Supplies of Labour," *Manchester School,* Vol. 22 (May 1954).

---

1 Japanese Wage Differentials before the Second World War

1. According to Alfred Marshall, the "net advantages" of an occupation are "the true reward which an occupation offers to labor" and "calculated by deducting the money value of all its disadvantages from that of all its advantages." *The Principles of Economics,* 8th ed. (1920), p. 73.

2. *The Evolution of Wage Structure* (New Haven, Conn.: Yale University Press, 1956), p. 364.

3. I presented parts of my findings to a session of the 1960 Conference of the Western Economic Association in August 1960. See "The Dynamics of Wage Differentials in Japanese Economic Development, 1880–1940," *Proceedings of the Thirty-Fifth Annual Conference of the Western Economic Association* (1960). In Tokyo, Shōwa Dōjin Kai, a research group, completed its study of Japanese wage structure about this time. See *Wagakuni chingin kōzō no shiteki kōsatsu* (A Historical Study of Japanese Wage Structure) (Tokyo: Shiseidō, 1960). Realizing the importance of this work, I contributed a brief review of it to *AER* (June 1962). This group's emphasis is on wage differentials after 1909 relying primarily on Factory Statistics (*KTH*), while I have tried to cover the last two decades of the nineteenth century as well. More recently, in connection with their work on long-term economic statistics of Japan (*ELTES*), the Hitotsubashi economists have been reviewing the whole stock of wage data. Some of their past data I have used are evidently superseded by their new estimates. But, hopefully, the broad pattern of wage differentials I am presenting in this chapter will not be affected to any great extent.

4. In this chapter the differential between a pair of wage series is always based on five-year moving averages of each series unless otherwise specified. The use of this smoothing process is expected to reduce the effect of imperfections or errors in the data which may not be distributed evenly over all the years in the series and the effect of irregular leads or lags between the two series which would spuriously magnify or diminish the ratios. Whenever two series of wages are compared, the differential is represented by the ratio of the higher to the lower wage so that an increase or decrease in the numerical value

may correspond to the widening or narrowing of the differential which the number represents.

5. Seiichi Tobata and Kazushi Ohkawa, ed., *Nihon no keizai to nōgyō* (The Japanese Economy and Agriculture), (2 vols., Tokyo: Iwanami, 1956), Vol. I, p. 196.

6. *The Agrarian Origins of Modern Japan* (Stanford, Calif.: Stanford University Press, 1959), pp. 120–23.

7. The formula for this measure of dispersion is

$$(1) \qquad \frac{\frac{1}{n} \sum_{1}^{n} |x_i - m|}{m}$$

where n is the number of industries involved, x_i the wage rate in the ith industry, m the simple average of wages of all the n industries, and i ranges from 1 to n. Another widely used measure of dispersion, coefficient of variation, is

$$(2) \qquad \frac{\sqrt{\frac{1}{n} \sum_{1}^{n} (x_i - m)^2}}{m}$$

where notations are the same as in Equation 1. Neither Equation 1 nor Equation 2 by itself is a sufficient measure of interindustry wage differentials. The question of what one should understand by "differential" or of what the "true" differential is has not been resolved to the satisfaction of all concerned. This question can become extremely philosophical, with no way out of the impasse. I have done a small amount of speculation on this question in my dissertation (*The Dynamics of Japanese Wage Differentials, 1881–1959*, Stanford University, 1961). See also Konosuke Odaka, "Chingin kakusa no sokutei ni tsuite" (On the measurement of wage differentials), *Keizai kenkyū* (Economic Review), Vol. 17 (April 1966), pp. 162–65.

8. Miyohei Shinohara, *Shotoku bunpai to chingin kōzō* (Income Distribution and Wage Structure) (Tokyo: Iwanami, 1953), pp. 22–26.

9. Hyoe Ouchi, ed., *Nihon keizai tōkei shū* (A Collection of Japanese Economic Statistics) (Tokyo: Nihon hyōron shinsha, 1958), pp. 280–81. Abbreviated NKTS hereafter.

10. "The Inter-Industry Wage Structure, 1899–1950," *AER*, Vol. XLV (June 1956), p. 363.

11. *The Conditions of Economic Progress*, 2nd ed. (London: Macmillan, 1951), pp. 467–69.

12. M. G. Kendall, *Rank Correlation Methods* (London: Charles Griffin, 1948).

13. Nishioka and Hattori, eds. *Nihon rekishi chizu* (A Historical Atlas of Japan) (Tokyo: Zenkoku kyōiku tosho, 1956).

14. *Dynamic Changes of Income and Its Distribution in Japan* (Tokyo: Kinokuniya, 1959), p. 58.

15. *Nōshōmu tōkei hyō* (Statistics of Agriculture and Commerce), annual, 1882–1925, succeeded by *Nōrinshō tōkei hyō* (Statistics of the Ministry of Agriculture and Forestry) and *Shōkōshō tōkei hyō* (Statistics of the Ministry of Commerce and Industry). There are also publications devoted to wages issued by these Ministries: Ministry of Agriculture and Commerce, *Tables on Wages,* 1920–1922; Ministry of Commerce and Industry, *Chingin tōkei hyō* (Wage Statistics), 1930, 1933–1939.

16. Tobata and Ohkawa, eds., *Nihon no keizai to nōgyō,* Vol. I, p. 203.

17. "A History of Money Wages in the Northern Kyushu Industrial Area, 1898–1939." *HJE,* Vol. 8 (February 1968), especially pp. 86–87.

---

2   Wage Differentials and
Economic Conditions

1. My earlier experiment with Japanese cycles is "Nihon keizai ni okeru junkan" (Cycles in Japanese Economy), in the University of the Ryukyus, Department of Economics, *Keizai kenkyū* (Economic Studies), No. 2 (1960).

2. Miyohei Shinohara, *Growth and Cycles in the Japanese Economy* (Tokyo: Kinokuniya, 1962), p. 79.

3. Kazushi Ohkawa and Henry Rosovsky, "Economic Fluctuations in Prewar Japan: A Preliminary Analysis of Cycles and Long Swings," *HJE,* Vol. 3 (1962), 10–33.

4. For business cycles in the 1870s and 1880s, see Shigeto Tsuru, *Essays in Japanese Economy* (Tokyo: Kinokuniya, 1958), Chapter 7.

5. Historians and economists generally agree that the 1890s were definitely a period of industrial progress in Japan. See W. W. Lockwood, *The Economic Development of Japan* (Princeton, N.J.: Princeton University Press, 1956), p. 18. However, the relative stagnation of the Japanese economy in the 1900s has not received much attention so far.

6. This has also been observed by Shinohara in his *Shotoku bunpai to chingin kōzō,* pp. 10–13.

7. For a competent summary of this issue, see Sho-Chieh Tsiang, *The Variations of Real Wages and Profit Margins in Relation to the Trade Cycle* (London: Pitman and Sons, 1947).

For the sake of completing the historical record, however, it may be added that the inverse relationship between real wages and price level was an entrenched phenomenon in Japan long before the emergence of modern economy and business cycles. Miss Yohko Sano examines the movements of wages for seven building trades between 1830 and 1894. Sharp price increases that occurred in the 1830s, 1860s, and around 1880 were accompanied by sharp reductions in real wages. See Yohko Sano, "The Changes in Real Wages of Construction Workers in Tokyo 1830–1894," *Managment and Labor Studies* (English Series No. 4) (Tokyo: Keio University, 1963). Similar swings are observed in building wages in Kyoto over a much longer period covering 1770 to 1870. See Mataji Umemura, "Kenchiku rōdōsha no jisshitsu chingin" (Real Wages of Construction Workers), *Keizai kenkyū* (Economic Review), Vol. 12 (April 1961).

8. Henry Rosovsky, *Capital Formation in Japan, 1868–1940* (New York: Free Press, 1961), p. 9.

9. G. Ranis, "Factor Proportions in Japanese Economic Development," *AER*, Vol. XLVII (September 1957).

10. M. W. Reder, "The Theory of Occupational Wage Differentials," *AER*, Vol. XLV (December 1955).

11. See, for example, Sylvia Ostry, "A Note on Skill Differentials," *Southern Economic Journal*, Vol. 29 (January 1963).

12. Reder, "The Theory of Occupational Wage Differentials," *AER*, Vol. XLV, p. 838.

13. W. C. Mitchell, *Business Cycles and Their Causes* (Berkeley: University of California Press, 1960), pp. 31–32.

14. J. R. Hicks, *The Theory of Wages* (London: Macmillan, 1932), pp. 86–87.

---

3   The Intersectoral and Interindustry Wage Differentials before the Second World War

1. The analysis of the intersectoral wage differential in this chapter draws heavily upon a previous article of mine, "The Intersectoral Wage Differential in Japan, 1881–1959," *Journal of Farm Economics,* Vol. XLIV (May 1962).

2. H. L. Parsons, *The Impact of Fluctuations in National Income on Agricultural Wages and Employment* (Cambridge, Mass.: Harvard University Press, 1952), pp. 42–43.

3. *Ibid.,* p. 42.

4. *Ibid.,* p. 46.

5. D. Gale Johnson, "The Nature of the Supply Function for Agricultural Products," *AER*, Vol. 40 (September 1950), p. 559.

6. M. W. Reder, "Wage Determination in Theory and Practice," *A Decade of Industrial Relations Research,* by the Industrial Relations Research Association (New York: Harper, 1958), p. 78. See also his "The Economic Consequences of Increased Immigration," *Review of Economics and Statistics,* Vol. XLV (August 1963).

7. This reversal of causation is nothing startling; it comes about naturally when the wage differential is regarded as something to be explained. But the proper recognition of the place of the intersectoral wage differential seems to have awaited the development of studies of other wage differentials and the need for consistent explanations for all of them. The treatment of the wage differential as a dependent, and migration as an independent, variable

is clearly developed by W. D. Weatherford, Jr., *Geographical Differentials of Agricultural Wages in the United States* (Cambridge, Mass.: Harvard University Press, 1957), pp. 65–67.

8. Reder, "Wage Determination in Theory and Practice" (*A Decade of Industrial Relations Research*), p. 79.

9. Weatherford somewhat picturesquely states that "farm laborers form a reserve of industrial labor which in good times is called forth into industrial jobs, but which in bad times is dammed up on farm, forcing farm wages down to pitifully low levels. In the course of time the influence of alternative opportunity on farm labor supply and wages is quite marked." (*Geographical Differentials of Agricultural Wages in the United States*, p. 67.)

10. The possibility of an adverse income effect on agricultural wages in the short run seems to have escaped general attention, but it could become a handy explanation in case agricultural wages failed to rise relative to industrial wages in association with an increase in aggregate demand.

11. For factor supplies to agriculture, see Johnson's "The Nature of the Supply Function," *AER*, Vol. 40. This work pursues the point that "the special characteristics of the behavior of agricultural output can be explained by the characteristics of the supply function of factors to agricultural firms" (p. 547). With respect to labor supply to industry, the whole Keynesian economics of employment can be drawn on.

12. There is a tendency to assume that the self-employed sector merely follows the course of events in the paid sector. This is the image of the intersectoral interdependence in W. Arthur Lewis's celebrated classic, "Economic Development with Unlimited Supplies of Labour," *Manchester School*, Vol. 22 (May 1954). I shall devote the last section of this chapter to the examination of the Lewisian concept of labor supply in relation to Japanese experience.

13. In recent years, there has been a substantial increase of attention given to the economics of the self-employed household economy. See, for example, Theodore W. Schultz, *Transforming Traditional Agriculture* (New Haven and London: Yale University Press, 1964). In Japan the Keio University economists have intensively cultivated this branch of economic analysis. See, for example, Keiichiro Obi and Iwao Ozaki, "Keizai hatten to shugyō kikō" (Economic Development and the Labor Supply Mechanism), *Management and Labor Studies Series* (No. 95). In this connection one should also recall two earlier studies of farm household economy and intersectoral labor transfer which have stood the test of time: Shinichi Watanabe, *Nihon nōson jinkō ron* (Rural Population in Japan) (Tokyo: Nangosha, 1938); Shigeo Nojiri, *Nōmin rison no jisshōteki kenkyū* (An Empirical Study of the Out-migration of the Farm Population) (Tokyo: Iwanami, 1942).

14. The intersectoral differences in the flexibility of the average product curve may be inferred from production function. Generally when the production function is of the Cobb-Douglas type and homogeneous of the first degree, that is, $\log O = A + a \log K + b \log L$, where O, K, L, and A are re-

spectively output, capital, labor, and a constant and a ($= 1 - $ b) is equal to capital's relative share in output, the elasticity of employment with respect to the average product of labor is equal to the reciprocal of the share of capital, that is, $1/a$ in the absolute value. In fitted production functions, the share of capital (including land) is larger in agriculture than in industry. Kazushi Ohkawa's agricultural production function, to be mentioned shortly in the text, puts the share of capital (and land) at 76 percent. The share of capital in Miyohei Shinohara's industrial production functions fitted for cross-sections of manufacturing for each year between 1929 and 1942 rarely rises to 45 percent. For the latter, see *Growth and Cycles in the Japanese Economy* (Tokyo: Kinokuniya, 1962), p. 331.

15. The covariation of intersectoral wage differential and migration has been tested differently by Ryoshin Minami. He uses the interwar population migration from farm households as the dependent variable and explains it by variables representing demand and supply factors. The industrial wage is a demand factor, while the agricultural wage is a supply factor. Labor is seen to be pulled by the industrial wage and pushed by the agricultural wage. See his "Population Migration Away from Agriculture in Japan," *EDCC,* Vol. 15 (January 1967).

16. The correlation coefficients between the intersectoral wage differential and trend-adjusted industrial employment of paid labor are: —0.84 for the period before the First World War and —0.98 (with the wage differential lagged behind employment by three years) for the period of 1915 to 1944. The employment of paid labor was just as flexible before as after the First World War. But the difference is that during the interwar period, overt unemployment became a serious problem in Japan for the first time. According to the analytical scheme of this chapter, unemployment is a factor that increases the elasticity of labor supply to mines and factories.

17. Lewis, "Economic Development with Unlimited Supplies of Labour." For a review of the controversy mentioned, see Ryoshin Minami, "The Turning Point in Japanese Economy," *Quarterly Journal of Economics,* Vol. 82. (August 1968).

18. Another person who tests the applicability of the Lewisian theory to Japan is Dale W. Jorgenson. However, it seems that Jorgenson has by-passed the issue of wage-productivity comparison, which is at the center of attention in the discussion of this chapter. While I agree with Jorgenson that economic development in Japan before the First World War was not Lewisian, I feel that his test is too roundabout. See Dale W. Jorgenson, "Testing Alternative Theories of the Development of a Dual Economy," in *The Theory and Design of a Dual Economy,* edited by Adelman and Thorbecke (Baltimore, Md.: The Johns Hopkins Press, 1966), pp. 45–60.

19. The economics of a self-employed family described here and on another occasion in this chapter may sound much like a rationalization of the economic behavior of the Japanese household, *ie.* For the labor market consequences of the *ie,* see Ezra F. Vogel, "Kinship Structure, Migration to the

City, and Modernization," *ASCMJ*, Chapter III. The fact that the behavior of the *ie* almost conforms to the analytical canons of standard micro-economic analysis is an additional support for the claim that Japan's so-called tradition was a peculiarly "modern" tradition indeed.

---

4   Japanese Wage Differentials
                                                       after the Second World War

1. For a general introduction to postwar Japanese economy, see G. C. Allen, *Japan's Economic Expansion* (London: Oxford University Press, 1965).

2. Nishikawa and Torii have also estimated agricultural production functions for different geographical areas of Japan and compared marginal products of labor with agricultural and construction wages for 1961. Everywhere the "stratification" of wages with the marginal products of labor as the floor is similar to Chart III. See Shunsaku Nishikawa and Yasuhiko Torii, "Nōgyō genkai sensanryoku no jōshō to hinōgyō chingin eno hakyū" (The Rise in the Marginal Productivity of Agriculture and Its Influence on Non-agricultural Wages), *NRKZ* (December 1967), pp. 13–24.

3. Since these concepts of wage payment are artifacts of the Ministry of Labor principally for the purpose of simplifying an enormous variety of wage payment practices in Japanese firms, any publication by this Ministry concerning wages carries notes explaining the concepts. See for example, *RH* (1957), pp. 156–57.

4. For the data and analysis of the labor force in postwar Japan, see Mataji Umemura, *Sengo nihon no rōdōryoku* (The Labor Force in Postwar Japan) (Tokyo: Iwanami, 1964). See also Tadao Ishizaki, *Tenkeiki no rōdō-keizai* (Labor Economy in the Period of Structural Transformation) (Tokyo: Toyo Keizai, 1967), pp. 57–72.

5. All kinds of wage differentials except for the intersectoral are exhaustively described with the use of various measures and indicators in the Ministry of Labor's annual publication, *The White Paper on Labor* (*RH*). Extensive analyses of specific topics that have to do with the labor market are presented by the research staff of the Ministry in the *Monthly Labor Statistics and Research Bulletin* (*MLSRB*) and in occasional publications devoted to selected problems. For a compendium of labor statistics, there is the bilingual *Yearbook of Labor Statistics* (*YLS*). The Economic Planning Agency (*EPA*) incorporates the Ministry of Labor data in a wider framework for the whole economy in its annual *White Paper on the State of the Economy* (*KH*). A quasi-official research institute, Japan Institute of Labor, publishes monthly bulletins. One of them is in Japanese, *Nihon rōdō-kyōkai zasshi* (*NRKZ*), and another in English, *Japan Labour Bulletin* (*JLB*). The contents are different.

6. For a fairly exhaustive analysis of wages and employment in the construction industry, see "Kensetsugyō rōmusha no chingin to koyō" (Con-

struction Workers' Wages and Jobs), *MLSRB* (May 1960); "Industrial Relations in the Construction Industry of Japan," *JLB* (June 1968). Village studies with an emphasis on the intersectoral labor transfer suggest how intensive the interactions in the labor market are among agriculture, construction, small businesses, and small-scale industries. See, for example, Shigeo Nojiri and Shiro Tatsuno, "Saikin ni okeru nōson jinkō-idō no seikaku" (The Character of Rural Population Mobility in Recent Years), *Nihon nōson jinkō mondai kenkyū* (Studies on the Problems of Rural Population in Japan), No. 3 (1954), pp. 237–67.

7. "Industrial Growth, Regional Structure and Differentials in Japan," *HJE*, Vol. 7 (February 1967), especially p. 5.

8. While direct test has not been done on this hypothesis, it has at least been shown that labor is more sensitively moving to high-wage from low-wage prefectures in postwar years than before the war. See Shunsaku Nishikawa, "Kenbetsuno rōdōryoku ryūshutsunyū to chingin shotoku" (Inter-Prefectural Flows of Labor, Wages and Incomes), *MGZ*, Vol. 55 (1962–1963), pp. 463–81.

9. The numbers are considerably larger after than before the war and fluctuate widely especially during the 1940s and early 1950s. For example, the flow of labor into agriculture in 1946 was nearly 1.5 million persons. The flow out of agriculture in 1951 was of that order. In the 1960s the net labor transfer from agriculture averages at about 650,000 persons, more than twice as high as the peak transfer that occurred before the war.

10. Ryoshin Minami's article on the statistical explanation of intersectoral population migration contains postwar as well as prewar data. See his "Population Migration Away from Agriculture in Japan." Masayoshi Namiki has done a similar experiment, using a concept akin to "unfilled vacancies" applied to the labor requirements of farm households in connection with labor transfer to nonagricultural employment. The proportion of farm households failing to fill the labor requirements by geographical area is inversely associated with the proportion of farm population obtaining employment in manufacturing establishments with 100 or more workers. See his "Chingin kōzō to nōka rōdōryoku" (Wage Structure and Farm Labor Force), *NCKK*, pp. 145–95.

11. For a review of literature on the structural characteristics of Japanese wages and employment, see Konosuke Odaka, "On Employment and Wage-Differential Structure in Japan: A Survey," *HJE*, Vol. 8 (June 1967), pp. 41–64.

12. For example, Seymour Broadbridge, *Industrial Dualism in Japan* (Chicago: Aldine, 1966).

13. For example, Kazushi Ohkawa, "Significant Changes in Japanese Agriculture Since 1945," *Journal of Farm Economics,* Vol. 43 (December 1961).

14. J. C. H. Fei and G. Ranis, *Development of the Labor Surplus Economy* (Homewood, Ill.: Richard Irwin, 1964).

15. Kazushi Ohkawa and Henry Rosovsky, "A Century of Growth," *SEEJ*, pp. 47–92.

16. Jorgenson, "Testing Alternative Theories of the Development of a

Dual Economy." Hugh T. Patrick and Peter Schran, "Economic Contrasts: China, India and Japan," *Journal of International Affairs*, Vol. 17 (No. 2, 1963), pp. 168–84.

17. Charles P. Kindleberger, *Europe's Postwar Growth* (Cambridge, Mass.: Harvard University Press, 1967).

---

5   The Labor Market Origins of
                                       Employer Paternalism

1. James C. Abegglen, *The Japanese Factory* (Glencoe, Ill.: The Free Press, 1958). By a curious historical accident this work gave me the much needed justification for investing my time in a historical study of Japanese labor market institutions. See, for example, Koji Taira, "The Characteristics of Japanese Labor Markets," *EDCC*, Vol. 10 (January 1962).

2. Abegglen, *The Japanese Factory*, p. 11.   3. *Ibid.*, p. 17.

4. *Ibid.*, pp. 67–68.   5. *Ibid.*, p. 68.

6. Clark Kerr, *Industrialization and Industrial Man* (Cambridge, Mass.: Harvard University Press, 1960).

7. *Ibid.*, Chapter 7.

8. Alexander Gerschenkron, "Economic Backwardness in Historical Perspective," *The Progress of Underdeveloped Areas*, edited by Bert F. Hoselitz (Chicago: University of Chicago Press, 1952).

9. Henry Rosovsky, *Capital Formation in Japan 1868–1940* (New York: Free Press, 1961), pp. 102–104.

10. Ronald Dore, "Sociology in Japan," *British Journal of Sociology*, Vol. 13 (June 1962), p. 120. Dore then refers to a very perceptive article by Hiroshi Hazama, who has since produced a substantial work on the subject. See Hiroshi Hazama, *Nihon rōmu kanrishi kenkyū* (Studies in the History of Work Force Management) (Tokyo: Daiyamondo, 1964). See also Michael Y. Yoshino, *Japan's Managerial System: Tradition and Innovation* (Cambridge, Mass.: MIT Press, 1968).

11. E. H. Phelps-Brown, *Economica*, Vol. 27 (February 1960), pp. 88–89.

12. S. B. Levine, *Industrial Relations in Postwar Japan* (Urbana: University of Illinois Press, 1958), p. viii. This book of Levine's leaves much to be desired in regard to the prewar industrial relations of Japan, which of course are not central to the thesis of the book. I have commented on that part of the book in my "Dynamics of Industrial Relations in Early Japanese Development," *Labor Law Journal* (July 1962). Since then Levine has clarified the issues involved and advanced valuable generalizations on the institutional dynamics of Japanese industrial relations. See his "Labor Markets and Collective Bargaining in Japan," *SEEJ*, Chapter 14. This work also appeared in Japanese in *NRKZ* (February 1964), which has called forth a valuable contribution by a research officer of a large Japanese firm. See Ryu Nibuya, "Nenkō seido no

kaiko to tenbō" (Diagnosis and Prognosis of *nenkō seido*), *NRKZ* (December 1964), pp. 34–44.

13. The role of *sankin-kōtai* in the evolution of the Japanese feudal economy is adequately discussed by Kee Il Choi, "Tokugawa Feudalism and the Emergence of the New Leaders of Early Modern Japan," *Explorations in Entrepreneurial History*, Vol. 9 (1956), pp. 72–90, and Gustav Ranis, "The Community-Centered Entrepreneur in Japanese Development," *idem*, Vol. 8 (1955), pp. 80–98.

14. For changing modes of utilization of labor in rural Japan during the Tokugawa period, see Smith, *The Agrarian Origins of Modern Japan*, Chapters 8–10.

15. For an over-all view of various types of employment relations during the Tokugawa period mentioned here and in the following paragraphs, see Hiroshi Hazama, "The Logic and the Process of Growth of the 'Familistic' Management in Japan," *Japanese Sociological Review*, Vol. 11 (1960), pp. 2–18 (Japanese text).

16. Kanji Maruyama and Sojiro Imamura, *Detchi seido no kenkyū* (A Study of the Apprenticeship Systems) (Tokyo: Seikosha, 1912); Economic Research Institute, Osaka Commercial College, *Osaka shōgyo shiryō* (Historical Materials on Osaka Commerce), 2 vols. (Osaka, 1934).

17. For an illuminating analysis of the characteristics of Japanese entrepreneurship during this period, see W. B. Burke, "Creative and Adaptive Response in Japanese Society," *American Journal of Economics and Sociology*, Vol. 21 (1962), pp. 103–12.

18. Biographical sketches, unless otherwise stated or supplemented, are based on the Association for the Study of Japanese Economic History, *Kindai nihon jinbutsu keizaishi* (Modern Japanese Economic History through Eminent Persons), 2 vols. (Tokyo: Toyo keizai, 1955).

19. For a detailed description of money changers' business, see S. Crawcour, "The Development of A Credit System in Seventeenth-Century Japan," *Journal of Economic History*, Vol. 21 (1961), pp. 342–60.

20. The "managerial revolution" has since been honored to this day as "bantōseiji." Ranis aptly remarks that "where it mattered, strangely enough, the Japanese were always able to elevate the rational over the traditional." "The Community-Centered Entrepreneur in Japanese Development," p. 96.

21. These "rules" are quoted in Kamekichi Takahashi, *Wagakuni kigyō no shiteki hatten* (The Historical Development of Japanese Enterprises) (Tokyo: Toyo keizai, 1956), pp. 180–81.

22. For a detailed description of these notorious labor problems, see Mikio Sumiya, *Nihon chinrōdōshi ron* (A History of Wage Labor in Japan) (Tokyo: Tokyo University Press, 1955), pp. 261–68.

23. E. Foxwell, "The Protection of Labour in Japan," *Economic Journal*, Vol. 11 (1901), p. 124.

24. In addition to the aforementioned works by Foxwell, Scalapino, and Sumiya, see Lockwood, *The Economic Development of Japan*, pp. 479–98;

NRUS, Vols. I and II; J. E. Orchard, *Japan's Economic Position* (New York: McGraw-Hill, 1930), Chapter 19; Kashiro Saito, *La protection ouvrière au Japon* (Paris: Librairie de la Société du Recueil général des Lois et des Arrêts, 1900); *SSU,* Chapter II; Mikio Sumiya, *Social Impact of Industrialization in Japan* (Tokyo: Japanese National Commission for UNESCO, 1963), Chapters I and II; Mikio Sumiya, ed., *Meiji zenki no rōdō mondai* (Labor Problems in the Early Meji Period) (Tokyo: Ochano mizu, 1960); Mataji Umemura, "Labor Market Structure and Inter-Industry Labor Mobility," *Keizai kenkyū* (Economic Review), Vol. 12 (1961), pp. 246–48.

25. *Shokkō jijō,* Vol. II, p. 10.

26. *Ibid.,* p. 12.

27. References cited in Note 24 above contain data and information on engineering industries as well. In addition, see Tsutomu Hyodo, "Tekkō kumiai no seiritsu to sono hōkai" (The Rise and Collapse of Metal Workers' Union), published in three parts in *Keizaigaku ronshū* (Journal of Economics) (January, July, and October 1966); Gennosuke Yokoyama, *Nihon no kasō shakai* (The Lower-Class Society of Japan) (originally in 1898, reprinted by Chūō Rōdō Gakuen, Tokyo in 1949).

28. *SSU,* pp. 734–735; Sumiya, *Nihon chinrōdoshi ron,* pp. 196–200.

29. Mitsuhaya Kajinishi et al., *Seishi rōdōsha no rekishi* (A History of Silk Industry Workers) (Tokyo: Iwanami, 1955), pp. 55–67; Yoshio Morita, *Wagakuni no shihonka dantai* (Employers' Association in Japan) (Tokyo: Toyo keizai, 1926), pp. 107–10; *SSU,* pp. 739–40.

30. This observation is based on comparison of the national total and the Okaya Federation registration at two different dates, the former referring to 1926 and the latter to 1922. The national total, together with the geographical distribution, of operations in the silk-reeling industry is from *SSU,* p. 54, while the Okaya Federation registration figures are from Takuji Sakura, *Jokō gyakutai shi* [*A History of the Maltreatment of Girl-Operatives*] (Tokyo: Kaihōsha, 1927), p. 40.

	Operatives in Silk Filatures	Operatives Registered with Okaya Federation	Those Registered as Percentage of Total
Nation	335,000	148,000	44.2%
Nagano Prefecture	92,000	51,000	55.8%

31. This episode may be of some interest from the point of view of industrial relations jurisprudence, when compared with the labor unions' efforts to attain what amounts to the workers' "property rights" over jobs.

32. Sakura, *Jokō gyakutai shi,* pp. 215–55.

33. Kajinishi et al., *Seishi rōdōsha no rekishi,* pp. 67–70; *SSU,* pp. 57–58; *KKN,* No. 2 (1917), pp. 85–86; Watanabe, *Nihon nōson jinkō ron,* pp. 332–47.

34. Based on a survey by the Mitsubishi Honsha in 1914; see the reproduction of this survey in *NRUS,* Vol. III, pp. 17–29.

35. For a detailed account of this incident and its aftermath, see Shuko

Shirayanagi, *Nakamigawa Hikojiro den* (The Life of Nakamigawa Hikojiro) (Tokyo: Iwanami, 1940), pp. 188–96.

36. Takashashi, *Wagakuni kigyō no shiteki hatten*, pp. 156–57.

37. This was the third session of a conference called *Nōshōkō Kōtō Kaigi* (Superior Council on Agriculture, Commerce, and Industry). There were changes in the membership of the conference between the first and third (final) sessions, the first consisting mainly of old-timers and the third of new men of business, like Shoda, engaged in the management of industrial establishments. With the changes in participants, the tone and content of arguments pro or con the proposed measures to regulate working conditions and employer-employee relations also changed. See Meiji bunka shiryō sōsho kankō kai (Society for the Publication of Meiji Cultural Materials), *Meiji bunka shiryō sōsho [Collection of Meiji Cultural Materials]* (Tokyo: Kazuma shobō, 1961), Vol. I.

38. *Ibid.*, pp. 118–19.

39. *Shokkō jijō*, Vol. I, p. 53.

40. D. W. Belcher, *Wage and Salary Administration* (Englewood Cliffs, N. J.: Prentice-Hall, 1962), p. 90.

41. In this section I draw mainly upon Riemon Uno, ed., *Shokkō mondai shiryō [Data on the Problems of Factory Operatives]* (Osaka: Kōgyō kyōiku kai, 1912). This work, comprising 16 pages of introduction, 84 pages of photographs of factory life, and 1,109 pages of text, was intended to be a systematic exposition of the problems of factory labor based on the first fifty issues of a journal, *Shokkō mondai shiryō A-gō* (Materials on the Labor Problem, Series A), started in January 1910 by the Kōgyō kyōiku kai (Society for Industrial Education), of which Uno was the chief editor. Owing to the publication date of the source used here (1912), the following description of employer behavior should be regarded as referring to a period several years prior to 1912.

42. Uno, *Shokkō mondai shiryō*, p. 10.   43. *Ibid.*, pp. 11–13.

44. *Ibid.*, pp. 165–67.   45. *Ibid.*, pp. 151–65.   46. *Ibid.*, pp. 167–71.

47. *Ibid.*, pp. 6–7.   48. *Ibid.*, pp. 88–101.   49. *Ibid.*, pp. 42–87.

50. *Ibid.*, pp. 171–94.   51. *Ibid.*, pp. 195–201.

52. This point was made by Gennosuke Yokoyama, *Nihon no kasō shakai*, p. 161.

53. Uno, *Shokkō mondai shiryō*, pp. 233–34.   54. *Ibid.*, pp. 254–58.

55. In this section, employers' rational responses are emphasized. How the measures undertaken by employers looked to workers to whom they were directed is another question. On this, there is the celebrated classic of Wakizo Hosoi, *Jokō aishi* (A Tragic History of Girl-Operatives) (originally in 1925, reprinted in 1954 by Iwanami with an interpretative note by Kazuo Okochi). Hosoi was a remarkable person. Raised in a poor deprived family, Hosoi did not even finish elementary school. He began to earn his keep at the age of 12 in 1908, starting his work in a weaving shed. Having moved about in the cotton textile labor market for 13 years, he sat down to write about the history of factory labor in the cotton textile industry. The book was an immediate suc-

cess. Management's new techniques in relation to the work force were in full swing when Hosoi was working. He captured with amazing vividness what these techniques were and how they looked from the point of view of employees. While I have no space to do justice to this important work in this book, I am aware that Japan's labor history cannot be complete without a full discussion of Hosoi's work and its implications.

56. Even in developed economies, "fair" pay conventionally accepted for a given job often collides with the market-determined pay. See Phelps-Brown, *The Economics of Labor*, Chapter 5.

57. The study of poverty, especially the poor, has always been a prominent feature of Japanese scholarship in labor and social policy. I have belatedly awakened to the importance of this subject. See, for example, "Ragpickers and Community Development: 'Ants Villa' in Tokyo," *ILRR*, Vol. 22 (October 1968).

---

6   The Labor Market, Group Power, and Public Policy

1. Here I condense and paraphrase generalizations about the past and present of capitalism advanced by several eminent scholars. Especially see Gunnar Myrdal, *Beyond the Welfare State* (New Haven: Yale University Press, 1960), Part 1; Clark Kerr, *Labor and Management in Industrial Society* (New York: Doubleday, 1964), and "Wage Relationships: The Competitive Impact of Market and Power Forces," *The Theory of Wage Determination,* edited by John T. Dunlop (London: Macmillan, 1957); Andrew Shonfield, *Modern Capitalism* (New York: Oxford University Press, 1965); J. K. Galbraith, *The New Industrial State* (Boston: Houghton Mifflin, 1967).

2. The evolutionary view of industrial relations presented here is admittedly old-fashioned. One of the fashionable frameworks today is the concept of "industrial relations system" which finds its most eloquent expression in John T. Dunlop, *Industrial Relations Systems* (New York: Holt, 1958). This work of Dunlop's was inspired by Talcott Parson's grand system of pattern variables and social equilibrium. I once used this type of theorizing to get at the nature of adjustment processes in the evolution of labor market institutions in Japan (*BJIR,* July 1964). I have since felt that the framework is both too abstract and too rigid to accommodate the concrete and dynamic developments in industrial relations over time. However, for a view of Japanese industrial relations in the Parsonsian and Dunlopian perspective, see Solomon B. Levine, "Postwar Trade Unionism, Collective Bargaining and Japanese Social Structure," *ASCMJ,* Chapter VIII.

3. *KKN,* No. 1 (1917), pp. 79–80.   4. *KKN,* No. 2 (1918), pp. 13–14.

5. *Ibid.,* pp. 67–70.   6. *KKN,* No. 3 (1919), pp. 15–16.

7. *KKN*, No. 4 (1920), pp. 49–51.

8. "Taisho demokurasii" is so well established as a clearly defined historical concept that it may hardly require qualifications. For information, see Robert A. Scalapino, "Elections and Political Modernization in Prewar Japan," *PDIMJ*, Chapter VIII.

9. Lockwood, *The Economic Development of Japan*, p. 512.

10. One may entertain a certain amount of sympathy toward the Meiji Government's "policy of inaction" concerning the labor market, although this sympathy wears thin as one proceeds to later years only to see the persistence of similar political preferences. I have expressed my own view of the Meiji Government's "inaction" vis-à-vis the labor market, which alone may be liable to misunderstanding, in "Market Forces and Public Power in Wage Determination: Early Japanese Experience," *Social Research*, Vol. 30 (Winter 1963).

11. T. C. Smith, *Political Change and Industrial Development in Japan: Government Enterprise 1868–1880* (Stanford: Stanford University Press, 1955), Chapter 8.

12. Saito, *La Protection ouvrière au Japon*, pp. 27–37.

13. This is an extremely subtle point. The provision in question is Article 17, Public Peace Police Law. The type of union that this article would tolerate was a spontaneous and voluntary association of workers using only the ideally peaceful approach to employment conditions which could in no way be interpreted as involving activities with any trace of "instigation," "temptation," or "violence." Such an impossible standard was of course tantamount to the prohibition of unionism. In his memorandum to the English Parliament, Oswald White, then Vice-Consul in Osaka, Japan, observed: "Trade unions are at the moment non-existent and under the present law would have little power if formed. They are not illegal, but there exists a clause in the Law of Public Security [now commonly translated as Public Peace Police Law] making it illegal to instigate a strike." *Report on Japanese Labour* (London: His Majesty's Stationery Office, 1920), p. 19.

14. For the history of preparatory actions taken by the Japanese Government during this long period, see MITI, *Shōkō seisaku shi* (A History of Commercial and Industrial Policies) (Tokyo, 1962), Vol. VIII, Chapter 1. For selected source materials, see also *NRUS*, Vol. III, Part I, Chapter 3. For the broader aspects of interactions between public power and private interest in historical perspective, see Lockwood, *The Economic Development of Japan*, Chapter 10.

15. Although not directly related to this particular event, Takeshi Ishida's article on the relationship between public policy and private interest groups is extremely helpful. See his "The Development of Interest Groups and the Pattern of Political Modernization in Japan," *PMIMJ*, Chapter IX.

16. See Yasoji Kazahaya, *Nihon shakai seisaku shi* (A History of Social Policy in Japan) (Tokyo: Aoki shoten, 1951), Vol. I, pp. 170–73.

17. MITI, *Shōkō seisaku shi,* p. 34.

18. For the reprints of parts of the Diet proceedings, see *NRUS,* Vol. III, pp. 206–209.

19. *Ibid.,* pp. 209–23.

20. *Ibid.,* pp. 225–31.

21. *Ibid.,* pp. 245–48. I mention this little detail here to illustrate how tricky the policy-making process was in prewar Japan. This will also be useful later for the appreciation of the economic planning process in postwar Japan to be discussed in Chapter 8.

22. MITI, *Shōkō seisaku shi,* pp. 80–92.

23. *Ibid.,* pp. 93–94. See also Harada, *Labor Conditions in Japan,* Chapter IX.

24. *SSU,* pp. 794–804. In view of the great difficulties that the Factory Law at its preparatory stage experienced with employer groups, it is somewhat mystifying that the Health Insurance Law despite its cost-raising effect on employers went through the Diet with absolutely no trouble. However, this was surely exceptional; it is safe to generalize about social legislation in Japan by saying that the Government tries to obtain a maximum of delay for any major piece of social legislation likely to put additional burden on employers or on public treasury. This happened to the Factory Law, the Trade Union Law, and the Relief and Protection Law. The socio-political problems attending the last-mentioned law are discussed in my "Public Assistance in Japan: Development and Trends," *JAS,* Vol. 27 (November 1967).

25. *SSU,* pp. 760–94.

26. Kazahaya, *Nihon shakai seisaku shi,* Vol. II, pp. 377–79.

27. *WCKSK,* pp. 292–97.

28. For Japan's relationship with the ILO Conventions, see Iwao F. Ayusawa, *A History of Labor in Modern Japan* (Honolulu: East West Center Press, 1966), Ch. 4, and Susumu Sato, *ILO jōyaku to nihon rōdōhō* (ILO Conventions and Labor Law in Japan) (Tokyo: Hosei University Press, 1957).

29. The brief run-down of the prewar labor movement in these few paragraphs is too short and too general to require documentation. But one would benefit from reading relevant sections in Levine, *Industrial Relations in Postwar Japan,* especially Chapters I–III; Robert A. Scalapino, "Labor and Politics in Postwar Japan," *SEEJ,* Chapter XV.

30. It may be noted at this point that the prewar principle of trade union organization appears so un-Japanese that one has great difficulty in applying Ishida's theory of Japanese organization to it. Ishida's hypothesis of "carte blanche leadership" fits postwar enterprise unionism very well. The prewar labor movement of Japan seems to be a material that challenges this hypothesis.

31. *RUN,* 1936, p. 150. For an illuminating discussion of prewar collective bargaining, see George O. Totten, "Collective Bargaining and Works

Councils As Innovations in Industrial Relations in Japan during the 1920s," *ASCMJ*, Chapter VII.

32. *NRUS*, Vol. 10, p. 432. See also *RUN*, 1936, pp. 149–59.

33. Totten in *ASCMJ*, and *NRUS*, Vol. 10, pp. 436–37.

34. *NRUS*, Vol. 10, p. 425.   35. *Ibid.*, pp. 522–32.   36. *Ibid.*, p. 495.

37. "Social minimum" as a parameter in the economic analysis of the labor market process is emphasized by Reder, *Labor in a Growing Economy*, pp. 324–26.

38. This is now a hoary issue, though it was very much alive in the early 1950s when I was a college student. See Benjamin Higgins, "Concepts and Criteria of Secular Stagnation," *Income, Employment and Public Policy*, edited Lloyd A. Metzler et al. (New York: Norton, 1948). In the late 1950s there was a neoclassical counter-revolution in American economic thought. One may well imagine through analogy and comparison that the "structuralist" views of Japanese economic processes will have to contend with the rising tide of a counter-revolution of a like nature.

39. Furthermore, a study of cross-section data indicates that labor turnover rates were inversely associated with wage levels of industries and sectors. See Shunsaku Nishikawa, "Rōdō no idōritsu to chingin suijun" (The Labor Turnover Rate and the Wage Level), *Management and Labor Studies Series*, No. 44 (1962–1963).

40. For a systematic theory of *nenkō joretsu*, see Masumi Tsuda, "Nenkō joretsu chingin to nenkō seido" (*Nenkō joretsu* wages and *Nenkō* System), *NCKK*, pp. 236–92. Tsuda develops his theory more fully in his *Nenkōteki rōshi kankei ron* (The *Nenkō*-type Industrial Relations) (Kyoto: Mineruva shobo, 1968). See also Sumiya, *Social Impact of Industrialization*, Chapter 3, especially Sections 4 and 5.

41. See Levine, "Labor Markets and Collective Bargaining in Japan," *SEEJ*, especially pp. 645–51.

42. See Haruo Shimada, "Nenkōsei no shiteki keisei ni tsuite" (A History of the Formation of the *Nenkō* System), *MGZ*, Vol. 61 (April 1968), especially pp. 61–63.

43. See the section on interfirm wage differentials in Chapter 1.

44. *NRUS*, Vol. 10, p. 516.   45. *Ibid.*, p. 488.   46. *NRUS*, Vol. 7, pp. 137–38.
47. *Ibid.*, pp. 130–32.   48. *Ibid.*, pp. 128–29.   49. *Ibid.*, p. 138.

---

7   Unionism, Wage Structure, and the Labor Market

1. This chapter in part updates my previous discussion of the subject: "Japanese 'Enterprise Unionism' and Inter-Firm Wage Structure," *ILRR*, Vol. 15 (October 1961).

2. Reynolds, *The Evolution of Wage Structure*, p. 167.

3. P. Ford, *The Economics of Collective Bargaining* (Oxford: Basil Blackwell, 1958), p. xii.

4. G. Rehn, "Unionism and the Wage Structure in Sweden," in *The Theory of Wage Determination,* ed. by J. T. Dunlop (London: Macmillan, 1957); Reynolds, *op. cit.;* B. C. Roberts, *National Wages Policy in War and Peace* (London: Allen and Unwin, 1958); A. Sturmthal, ed., *Contemporary Collective Bargaining in Seven Countries* (Ithaca, N. Y.: New York State School of Industrial and Labor Relations, 1957).

5. For a discussion of international data, see my *ILRR* article and "Wage Differentials in Developing Countries: A Survey of Findings," *ILR,* Vol. 93 (March 1966). For an intensive discussion of American data, see Richard Lester, "Pay Differentials by Size of Establishment," *Industrial Relations,* Vol. 7 (October 1967).

6. G. Rehn, "Unionism and the Wage Structure in Sweden," p. 236.

7. *Ibid.,* pp. 236–37.

8. The remaining 20 percent is distributed by type of union as follows: industrial, 11.3 percent; occupational, 4.9 percent; regional, 0.6 percent; and others, 3.3 percent. *RH* (1957), p. 245.

9. Solomon B. Levine, *Industrial Relations in Postwar Japan,* p. 90.

10. *Ibid.,* p. 117.

11. The analytical method tried here is adapted from the standard practice in price theory applied to the analysis of the impact of unionism. See M. Bronfenbrenner, "The Incidence of Collective Bargaining Once More," in *Labor and Trade Unionism: An Interdisciplinary Reader,* ed. by W. Galenson and S. M. Lipset (New York: John Wiley, 1960), pp. 170–77.

12. For facts and data on the advantages of large firms in the capital market, see Kojiro Niino, "Size of Firm and Credit Availability," *Kōbe University Economic Review,* No. 4 (1958). See also Miyohei Shinohara, "Shihon shūchū to chingin kōzō" (Capital Concentration and Wage Structure), *NCKK,* pp. 3–55.

13. Establishment and firm are not synonymous, for a firm may include more than one establishment. But an overwhelming majority of Japanese firms are one-establishment firms. In 1956, for instance, there were 195,566 manufacturing establishments with four or more employed persons operated by 188,350 firms (Prime Minister's Office, Bureau of Statistics, *Establishment Census,* 1947, 1951, 1954, 1957, 1960).

14. The wage differentials for 1909 and 1910 in Table 15 are based on the earnings of male operatives. Similar differentials are also observed in female earnings. But the weighted average earnings of male and female operatives in 1909 and 1910 were lower in the large establishments than in the small. This was due to the fact that large manufacturing establishments in those days were mostly in the textile industries where low-wage, female workers predominated.

15. For the growth and fluctuations of the postwar economy of Japan, see

Shigeto Tsuru, "Business Cycles in Postwar Japan," in *The Business Cycle in the Postwar World*, ed. Erik Lundberg (London: Macmillan, 1955), pp. 178–200; also, see his "Growth and Stability of the Postwar Japanese Economy," *American Economic Review Proceedings*, May 1960, pp. 400–11.

16. Other sources (Ministry of Labor's employment indices, for instance) suggest that a decrease in manufacturing employment occurred only between 1949 and 1950. Table 18 compares 1947 and 1951 because the *Census of Establishments* was so spaced, and because this census was the most reliable for employment data by size of establishment. As for 1928 and 1931, they were the years of highest and lowest factory employment, respectively.

17. This might be taken as another piece of evidence to substantiate the widely believed idea that "youthful unionism [the early organizational stage] is more potent wage-wise than mature unionism" (Richard A. Lester, *As Unions Mature* [Princeton, N. J.: Princeton University Press, 1958], p. 133).

18. For the background of general economic conditions after the Second World War, see G. C. Allen, *Japan's Economic Recovery* (London: Oxford University Press, 1958), and J. B. Cohen, *Japan's Postwar Economy* (Bloomington: Indiana University Press, 1958).

19. Kozo Yamamura, *Economic Policy in Postwar Japan* (Berkeley and Los Angeles: University of California Press, 1967).

20. M. S. Farley, *Aspects of Japan's Labor Problems* (New York: John Day, 1950), pp. 92–95. This dispute technique was known as "production control" and was quite fit for a time of general scarcity when the loss of income through strikes was unwise. On the effect of this technique on production, Farley says that "an abundance of reliable testimony confirms the fact that in many cases output was greatly expanded not only because the employees worked harder under their own leaders . . . but because they introduced administrative improvements" (pp. 92–93).

21. *Ibid.*, Chap. 15.

22. Kazuo Okochi, *Labour in Modern Japan* (Tokyo: The Science Council of Japan, 1958), pp. 73–109.

23. Of course, not all unions were aggressive enough to engage in "production control" in the first place, or active enough to set up joint councils later. The unions having these councils were about 40 percent of all the unions in 1949, but in 1957 had decreased to 34 percent. *RH* (1957), p. 250.

24. *KH* (1960), p. 245.

25. Gerald G. Somers and Masumi Tsuda, "Job Vacancies and Structural Change in Japanese Labor Markets," in *The Measurement and Interpretation of Job Vacancies*, by National Bureau of Economic Research (New York: Columbia University Press, 1966), p. 215. For a fuller study of "temporary workers," see Hokkaido Labor Research Institute, *Rinjikō* (Temporary Workers) (1956), 2 vols.

26. *YLS* (1961), p. 34.

27. Masao Yamamoto, *Nihon no kōgyō chitai* (Japan's Industrial Areas) (Tokyo: Iwanami, 1959), p. 166.

28. Tokutaro Yamanaka and Yoshio Kobayashi, *The History and Structure of Japan's Small and Medium Industries* (Tokyo: The Science Council of Japan, 1957), p. 45.

29. For an important aspect of trade union democracy and solidarity in Japan, see S. B. Levine, "Japan," in A. Sturmthal, ed., *White Collar Trade Unions* (Urbana: University of Illinois Press, 1967), pp. 205–60.

30. Teisuke Hayashida, "Seikatsukyū to nōryokukyū" (Living Wage versus Pay by Ability), *CKC*, pp. 936–51.

31. *RH* (1962), pp. 362–63.

32. Somers and Tsuda, "Job Vacancies and Structural Change in Japanese Labor Markets," p. 215.

33. The age gradient of pay has also given rise to a speculation that younger workers are paid less than their marginal products. If so, workers may be considered as being forced to lend parts of their pay to the company. Some of them recover the loans with interest when they become old and get paid more than their marginal products. This arrangement is seen to be contributory toward company expansion. See Kang Chao, "Labor Institutions in Japan and Her Economic Growth," *JAS*, Vol. 27 (November 1968). While I do not agree with the presumption of "exploitation," I recognize that Chao's viewpoint is rather widely shared by many observers of Japanese industrial relations.

34. Kazuo Okochi et al., *Nihon no yunion riidaa* (Trade Union Leaders in Japan) (Tokyo: Toyo keizai, 1965).

35. In this account of the continuity of wartime and postwar industrial relations, I paraphrase Ryohei Magota's powerful article, "Senji rodoron eno gimon" (Doubts about the Accepted Presumptions about Wartime Industrial Relations), *NRKZ*, Vol. 7 (July 1965). See also a full account of the development of the wartime labor economy in Sumiya, *Social Impact*, Chapter 4. For a thorough treatment of Japan's controlled economy during the war, see J. B. Cohen, *Japan's Economy in War and Reconstruction* (Minneapolis: University of Minnesota Press, 1949).

36. *RH* (1968), p. 201. *CH* (1968), p. 41.

37. Robert Evans, Jr., "Shunto: Japanese Labor's Spring Wage Offensive," *Monthly Labor Review* (October 1967). Taishiro Shirai, "The Changing Pattern of Collective Bargaining in Japan," *BJIR*, Vol. 3 (July 1965).

38. The information presented here is from *CH* (1968), Chapter 2.

39. *Ibid.,* p. 48.

40. Which trade union federation really sets the pace is not an easy question. I have followed the judgment of the EPA economists in considering these federations as pace-setters. See EPA, *Bukka antei to shotoku seisaku* (Price Stabilization and Incomes Policy) (Tokyo, 1968), p. 160.

41. For an attempt to rate trade unions by criteria like strike funds, solidarity, wage gains, etc., see Wakao Fujita and others, "Anatano kumiai o saitensuru" (We Rate Your Unions), *Gendai* (October 1968), pp. 56–75.

42. EPA, *op. cit.,* pp. 160–70. Haruo Shimada and Miss Yoko Sano also test

the role of the wage leadership in the Spring Offensive. Their conclusions agree with those of the EPA experiments. See Haruo Shimada, "Wagakuni chingin kettei kikō no keiryō bunseki (1)" (An Econometric Analysis of the Wage Determination Mechanism in Japan), *MGZ*, Vol. 61 (May 1968) and Yoko Sano under the same title (2), *idem.*, (July 1968).

43. *RH* (1968), p. 15.

44. The enterprise union's collective egoism makes an odd contrast to the progressive stance of the national trade union centers. Hence the paradox lucidly put by Shigeto Tsuru: ". . . Here is a paradoxical situation of organized workers in large firms sharing in the productivity rise with the monopoly capitalists who tend to exploit their small subsidiary firms, which in turn can survive only by exploiting their nonunion workers to the utmost. This is a paradoxical situation, indeed, especially when we reflect upon the fact that the organized workers in large firms are the most radical elements in Japanese politics, while the unorganized workers in small firms have been shown generally to share the politically conservative views of their employers." "Survey of Economic Research in Postwar Japan—Major Issues of Theory and Public Policy Arising Out of Postwar Economic Problems," *AER*, Vol. 54 (June 1964), Part II, p. 96.

45. Observations based on statistical information in *RH* (1968), p. 181 and p. 201.

46. See also Kozo Yamamura, "Wage Structure and Economic Growth in Postwar Japan," *IIRR*, Vol. 19 (October 1965).

47. Akira Takanashi, *Gendai nihon no rōdō mondai* (Labor Problems in Modern Japan) (Tokyo: Toyo keizai, 1965), Chapter 5, Section 5.

48. My attention throughout this chapter is on wage structure. Whether unions can raise the general level of wages for the whole paid sector is a different question. A related question is whether unions can raise labor's share in output either in individual industries or in the whole paid sector. During the 1950s, union power represented by the rate of unionization declined. Fortuitously, labor's share in output in manufacturing also declined. For a discussion of this interesting correlation, see Masao Baba, "Economic Growth, Labor Unions and Income Distribution," in *Postwar Economic Growth in Japan,* edited by Ryutaro Komiya and translated by Robert Ozaki (Berkeley and Los Angeles: University of California Press, 1966), Chapter 7.

49. Based on an EPA report (noted in connection with Table 28). See Ishizaki, *Tenkeiki no rōdō keizai,* p. 154.

50. Ishizaki also interprets the data roughly in line with my observations. *Ibid.*, pp. 154–56.

8   Labor, Management,
                                                                and Participatory Democracy

1. For an extremely useful insight into the significance of the institutional aspects of planning in general, see Jan Tinbergen, *Central Planning* (New Haven and London: Yale University Press, 1964).

2. Much of this chapter is drawn from my "Participation by Workers' and Employers' Organizations in Economic Planning in Japan," *ILR*, Vol. 94 (December 1966). I have also utilized portions of my thoughts expressed in my "Bunmei, kokka, minshu-shugi" (Civilization, the State and Democracy), *Chūō kōron* (Central Review) (January 1968).

3. This is also a major concern in welfare economics. See M. W. Reder, *Studies in the Theory of Welfare Economics* (New York: Columbia University Press, 1947) and I. M. D. Little, *A Critique of Welfare Economics* (London: Oxford University Press, 1957).

4. These statistics are taken from statements in the letters of transmission covering the reports of the Council on draft economic plans submitted to the Prime Minister. There are some discrepancies between these and the figures presented in Table 30.

5. The following description of the working arrangements of the Council is based on the introductory statements and membership lists contained in various plan documents.

6. Particularly enlightening on the administrative setup of the EPA is Satoru Yoshiue, "The Experience of National Economic Planning in Japan," *Planning for Economic Development,* Vol. II, by the United Nations (New York, 1965), pp. 125–30.

7. Law No. 263 concerning the establishment of the Economic Planning Agency (1952 and revised frequently since), Article 11.

8. In the Prime Minister's Office there are seven "agencies," of which four (including the EPA) are headed by Ministers of State.

9. Law No. 263, Art. 3, Para. 3.

10. Shigeto Tsuru, "Formal Planning Divorced From Action: Japan," in *Planning Economic Development,* ed. by Everett E. Hagen (Homewood: Irwin, 1963), p. 143.

11. Saburo Okita, *Keizai keikaku* (Economic Planning) (Tokyo: Shiseido, 1962), p. 42.

12. "Kokai toronkai—chuki keizai keikaku o megutte" (Symposium on the Medium-Term Economic Plan), *NKKSK* (December 1964), pp. 7–8.

13. See also Miyohei Shinohara, "Evaluation of Economic Plans in the Japanese Economy," *Weltwirtschaftliches Archiv,* Vol. 92 (1964), pp. 208–21.

14. Okita, *Keizai keikaku,* Part I, Chapter 2.

15. Tadao Uchida, "Atarashii chōki keikaku eno teigen" (Advice Concerning a New Long-Term Plan), *Chūō kōron* (January 1964), pp. 225–26.

16. Takayuki Yamamoto, "Shotoku baizō to kigyō keiei" (Income Doubling and Business Management), *Keieisha* (The Manager) (January 1961), p. 30.

17. This is the view of Tadao Uchida, "Atarashii chōki keikaku eno teigen," pp. 229–30.

18. For a discussion of social security in the National Income Doubling Plan, see "Social Security in Japan," *ILR,* Vol. 84 (October 1961), especially pp. 300–301.

19. This part of a plan is commonly known as "projection" or "forecasting." Some plans are no more than projections, in which case it is meaningless to speak of implementation.

20. This is what differentiates a plan from a projection. In other words, a plan creates a new trend of economic conditions rather than following the past trend. See Okita, *Keizai keikaku,* especially pp. 42–45. For examinations of plan targets from the point of view of logical consistency, see Hiroshi Kitamura, "Long-run Projection of the Japanese Economy—A Critical Evaluation," *Kyklos,* Vol. 9 (1956), pp. 135–63.

21. In the middle 1950s the predominant feeling among the ablest Japanese economists was that the maximum long-term rate of growth could not exceed 5 percent per annum. Since that time, the unknown, true potentiality of the Japanese economy has been a subject of lively controversy among Japanese economists. See Miyohei Shinohara, *Growth and Cycles in Japanese Economy,* Chapter 5 and Shigeto Tsuru, "Survey of Economic Research in Postwar Japan," pp. 92–95. See also Leon Hollerman, "Some Doubts About the 'Overfulfillment' of Japan's New Long-Range Economic Plan," *Kyklos,* Vol. 14 (1961), pp. 73–80.

22. For an evaluation of the Japanese economy's performance and prospects under the National Income Doubling Plan, see M. Bronfenbrenner, "Economic Miracles and Japan's Income Doubling Plan," *SEEJ,* Chapter 11; M. Fujioka, "Appraisal of Japan's Plan to Double Income," *I.M.F. Staff Papers,* Vol. 10 (March 1963), pp. 150–85; Saburo Okita, "Japan's Seventh-Inning Stretch," *Columbia Journal of World Business,* Vol. 1 (Winter 1966), pp. 123–29; Robert S. Ozaki, "Japan's 'Price Doubling' Plan?" *Asian Survey,* Vol. 5 (October 1965).

23. Allen, *Japan's Economic Expansion,* p. 39. See also Shinohara, "Evaluation of Economic Plans in the Japanese Economy," p. 213.

24. Most of the works so far cited agree on this point. See also "Consider Japan," in *The Economist* (September 1 and September 8, 1962).

25. Satoshi Kawai, Akihito Kanai and Yoshitaka Uchiki, "Daikigyō ni okeru setsubi tōshi kettei no jittai," (The Truth About Investment Decisions in Large Firms), *NKKSK,* No. 13 (June 1965), pp. 29–41.

26. Saburo Okita and Isamu Miyazaki, "The Impact of Planning on Economic Growth in Japan," *Development Plans and Programs* (Paris: O. E. C. D.,

1964), pp. 41–66. See also Eugene Rotwein, "Economic Concentration and Monopoly in Japan," *Journal of Political Economy*, Vol. 72 (June 1964). On the other hand, Kozo Yamamura sounds an alarm about recent trends for concentration of economic power. See his *Economic Policy in Postwar Japan*, Chapters 4–7.

27. Here I make use of Hirschman's felicitous dichotomy and abbreviations with a little twist. See Albert O. Hirschman, *The Strategy of Economic Development* (New Haven: Yale University Press, 1958), Chapter 5.

28. EPA, *Keizai shakai hatten keikau no kaisetsu* (A Primer on the Economic and Social Development Plan) (1967), p. 151.

29. Saburo Okita, "Keizai seichō no keizaigaiteki jōken," (Extra-Economic Dimensions of Economic Growth), *Chūō kōron* (May 1967), p. 122.

30. On this point, I fully agree with Hisao Kanamori. But my view of what the government should or can do on the basis of correct understanding of Japan's growth potential is the complete reverse of what Kanamori advocates. Kanamori seems to be saying that since the Japanese economy is essentially capable of growing at a very high rate (on which I agree), the government should also be equally aggressive in SOC formation (for which I have reservations). I feel that the very vigor of the private sector leaves little room for the government's spending on capital or on consumption if (and indeed if) the overheating of the economy should be avoided. See his *Chikarazuyoi taiyō* (The Strong Sun) (Tokyo: Daiyamondo, 1968).

31. *KH* (1968), p. 222 and p. 309.

32. The authors of the National Income Doubling Plan were aware of this type of obstacle to plan implementation. See also Hirotatsu Fujiwara, *Kanryō: Nihon no seiji o ugokasu mono* (Bureaucrats: Prime Movers in the Japanese Government) (Tokyo: Kodansha, 1964), Chapter 5, Section 4.

33. The information presented here is mainly culled from reports in the leading dailies like the *Asahi* and the *Nihon keizai*. For a more substantial reading, see Yoshihara Yamamura, "Shinnendo yosan hensei no budaiura" (Budget for the New Fiscal Year Seen From Behind the Scenes), *Ekonomisto* (19 January 1965), pp. 78–81.

34. See a participant's reminiscences: Yasuo Takeyama, "Keizai shakai hatten keikaku o meguru mondaiten" (Problems about the Economic and Social Development Plan), *NKKSK* (April 1, 1967), pp. 40–45.

35. EPA, *Keizai shakai hatten keikaku no kaisetsu*, p. 198.

36. *Ibid.*, p. 28.

37. *KH* (1968), pp. 1–5.

38. See Yukio Suzuki, *Seiji o ugokasu keieisha* (Businessmen behind Politics) (Tokyo: Nihonkeizai, 1965). Extremely useful for historical perspective is Takeshi Ishida, "The Development of Interest Groups and the Pattern of Political Modernization in Japan," *PDIMJ*, Chapter 9.

39. The following description of these four organizations, unless otherwise noted, is taken primarily from *Information Bulletin* (Consulate-General of Japan, Geneva), Vol. 9 (December 15, 1963).

40. For a brief history of Doyukai, see also its own statement appended to CED, *Japan in the Free World Economy* (New York, 1963).

41. Kazutaka Kikawada, "Kyōchōteki kyōso eno michi" (Toward Harmonious Competition), *Chūō kōron*, Supplement (Summer 1964), pp. 50–53.

42. Most outspoken among them is Masahiro Tatemoto of Kyoto University. See, for example, his "'Keizai ni yowai' naikaku no keizai keikaku" (Economic Planning by the Government "Weak in Economics"), *Chūō kōron* (May 1967), pp. 152–63.

43. Uchiki, Kanai and Kawai, "Toppu manējimentono ishiki to kōdō" (Ideology and Action of Japanese Top Management), *NKKSK* (September 1965), pp. 89–99.

44. Suzuki, *Seiji o ugokasu keieisha.*

45. Fujiwara, *Kanryo,* Chapter 9.

46. Saburo Okita in *Chūō kōron* (May 1967), p. 127. How lively the entrepreneurial activities were during the 1950s can be seen from Kazuo Noda, "Postwar Japanese Executives," *Postwar Economic Growth in Japan,* ed. by Komiya, Chapter 11.

47. Ministry of Labor, *Rōdō kumiai kihon chōsa hōkoku* (Basic Surveys of Trade Unions) (1967).

48. See, for example, Sōhyō's evaluation of the National Income Doubling Plan, "Background of Government Plan to 'Double the National Income,'" *Sōhyō News,* No. 187 (February 25, 1961).

49. Toshiro Kato, "Chūki keizai keikaku o hihansuru. Dōmei chōki chingin keikaku no kakuritsu e" (A Critique of the Medium-Term Economic Plan and A Contribution Toward Domei's Long-Term Wage Policy), *Domei* (January 1965).

50. These figures are derived from the membership lists of the Ministry of Labor's advisory councils as of November 1963.

51. Ishida, "The Development of Interest Groups and the Pattern of Political Modernization in Japan," p. 326.

52. For the trade union view of this situation, see Haruo Wada, "Rōdō kumiai ni okeru kakushin towa nanika" (New Lines for Trade Unions?), *Chūō kōron* (May 1967), pp. 288–97.

53. Kiyoshi Ebata, "Sangyō saihensei to rōdō mondai" (Industrial Reorganization and Labor Problems), *Chūō kōron* (July 1968), p. 160.

54. *Ibid.,* p. 161.

55. Susumu Sato, *ILO jōyaku to nihon rōdōhō,* p. 40. See also *JLB* (July 1965).

56. ILO, *Report of the Fact-Finding and Conciliation Commission on Freedom of Association Concerning Persons Employed in the Public Sector in Japan* (Geneva, 1965). See also Alice H. Cook, "The International Labor Organization and Japanese Politics," *ILRR,* Vol. 19 (October 1965).

57. ILO, *Report,* p. 705.   58. *Ibid.,* p. 725.

59. I have drawn heavily upon reports in various issues of *JLB* in tracing the events related to the advisory council in question.

60. *Ibid.* (August 1968), p. 4.
61. *Ibid.* (September 1968), p. 3.
62. *Ibid.* (December 1968), p. 4.

Conclusion   The Labor Market, Individual Freedom
and Organized Effort

1. E. H. Phelps-Brown, "Wage Policy and Wage Differences," *Labor and Trade Unionism,* ed. by Galenson and Lipset, pp. 21–22. For an extremely illuminating view of the individual-market relationship, see Gary S. Becker, "Irrational Behavior and Economic Theory," *Journal of Political Economy,* Vol. 70 (February 1962).

Selected Bibliography

THIS LISTING IS LIMITED to references which are principally concerned with, or devote substantial space to, the labor market, industrial relations, and social policy in Japan.

A — Western Language Books and Articles

Abegglen, J. G. *The Japanese Factory*. Glencoe, Illinois, 1958.

Allen, G. C. *Japan's Economic Expansion*. New York, 1966.

Ayusawa, Iwao F. *A History of Labor in Modern Japan*. Honolulu, 1966.

Baba, Masao. "Economic Growth, Labor Unions and Income Distribution." *Postwar Economic Growth in Japan*. Ed. Ryutaro Komiya. Tr. Robert S. Ozaki. Berkeley and Los Angeles, 1966.

Chao, Kang. "Labor Institutions in Japan and her Economic Growth." *Journal of Asian Studies,* 28 (November 1968).

Cook, Alice H. "The International Labor Organization and Japanese Politics." *Industrial and Labor Relations Review,* 19 (October 1965).

Dore, R. P. "Sociology in Japan." *British Journal of Sociology,* 13 (June 1962).

———, ed. *Aspects of Social Change in Modern Japan*. Princton, 1967.

Evans, Jr., Robert. "Shuntō: Japanese Labor's Spring Wage Offensive." *Monthly Labor Review,* 90 (October 1967).

Foxwell, Ernest. "The Protection of Labour in Japan." *Economic Journal,* 11 (March 1901).

Harada, Shuichi. *Labor Conditions in Japan*. New York, 1928.

Hotani, Rokuro and Takeshi Hayashi. "The Evolution of Wage Structure in Japan." *Industrial and Labor Relations Review,* 15 (October 1961).

Ishida, Takeshi. "The Development of Interest Groups and the Pattern of Political Modernization in Japan." *Political Development in Modern Japan.* Ed. Robert E. Ward. Princeton, 1968.

Karsh, Bernard and Solomon B. Levine. "Present Dilemmas of the Japanese Labor Movement." *Labor Law Journal,* 13 (July 1962).

Levine, Solomon B. *Industrial Relations in Postwar Japan.* Urbana, Illinois, 1958.

———. "Labor Markets and Collective Bargaining in Japan." *The State and Economic Enterprise in Japan.* Ed. W. W. Lockwood. Princeton, 1965.

———. "Japan." *White Collar Trade Unions.* Ed. A. Sturmthal. Urbana, Illinois, 1967.

———. "Postwar Trade Unionism, Collective Bargaining, and Japanese Social Structure." *Aspects of Social Change in Modern Japan.* Ed. R. P. Dore. Princeton, 1967.

Lockwood, W. W. *The Economic Development of Japan.* Princeton, 1954.

———, ed. *The State and Economic Enterprise in Japan.* Princeton, 1965.

Minami, Ryoshin. "Population Migration Away from Agriculture in Japan." *Economic Development and Cultural Change,* 15 (January 1967).

———. "The Turning Point in Japanese Economy." *Quarterly Journal of Economics,* 82 (August 1968).

Minemura, Teruo. "The Role of the Government in Industrial Relations: An Outline." *British Journal of Industrial Relations,* 3 (July 1965).

Nakayama, Ichiro. "The Modernization of Industrial Relations in Japan." *British Journal of Industrial Relations,* 3 (July 1965).

Odaka, Konosuke. "On Employment and Wage-Differential Structure in Japan: A Survey." *Hitotsubashi Journal of Economics,* 8 (June 1967).

———. "A History of Money Wages in the Northern Kyushu Industrial Area, 1898–1939." *Hitotsubashi Journal of Economics,* 8 (February 1968).

Okochi, Kazuo. *Labor in Modern Japan.* Tokyo, 1958.

Orchard, John E. *Japan's Economic Position.* New York, 1930.

Saito, Kashiro. *La protection ouvrière au Japon.* Paris, 1900.

Sano, Yohko. "The Change in Real Wages of Construction Workers in Tokyo 1830–1894." *Management and Labor Studies* (English Series), No. 4 (1963).

Scalapino, Robert A. "Japan." *Labor and Economic Development.* Ed. W. Galenson. New York, 1959.

Shirai, Taishiro. "The Changing Pattern of Collective Bargaining in Japan." *British Journal of Industrial Relations,* 3 (July 1965).

Somers, G. G. and Masumi Tsuda. "Job Vacancies and Structural Change in Japanese Labor Markets." *The Measurement and Interpretation of Job Vacancies.* Ed. National Bureau of Economic Research. New York, 1966.

Sumiya, Mikio. *Social Impact of Industrialization in Japan.* Tokyo, 1963.

———. "The Impact of Technological Change on Industrial Relations in Japan." *British Journal of Industrial Relations,* 3 (July 1965).

Taira, Koji. "The Dynamics of Wage Differentials in Japanese Economic Development." *The Proceedings of the 35th Annual Conference of the Western Economic Association,* 1960.

———. "Japanese 'Enterprise Unionism' and Inter-Firm Wage Structure." *Industrial and Labor Relations Review,* 15 (October 1961).

————. "The Characteristics of Japanese Labor Markets." *Economic Development and Cultural Change,* 10 (January 1962).

————. "The Inter-Sectoral Wage Differential in Japan, 1881–1959." *Journal of Farm Economics,* 44 (May 1962).

————. "The Dynamics of Industrial Relations in Early Japanese Development." *Labor Law Journal* (July 1962).

————. "Trade, Wages and Employment in Textiles." *International Labor Review,* 87 (January 1963).

————. "Market Forces and Public Power in Wage Determination: Early Japanese Experience." *Social Research,* 30 (Winter 1963).

————. "The Labour Market in Japanese Development." *British Journal of Industrial Relations,* 2 (July 1964).

————. "Wage Differentials in Developing Countries: A Survey of Findings." *International Labor Review,* 93 (March 1966).

————. "The Participation of Workers' and Employers' Organizations in Economic Planning in Japan." *International Labor Review,* 94 (December 1966).

————. "Japan." *Low Income Groups and Methods of Dealing with Their Problems.* Ed. Organization for Economic Cooperation and Development. Paris, 1966.

————. "Public Assistance in Japan: Development and Trends." *Journal of Asian Studies,* 27 (November 1967).

————. "Ragpickers and Community Development: 'Ants' Villa' in Tokyo." *Industrial and Labor Relations Review,* 22 (October 1968).

Tsuda, Masumi. "Japanese Wage Structure and Its Significance for International Comparisons." *British Journal of Industrial Relations,* 3 (July 1965).

Vogel, Ezra F. "Kinship Structure, Migration to the City, and Modernization." *Aspects of Social Change in Modern Japan.* Ed. R. P. Dore. Princeton, 1967.

White, Oswald. *Report on Japanese Labor.* London, 1920.

Yamamura, Kozo. *Economic Policy in Postwar Japan.* Berkeley and Los Angeles, 1967.

Yoshino, Michael Y. *Japan's Managerial System: Tradition and Innovation.* Cambridge, Mass., 1968.

B   Japanese Language Books and Articles

Ebata, Kiyoshi. "Sangyō saihensei to rōdō mondai" (Industrial Re-organization and Labor Problems). *Chūō kōron* (Central Review), July 1968.

Hazama, Hiroshi. *Nihon rōmukanrishi kenkyū* (Studies in the History of Work Force Management in Japan). Tokyo, 1964.

Hokkaido rōdō kagaku kenkyūjo (Hokkaido Institute of Labor Studies). *Rinjikō* (Temporary Workers). 2 vols. Sapporo, 1955.

Hosoi, Wakizo. *Jokō aishi* (A Tragic History of Girl-Operatives). Tokyo, 1925.

Hyodo, Tsutomu. "Tekkō kumiai no seiritsu to sono hōkai" (The Formation and Collapse of the Metal Workers' Union). 3 parts. *Keizaigaku ronshū* (Journal of Economics), 31 (January 1966); 32 (July 1966); 32 (October 1966).

Ishizaki, Tadao. *Tenkeiki no rōdō keizai* (Labor Economy in the Period of Structural Transformation). Tokyo, 1967.

Kazahaya, Yasoji. *Nihon shakai seisakushi* (A History of Social Policy in Japan). 2 vols. Tokyo, 1951.

Magota, Ryohei. "Senji rōdōron eno gimon" (Doubts About the Accepted Presumptions About Wartime Industrial Relations). *Nihon rōdō kyōkai zasshi* (The Monthly Journal of the Japan Institute of Labor), 7 (July 1965).

Maruyama, Kanji and Sotaro Imamura. *Detchi seido no kenkyū* (A Study of the Apprenticeship Systems). Tokyo, 1912.

Nakayama, Ichiro, ed. *Chingin kihon chōsa* (Basic Surveys of Wages). Tokyo, 1956.

Nibuya, Ryu. "Nenkō seido no kaiko to tenbō" (Diagnosis and Prognosis of *nenkō seido*). *Nihon rōdō kyōkai zasshi* (The Monthly Journal of the Japan Institute of Labor), 6 (December 1964).

Nishikawa, Shunsaku. *Chiikikan rōdō idō to rōdō shijo* (Inter-Regional Labor Mobility and the Labor Market). Tokyo, 1966.

————. "Rōdō no idōritsu to chingin suijun" (The Labor Turnover Rate and the Wage Level). *Management and Labor Studies* (Japanese Series), No. 44 (1962–1963).

Nishikawa, Shunsaku and Yasuhiko Torii. "Nōgyō genkai seisanryoku no jōshō to hinōgyō eno hakyū" (The Rise in the Marginal Productivity of Labor in Agriculture and Its Influence on Non-Agricultural Wages). *Nihon rōdō kyōkai zasshi* (The Monthly Journal of the Japan Institute of Labor), 9 (December 1967).

Nojiri, Shigeo. *Nōmin rison no jisshōteki kenkyū* (An Empirical Study of the Out-Migration of the Farm Population). Tokyo, 1942.

Obi, Keiichiro and Iwao Ozaki. "Keizai hatten to shūgyō kikō" (Economic Development and the Labor Supply Mechanism). *Management and Labor Studies* (Japanese Series), No. 95 (1963–1964).

Okochi, Kazuo, Shojiro Ujihara, Ko Takahashi, and Akira Takanashi. *Nihon no yunion riidaa* (Trade Union Leaders in Japan). Tokyo, 1965.

Sakura, Takuji. *Jokō gyakutaishi* (A History of the Maltreatment of the Girl-Operatives). Tokyo, 1927.

Sano, Yoko. "Wagakuni chingin kettei kikō no keiryo bunseki - 2" (An Econometric Analysis of the Wage Determination Mechanism in Japan). *Mita gakkai zasshi* (The Journal of the Mita Academy), 61 (July 1968).

Sato, Susumu. *ILO jōyaku to nihon rōdōhō* (ILO Conventions and Labor Laws in Japan). Tokyo, 1957.

Shimada, Haruo. "Nenkōsei no shiteki keisei ni tsuite" (A History of the

Formation of the *Nenko* System). *Mita gakkai zasshi* (The Journal of the Mita Academy), 61 (April 1968).

————. "Wagakuni chingin kettei kikō no keiryō bunseki - 1" (An Econometric Analysis of the Wage Determination Mechanism in Japan). *Mita gakkai zasshi* (The Journal of the Mita Academy), 61 (May 1968).

Shinohara, Miyohei. *Shotoku bunpai to chingin kōzō* (Income Distribution and Wage Structure). Tokyo, 1953.

Shinohara, Miyohei and Naomichi Funahashi, eds. *Nihongata chingin kōzō no kenkyū* (Studies on Japanese Wage Structure). Tokyo, 1961.

Showa dojin kai, ed. *Wagakuni chingin kōzō no shiteki bunseki* (A Historical Study of Japanese Wage Structure). Tokyo, 1960.

Sumiya, Mikio. *Nihon chinrōdō shi ron* (A History of Wage Labor in Japan). Tokyo, 1955.

————, ed. *Sangyō to rōdō kumiai* (Industry and Trade Unions). Tokyo, 1959.

————, ed. *Meiji zenki no rōdō mondai* (Labor Problems in Earlier Meiji Period). Tokyo, 1960.

————. "Chūshō kigyō rōdō mondai no honshitsu" (The Fundamental Problems of Medium and Small Industries). *Nihon rōdō kyōkai zasshi* (The Monthly Journal of the Japan Institute of Labor), 3 (September 1961).

Taira, Koji. "Nijūnengo no rōshi kankei" (Industrial Relations 20 Years From Now). *Sekai no rōdō* (Labor of the World), 16 (August 1966).

Takanashi, Akira. *Gendai nihon no rōdō mondai* (Labor Problems in Modern Japan). Tokyo, 1965.

Tsuda, Masumi. *Nenkōteki rōshi kankei ron* (The *Nenkō*-Type Industrial Relations). Kyoto, 1968.

Umemura, Mataji. *Chingin, koyō, nōgyō* (Wages, Employment and Agriculture). Tokyo, 1961.

————. *Sengo nihon no rōdōryoku* (The Labor Force in Postwar Japan). Tokyo, 1964.

Uno, Riemon. *Shokkō mondai shiryō* (Data on the Problems of Factory Operatives). Osaka, 1912.

Wada, Haruo. "Rōdō kumiai ni okeru kakushin towa nani ka" (New Lines for Trade Unions?). *Chūō kōron* (Central Review), May 1967.

Watanabe, Shinichi. *Nihon nōson jinkō ron* (Rural Population in Japan). Tokyo, 1938.

Yokoyama, Gennosuke. *Nihon no kasō shakai* (The Lower-Class Society of Japan). Tokyo, 1898.

C Governmental Publications, Statistical Compendia, and Source Books

Bank of Japan. *Hundred-Year Statistics of the Japanese Economy.* Tokyo, 1966.

Hitotsubashi University. Institute of Economic Research. *Estimates of Long-Term Economic Statistics.* 13 vols. Date varies. Some are unpublished.

International Labor Office. *Report of the Fact-Finding and Conciliation Commission on Freedom of Association Concerning Persons Employed in the Public Sector in Japan.* Geneva, 1965.

Japan Institute of Labor. *Japan's Labor Statistics.* Tokyo, 1967.

Japanese Goverment. Economic Planning Agency. *Bukka antei to shotoku seisaku.* (Price Stabilization and Incomes Policy). Tokyo, 1968.

————. Ministry of Agriculture and Commerce. *Shokkō jijō* (Conditions of Factory Workers). 3 vols. Tokyo, 1903.

————, ————. *Nōshōmu tōkei hyō* (Statistics of Agriculture and Commerce). Tokyo, 1882–1925.

————, ————. *Tables on Wages.* Tokyo, 1920–1922.

————, ————. *Kōjō kantoku nenpō* (Annual Report on Factory Supervision). Tokyo, 1916–1922.

————. Ministry of Commerce and Industry. *Chingin tōkei hyō* (Statistics of Wages). Tokyo, 1930, 1933–1939.

————, ————. *Kōjō or Kōgyo tōkei hyō* (Factory Statistics or Census of Manufacture). Tokyo, 1909, 1914, 1919 to date.

Japanese Government. Ministry of International Trade and Industry. *Nihon sangyō no genjō* (The Current Conditions of Japanese Industries). Tokyo, 1959.

————, ————. *Shōkō seisaku shi* (A History of Commercial and Industrial Policies), Vol. 8. Tokyo, 1962.

————, ————. *Kōgyō tōkei hyō* (inherited from the Ministry of Commerce and Industry).

————. Ministry of Labor. *Yearbook of Labor Statistics.* Tokyo, 1948 to date.

————, ————. *Monthly Labor Statistics and Research Bulletin.* Tokyo, 1948 to date.

————, ————. *Rōdō hakusho* (White Paper on Labor). Tokyo, 1948 to date.

————, ————. *Nihon no rōdō keizai* (Labor Economy of Japan). Tokyo, 1957.

————, ————. *Nihon no chinguin kōzō* (Japanese Wage Structure). Tokyo, 1960.

————. Ministry of Welfare. *Rōdōsha chingin chōsa hōkoku* (Report on the Investigation of Wages). Tokyo, 1939.

————. Prime Minister's Office. *Nihon teikoku tōkei nenkan* (The Statistical Yearbook of the Empire of Japan). Tokyo, 1822–1941.

————, ————. *Rōdō tōkei yōran* (Handbook of Labor Statistics). Tokyo, 1924–1939.

————, ————. *Rōdō tōkei jitchi chōsa hōkoku* (Field Surveys of Labor Statistics). Tokyo, 1924–1935.

————, ————. *Establishment Census.* Tokyo, 1947 to date.

Japan Productivity Center. *Chingin hakusho* (White Paper on Wages). Tokyo, 1968.

Kyōchō kai. *Saikin no shakai undō* (The Social Movements in the Recent Years). Tokyo, 1930.

Meiji bunka shiryō sōsho kankō kai (Society for the Publication of Meiji Cultural Materials), ed. *Meiji bunka shiryō sōsho* (Collection of Meiji Cultural Materials), Vol. II. Tokyo, 1961.

Ohkawa, Kazushi and Associates. *The Growth Rate of the Japanese Economy Since 1878*. Tokyo, 1957.

Osaka Commercial College. Institute of Economic Research. *Osaka shōgyō shiryō shūsei* (Historical Materials on Osaka Commerce). 2 vols. Osaka, 1934.

Ouchi, Hyoe, ed. *Nihonkeizai tōkeishu* (A Collection of Japanese Economic Statistics). Tokyo, 1958.

Rōdō undō shiryō iinkai (Committee for Historical Materials on the Japanese Labor Movement), ed. *Nihon rōdō undō shiryō* (Historical Materials on the Japanese Labor Movement). 11 vols. Date varies. Some are unpublished.

Tōyō keizai shinpōsha (Oriental Economist, Inc.), ed. *Meiji taishō kokusei sōran* (A Comprehensive Survey of the State of the Nation During the Meiji and Taisho Periods). Tokyo, 1926.

Index

Studies of the
East Asian Institute

The Ladder of Success in Imperial China by Ping-ti Ho. New York: Columbia University Press, 1962.

The Chinese Inflation, 1937–1949 by Shun-hsin Chou. New York: Columbia University Press, 1963.

Reformer in Modern China: Chang Chien, 1853–1926, by Samuel Chu. New York: Columbia University Press, 1965.

Research in Japanese Sources: a Guide, by Herschel Webb with the assistances of Marleigh Ryan. New York: Columbia University Press, 1965.

Society and Education in Japan, by Herbert Passin. New York: Bureau of Publications, Teachers College, Columbia University, 1965.

Agricultural Production and Economic Development in Japan, 1873–1922, by James I. Nakamura. Princeton, N. J.: Princeton University Press, 1966.

Japan's First Modern Novel: Ukigumo of Futabatei Shimei, by Marleigh Ryan. New York: Columbia University Press, 1967.

The Korean Communist Movement: 1918–1948, by Dae-Sook Suh. Princeton, N. J.: Princeton University Press, 1967.

The First Vietnam Crisis, by Melvin Gurtov. New York: Columbia University Press, 1967.

Cadres, Bureaucracy and Political Power in Communist China, by A. Doak Barnett. New York: Columbia University Press, 1967.

The Japanese Imperial Institution in the Tokugawa Period, by Herschel Webb. New York: Columbia University Press, 1968.

The Recruitment of University Graduates in Big Firms in Japan, by Koya Azumi. New York: Teachers College Press, Columbia University, 1968.

The Communists and Chinese Peasant Rebellion: a Study in the Rewriting of Chinese History, by James P. Harrison, Jr. New York: Atheneum Publishers, 1969.

How the Conservatives Rule Japan, by Nathaniel B. Thayer. Princeton, N. J.: Princeton University Press, 1969.

Aspects of Chinese Education, edited by C. T. Hu. New York: Teachers College Press, Columbia University, 1969.

Imperial Restoration in Medieval Japan, by Paul Varley. New York: Columbia University Press (forthcoming).

Economic Development and the Labor Market in Japan, by Koji Taira. New York: Columbia University Press, 1970.

Li Tsung-Jen, A Memoir. Edited by T. K. Tong. University of California Press (forthcoming).

Documents on Korean Communism, by Dae-Sook Suh. Princeton, N. J.: Princeton University Press (forthcoming).

The Japanese Oligarchy and the Russo-Japanese War, by Shumpei Okamoto. New York: Columbia University Press (forthcoming).